PLATO AND POSTMODERNISM

Steven Shankman, Editor

PLATO AND POSTMODERNISM

duBois
Shankman
Webb
Halperin
Berger
Kadir
Thomson
Orsini
Kintz
Larisch

WIPF & STOCK · Eugene, Oregon

Wipf and Stock Publishers
199 W 8th Ave, Suite 3
Eugene, OR 97401

Plato and Postmodernism
By Shankman, Steven

ISBN 13: 978-1-60608-809-8
Publication date 6/11/2009
Previously published by Aldine Press, 1994

PLATO AND POSTMODERNISM

CONTENTS

by Page duBois

Foreword

What would it mean to think about Plato in the context of postmodernism? The papers in this volume on "Plato and Postmodernism" address this matter from many different locations. My first question is: Whose postmodernism? In contrast to Hal Foster's distinction between a postmodernism of resistance and a postmodernism of reaction, E. Ann Kaplan distinguishes between a commercial or co-opted postmodernism and a utopian postmodernism.[1] Resistance to what, reaction to what, utopia of what? Susan Bordo has argued that postmodernism can be used to collapse gender categories, to erase alterity and historical difference.[2] Postmodernism can be condemned from the point of view of traditional Marxism, as the loss of the coherent subject, the agent of political action, or from the view of cultural feminism, as the abandonment of a dream of wholeness and fusion, or regarded ambivalently as the "cultural logic of late capitalism."[3] But if postmodernism is the logic of late capitalism, or a reaction to modernism, the regime of infinitely proliferating simulacra, or some utterly new and unknowable beast, it may represent an opportunity as well as something to be deplored. I would want to argue for a utopian anti-sexist, anti-racist postmodernism, one that celebrates heterogeneity and difference, the fragmentary and erotic always until now kept at the boundaries of Western culture. What I would not want to see is a postmodernism that rehabilitates the classical authors, that sees postmodernism in Plato and argues that we should return to him because he is us.

It is fashionable to argue that Plato is more rhetorical, literary, ironic, self-reflexive than we have always thought, we of the Western metaphysical tradition. Plato does not present, in this view, a systematic philosophy, nor does he argue for specific doctrines. He is engaged in a truly dialogic practice, writing open texts that turn on each other, that commit conspicuous logical errors, that call attention to their own arbitrariness and to the difficulties inherent in any model of mastery and discipleship. This may well be, although I have not yet been convinced that there is no doctrinal substance presented in the form of these dialogical texts.

Post-structuralist readings, new critical, formalist readings, even of Plato, sever the textual object from the content of its production and reproduction, and therefore obscure the conditions under which the text is produced. If there is "nothing outside the text," the text for me is not just one dialogue, not just the Platonic corpus, or even all of the social text of ancient Greek society, but also the persistent exclusion of women from philosophical pleasure and labor, and I believe such matters should enter into the debates concerning "Plato and Postmodernism."

Foreword

There is a moment in the *Symposium* in which Socrates speaks of the disruptive, troubling presence of the women at the scene of philosophy, invoking a creature from mythology. In response to Agathon's speech, he says:

> his speech reminded me so strongly of that master of rhetoric, Gorgias, that I couldn't help thinking of Odysseus, and his fear that Medusa would rise from the lower world among the ghosts, and I was afraid that when Agathon got near the end he would arm his speech against mine with the Gorgon's head of Gorgias' eloquence, and strike me as dumb as a stone. (198c)

Of course this is a witty little joke, using the elements of a shared vocabulary among men, and of course I exhibit the heavy handed literalism of the humorless feminist when I point it out. But I am enough of a Freudian, or even of a new critic, to believe that even jokes can be interpreted. Here the woman who threatens to rise up from the underworld, like the dead mother of Odysseus, endangers speech and the philosophical occasion, the ecstatic contemplation of pederastic love: she threatens to impose silence.

This is not a lament, a call for reading Sappho instead of Plato. But let us not use whatever break the entry into the postmodern means merely to reread and reinscribe the canonical texts of our history. I think the exclusion of women from philosophy should figure in our readings, that if "the female" is included, through metaphor or appropriation, but left out of the dialogical participation that is the philosophical life, then we need to talk about that. One of the difficulties I have always had with the Habermassian ideal speech situation is that it fails to acknowledge and address the inequalities of power, of silences, of some of those I would assume he intends to include in democratic conversation. One of the mechanisms of exclusion, especially in universities, in academic discourse in general, is the weight of a tradition that overlooks traditional exclusions, that sets those aside as irrelevant to the real work of intellectuals. Postmodernist theory can perpetuate this exclusion by pretending that gender has definitively erased, that there are no inequities, no differences, that we are all simulacra, all equally absent from discourse, present only as polyvalent, polymorphous signs. That discourse can be just the same old story, a refusal of the material world, of historically gendered bodies, that serves the perpetuation of injustice and exclusion. We cannot pretend that others do not essentialize race and gender, even if we wish to inhabit a deterritorialized utopia free of homophobia, racism and sexism. I still believe that Plato yearns for a disembodied sojourn among the forms, and that some of us might want to contest his sovereign place in the history of Western civilization.

NOTES

[1]Hal Foster, "Postmodernism: A Preface," in Hal Foster, ed. *The Anti-Aesthetic: Essays on Postmodern Culture* (Port Townsend, Wa.: Bay Press, 1983), ix-xvi; E. Kaplan, "Introduction," in E. Kaplan, *Postmodernism and Its Discontents* (London and New York: Verso, 1988), 4.

[2]Susan Bordo, "Feminism, Postmodernism and Gender-Skepticism," unpublished paper.

[3]See Fredric Jameson, *Postmodernism or The Cultural Logic of Late Capitalism* (Durham, North Carolina: Duke University Press, 1991)

by Steven Shankman

Preface

Much contemporary literary criticism explicitly questions the assumptions of so-called Western "metaphysics," whose founder is reputed to be Plato. The kinds of issues raised in contemporary theory are, however, often precisely those raised by Plato. Plato explored such problems as the ontological status of the "transcendental signified"; the question of gender in relation to the problem of universal philosophical truth; difference and sameness; problems of language, speech, and writing; the chimera of the disinterested subject. Indeed, as David Halperin suggests in his essay in this volume, Plato can be viewed not as "a metaphysical dogmatist" but rather as "a kind of deconstructionist *avant la lettre,* a cunning writer fully alive to the doubleness of his rhetoric . . . and who actively courts in his writing an effect of undecidability" (*infra,* 62). Or, as Harry Berger, Jr. puts it in his contribution to this volume, if Derrida were to look for it, "he would find inscribed in the dialogues a critique of Platonism very similar to his [i.e. Derrida's] own" (*infra,* 76).

In reading some contemporary criticism, I became concerned that Plato was perhaps being used as a straw man by sceptics or ideologically-oriented theorists who wished to attack classical "metaphysics" and its alleged founder, Plato, without attending sufficiently to the richness, complexity, and ambiguities (many of them intentional) of his writings. I knew that the very word "metaphysics," for example, was foreign to Plato's philosophical vocabulary and I thought that we should let Plato—the "Other"—speak for himself. Jacques Derrida is a learned man and reads the Platonic texts, as does Julia Kristeva, Luce Irigaray, and Michel Foucault. But I was concerned that, for many graduate students who were familiar with Derrida, Kristeva, Irigaray, and Foucault, Plato was just a name.

So I proposed to teach a graduate seminar in which Plato would not be just a name, but a concrete presence whose texts could directly confront postmodernism (or, perhaps more accurately but less pleasing to the ear, poststructuralism). The idea was to read the Platonic texts side by side with contemporary theory, to let the sparks fly and hope that we could control the resulting fire. We were almost consumed by the blaze the first week, after our discussion of Plato's parable of the cave read in the context of Luce Irigaray's critique of Plato's symbolism in the section entitled "Plato's Hystera" in *Speculum: Of the Other Woman.* But tempers calmed, and we more or less politely—and generally with good (and sometimes with outrageous) humor—proceeded with the course. The confrontations between Plato and Postmodernism continued in the following weeks, as we read Plato's critique of rhetoric in the *Gorgias* and *Protagoras* in the light of Paul de Man's essays "The Rhetoric of Temporality" and "Semiology and Rhetoric"; the *Cratylus* and *Phaedrus* alongside Derrida's famous essay "Plato's

Pharmacy" and the first chapter in *Of Grammatology* ; the *Symposium* in the light of Helène Cixous' "The Laugh of the Medusa" and David Halperin's "Why is Diotima a Woman?"; Plato on difference and sameness in his late dialogue *The Sophist* and Derrida on "Différance"; Aristotle's conception of *katharsis* in the *Poetics* as glossed by Julia Kristeva in *Powers of Horror* ; Plato's reflections on aesthetic pleasure in the *Philebus* alongside Kant's descriptions of aesthetic distinterestedness and Derrida's reflections, in "The Parergon," on Kant's reflections.

At times in my efforts to fashion an intelligible response for the students about the week's reading I felt like a lesser John Donne trying to construct a huge metaphysical pun: there was Plato on one side and Derrida or Paul de Man or Helène Cixous on the other, one side the equivalents of Donne's lovers and the other of Donne's compasses, and the task at hand was to make mutually illuminating connections between the two sides of the equation. But out of that seminar came some outstanding presentations and papers from the students, along with the desire to continue the dialogue between Plato and Postmodernism in a conference held at the University of Oregon in the Fall of 1991. All of the essays in this volume, with the exception of the piece by Harry Berger, Jr., are revisions of papers given at that conference.

There are many people to thank for making the symposium and this subsequent volume possible. Generous support for the symposium came from many directions at the University of Oregon. I wish to thank the Department of English, the Humanities Center, the College of Arts and Sciences, the Center for the Study of Women in Society, the Program in Comparative Literature, the Provost's Office, and the Department of Classics. I wish also to thank all the students who participated in my seminar, who did not know what they were getting themselves into but who persevered and made the class such a stimulating experience for me and, I hope, for them. For organizing the symposium with flair and precision, I am extremely grateful to BethAnn Lindell, Laurence Musgrove, and Paige Price. The symposium would not have happened without their initiative, imaginative ideas, and constant effort. Special thanks are due to John T. Mosely, vice-president of research at the University of Oregon, for his generous and timely support of our efforts. I would like to thank Steven Shurtleff for his help in composing the index and bibliography, and reading proofs. Gerald Harnett of the Aldine Press has been very helpful in the many stages of the evolution of this book.

Because my own essay is an expansion of the of the introductory remarks I made at the symposium and explicitly addresses the topic of Plato and Postmodernism in a general way, I thought that it would serve as an appropriate introduction to the other essays in this volume.

Preface

What is the relation of Plato to Postmodernism? How compatible are Plato's views with modern theoretical preoccupations? Are they at odds or secretly connected? Is the relationship one of schism or symbiosis? The essays in Part I specifically address the issue of whether this volume should be entitled "Plato and Postmodernism," or "Plato *or* Postmodernism." Part II contains essays investigating the relation between specific dialogues of Plato—the *Symposium* in Chapter 3, the *Phaedrus* in Chapter 4, the *Cratylus* in Chapters 5 and 6, and the *Parmenides* in Chapter 7—and contemporary theoretical concerns. Part III is addressed to the issue of Plato and the Feminine.

I regret that Page duBois' stimulating keynote address, "Sappho in the Text of Plato," could not be included in this book due to a commitment to another publisher. I am grateful for writing the "Foreword" to this volume and for summarizing the contents of her paper there.

Steven Shankman

Part One: Plato and/or Postmodernism?

by Steven Shankman

Plato and Postmodernism

As I remarked in the Preface, much critical theory that we associate with postmodernism explicitly questions the assumptions of western metaphysics. This is perhaps especially true of deconstruction. In his well-known essay "La Pharmacie de Platon," for example, Jacques Derrida refers to "Platonisme" as "la structure dominante de l'histoire de la métaphysique"[1] and he then attempts to expose what he considers to be the rickety foundations of this Platonism. I wish to rescue Plato from what Derrida calls Platonism; to allow Plato's texts to speak for themselves, unencumbered by the "tradition," so often lamented in today's critical climate, that they have initiated; and then to measure some of contemporary criticism's hallowed presuppositions against what Plato actually has to say. As Harry Berger, Jr. will argue in Chapter 4 of this volume (*infra*, 76), "the closure and commitment Derrida deconstructs should be ascribed to Platonism, but not to Plato; that the metaphysics of presence is reflected back into the text of Plato's both by Platonism and by its rivals or critics (including Derrida)." I will be arguing that Plato in fact shares some of the concerns of "postmodern" theory; and that Plato anticipated,[2] and attempted to protect his work against, many of the kinds of criticisms that were to be made by later thinkers, including some of today's literary theorists.

"Postmodernism" is admittedly a slippery and unsatisfying term.[3] Nonetheless, the kinds of concerns I will be suggesting that Plato anticipates *and goes well beyond* can usefully be grouped under its general rubric, or under the rubric of "poststructuralism." The specific currents I shall place under the heading of postmodernism are Derridean and de Manian deconstruction; Foucauldian social constructionism and the New Historicism that it ushered in; and that side of feminist thought, following in the tradition of Derrida and Lacan, that is represented by Luce Irigaray.

In the course of my thinking about the topic of Plato and Postmodernism in regard to issues raised by some recent feminist theory, I felt compelled to coin a critical term that I introduce here, with no small degree of Socratic irony, as a specific example of what I take to be a general Platonic strategy: *prophylactic phallocentrism*. I realize that this takes some explanation, and I shall elucidate in more detail what I mean by this term when I come to discuss the *Symposium*. For now suffice it to say that Plato, while certainly not a feminist in the postmodern or even modern sense, virtually anticipates the charge of "phallocentrism" and protects himself in advance against it. Perhaps "protection" is the wrong word, for it connotes a defensiveness that tends to be absent from the Socratic stance and is more accurately associated with a sophist such as Thrasymachus in the *Republic*—whose emotional investment in his opinions and determination to save face make him an often edgy and aggressive opponent—rather than with the gentleness of the philosopher. Plato protects or grants himself immunity from such a charge in this instance and in analogous instances, I shall argue, by attempting to articulate a notion of language and of truth that resists being deformed into an ideologically airtight or absolutist "position." I hope that my discussion of the similarities between the concerns of Platonic thought and postmodern criticism will help to call into question the insidious and ideologically motivated opposition between the conservatives who wish to enlist Plato as a traditionalist and the radicals for whom Plato is a repressive reactionary.

Problems of Language

Probably the most striking resemblance to Jacques Derrida in the Platonic corpus can be found in the person of Cratylus, from whom the dialogue takes it name. I shall elaborate this resemblance in the section that follows, but first it is necessary to remark upon what makes the *Cratylus*—a dialogue that is the subject of two of the essays in this volume—so relevant to postmodernism. The dialogue is concerned with the question whose answer has decided, to a large degree, the direction in which contemporary critical theory, since the days of structuralism, has gone; and that question is: are names—and, by implication, are linguistic signs—natural or conventional? We have long since decided that signs are merely conventional, that there is no necessary relation between signs and what they signify. Plato asks us to reconsider the answers we have given.

The antagonists of the dialogue are Cratylus and Hermogenes. Cratylus believes in the reality of the natural sign, Hermogenes of the conventional, that reality is completely "constructed," in Foucauldian and New Historicist terms. It is the role of Socrates in this dialogue to question these ideological positions and to suggest a solution to the problem articulated from a philosophical perspective. In Cratylus we find a paradox that may strike us as strange, and yet I would argue that it is remarkably postmodern. Cratylus is a believer in the reality of the natural sign and yet is a follower of the Heraclitean doctrine that all is flux. One would think that these attitudes are incompatible, that the believer in the natural sign would be an absolutist rather than a relativist. What the dialogue reveals, however, is that it is precisely the relentless demand for identity between signified and signifier that results in the kind of radical scepticism indulged in by Cratylus. As M. H. Abrams has said of Derrida, Cratylus is "an absolutist without absolutes."[4]

Socrates begins his investigation—or mediation, as Djelal Kadir and Douglass H. Thomson will suggest in Chapters 5 and 6 respectively[5]—by having Hermogenes concede that a completely arbitrary relation between names and things would imply a Protagorean relativism that is unacceptable even to Hermogenes. Names cannot simply fluctuate according to our fancy (386d), some hint of the essence of a thing is surely suggested by its name. The elaborate etymologies indulged in by Socrates have two functions in the dialogue. On the one hand, these etymologies suggest that one can indeed argue for a natural relation between things and their names. On the other hand, the intricacy of the arguments and their sometimes questionable veracity undercut the very point Socrates is attempting to make about the completely natural relations between names and things. Hermogenes, at any rate, appears to be convinced by Socrates' arguments to abandon his radically nominalist position. But then Cratylus must be shaken of his ideological certainty that there must be a purely natural relation between names and things.

Plato begins along this road by showing the incompatibility of ideological fervor with common sense. Socrates says:

> Well, what do you say to the name of our friend Hermogenes, which was mentioned before—assuming that he has nothing of the nature of Hermes in him, shall we say that this is a wrong name, or not his name at all?[6]

To which Cratylus answers:

> I should reply that Hermogenes is not his name at all, but only appears to be his, and is really the name of somebody else, who has the nature which corresponds to it. (429c)

Hermogenes clearly believes that his name is Hermogenes. But if Hermogenes has in him nothing of the nature of Hermes, Cratylus would deny the reality of the fact that Hermogenes' name is Hermogenes rather than give up on his theory that only natural names are truly names. According to Cratylus, Hermogenes must be wrong about his own name. Derrida appears to share Cratylus' insistent scepticism on this very point. For, as Vicki Hearne informs us, "the French philosopher Jacques Derrida, in a lecture on memory and mourning, remarked that we never know, that we die without ever being sure, what our proper names are".[7]

Socrates then attempts to articulate a notion of language based on likeness rather than identity. Although Plato has been taken—wrongly, in my view—as an enemy of the notion of imitation (*mimêsis*), in this dialogue it is clear that he is valuing imitation as a necessary mediator between words and things, especially when we are dealing with qualitatively rather than quantitatively describable experience. It is here that Socrates puts forth his argument for the necessity of the distinction between resemblance (which works through imitation) and identity in a famous passage. That a thing and what nominally represents it must be identical, Socrates says,

> may be true about numbers, which must be just what they are, or not be at all. For example, the number ten at once becomes other than ten if a unit be added or subtracted, and so of any other number, but this does not apply to what is qualitative or to anything which is represented under an image (*eikôn*). I should say rather that the image, if expressing in every point the entire reality, would no longer be an image. Let us suppose the existence of two objects. One of them shall be Cratylus, and the other an image (*eikôn*) of Cratylus, and we will suppose, further, that some god makes not only a representation such as a painter would make of your outward form and color, but also creates an inward organization like yours, having the same warmth and softness, and into this infuses motion, and soul, and mind, such as you have, and in a word copies all your qualities and places them by you in another form. Would you say that this was Cratylus and the image of Cratylus, or that there were two Cratyluses?
> (432b-c)

Names, therefore, cannot be exactly identical with things, or they would be identical copies of the things themselves. What is important in names is that "the general character [of the thing named] be preserved" (433a), even if there is not correspondence at every point, for the thing will nevertheless be signified (*lexetai ge to pragma*) through resemblance.

The word *sklêros* ("hard") contains the letter lambda, which is a liquid and thus, because of its softness, contradicts the meaning of the word which it helps to constitute. Cratylus suggests to Socrates that perhaps the letter should indeed be changed to one more appropriate to the meaning of the word, but Socrates gets Cratylus to admit that the word is nonetheless intelligible as it is conventionally spelled. Socrates thus gets Cratylus to agree that custom or convention does in fact contribute to our understanding of language.

In an essay such as "Plato's Pharmacy" Jacques Derrida appears to have mistaken Cratylus's view of language, which seeks a consistent and transparent identity between signifier and signified, for Plato's own. Derrida's strategy in that essay is concisely stated by Charles L. Griswold, Jr.:

> Derrida deconstructs the *Phaedrus* by concentrating on the ambiguity of the pivotal word "pharmakon," a word which can mean both "cure" and "poison." He grants that Plato has led himself to the brink of a *topos* in which metaphysical distinctions cannot be sustained. Plato reveals this difficulty even as he attempts to distinguish between spoken and written discourse, for he uses the the latter to articulate the former: true spoken dialectic will, Socrates suggests, be "written" in the soul of the learner.[8]

The more rigorously one wants to define distinctions, the more quickly one becomes entangled within those distinctions' actual denials of their own validity. Derrida, in his own words, wishes "appeler la suspicion sur le droit à poser de telle limites" ("to put in doubt the right to posit such [definitional] limits in the first place"). He continues:

> En un mot, nous ne croyons pas qu'il existe en toute rigeur une texte platonicien, clos sur lui-même, avec son dedans et son dehors.
>
> In a word, we do not believe there exists, in all rigor, a Platonic text, closed upon itself, complete with its inside and its outside.

Definitional limits in Plato's texts, for Derrida, are always blurring, turning into their opposites, despite the author's efforts to distinguish them from each other. How, then, are we to understand what Plato is saying? Is the text then simply a kaleidoscope of free-playing signifiers? Derrida is careful to guard himself against this conclusion:

> Non qu'il faille dès lors considérer qu'il fait eau de toute part et qu'on puisse le noyer confusément dans la généralité indifférencié de son élément.
>
> Not that one must then consider that it is leaking on all sides and can be drowned confusedly in the undifferentiated generality of its elements.

But what, precisely, is the alternative to free play? One need not resort to the extreme view that the text is leaking on all sides, Derrida states, but "simplement"—and with this "simplement" comes the mediating solution to the either/or predicament:

> Simplement, pourvu que les articulations soient rigoureusement et prudemment reconnues, on doit pouvoir dégager des forces d'attraction cachées reliant un mot présent et un mot absent dans le texte de Platon. Une telle force, étant donné le *système* de la langue, n'a pas pu ne pas peser sur l'écriture et sur la lecture de ce texte.
>
> Rather, provided the articulations are rigorously and prudently recognized, one should simply be able to untangle the hidden forces of attraction linking a present word with an absent word in the text of Plato. Some such force, given the *system* of the language, cannot *not* have acted upon the writing and the reading of this text.[9]

This "simplement" leaves me confused; the prose that offers up the alternative is very difficult, but I will make an effort. It seems that somehow, independent of the author Plato, The System of Language Itself is establishing the meaning of Plato's text. But what is this system, and how can one gain access to it? Despite Derrida's claim to the contrary, it appears that we are indeed left with an either/or situation. Either Plato must define precisely what he means, in a noncontradictory way, each time he uses the word *pharmakon;* or, if he does not, then the text is perceived to be "leaking on all sides" ("il fait eau de toute part") and drowns in its own internal contradictions. I know that Derrida suggests a middle ground introduced by that "simplement," but the alternative that follows the "simplement" is articulated in such leaky prose that a serious attempt at grasping its meaning is frustrated.

If Plato really knew what he was doing, if he was in control of his language rather than being in the inevitable position of having his language control him, Derrida implies, he would have made sure that the word *pharmakon* everywhere and unambiguously referred to the same specific thing: he could not have allowed it to mean both poison *and* remedy at the same time. Derrida's impressively learned, agile, but overly long and meandering essay then consists—to a large degree—of a relentless scholasticism that points out the often contradictory nature of the various things referred to chiefly by the word *pharmakon* and its cognates as Derrida ultimately argues that "La pharmacie n'a pas de fond" ("The pharmacy has no foundation").[10] Derrida, however, appears to be confusing the philosopher Plato's views about language with the views of the ideologist Cratylus. The philosopher knows that words need not always mean the same thing, that ambiguity is intrinsic to the linguistic process. It is not Plato's pharmacy that has no foundation. It is rather Derrida's reading of Plato's pharmacy that has no foundation, because Derrida has made the fundamental mistake of assuming that, for Plato, being a philosopher means, above all, achieving systematic terminological consistency.[11] As David Halperin asserts, however, Plato is not "a metaphysical dogmatist" (*infra*, 62). And Plato was, moroever, profoundly aware of the capacity of language both to reveal and to conceal reality. In the *Cratylus,* Socrates—half jokingly—explains to Hermogenes the etymology of his near namesake, the god Hermes who, he says, is both an "interpreter (*hermeneus*), or messenger" as well as a "thief." Similarly, Pan, who is the son of Hermes, is "smooth in his upper part, and rough and goatlike in his lower regions." And this kind of powerful ambivalence, he adds, "has a great deal to do with language" (408a). Derrida's mistake is that he assumes that Plato does not accept the inherently ambiguous and analogical nature of language and that in the *Phaedrus* the philosopher intended that there consistently be an identity between the word *pharmakon* and all the signifieds to which this word refers. If there is no identity, for Derrida, then we are left only with difference.

The preceding analysis was not meant as a point by point critique of Derrida. My aim has been rather to suggest not only that Plato anticipates some of Derrida's concerns, but that Plato abandons Derrida's nominalist deconstructions as impediments to true philosophical enquiry. In response to Derrida's essay, I therefore cannot resist recalling what Plato has to say about difference in the *Sophist*: "Merely to show that in some unspecified way the same is different or the different is the same, the tall short, the like unlike, and to take pleasure in perpetually parading such contradictions in argument—that is not genuine criticism, but may be recognized as the callow offspring of a too recent contact with reality. . . . Yes, my friend, and the attempt to separate everything from every other thing not only strikes a discordant note but amounts to a crude defiance of the philosophical muse... *The isolation of everything from everything else means a complete abolition of all discourse"* (*Teleiotatê pantôn logôn estin aphanisis,* 259b-e). The perpetual parading of contradictions in argument—such as Derrida often indulges in in "Plato's Pharmacy"—is, from Plato's perspective, just so much nominalist nitpicking that finally renders all speech meaningless and all philosophical enquiry impossible.

Derrida's linguistic inheritance appears to be Lockian/Enlightenment nominalism, against which he is rebelling. As in the nominalist view of language, there is an unstated expectation in Derrida's assumptions about the Platonic use of language that technical philosophical terms should, optimally, always and unambiguously refer to discrete particulars. Derrida's rebellion, however,—by implicitly rejecting an ambiguous or analogical view of language—implicitly accepts the assumptions of the very nominalism it allegedly rejects. It is worth contrasting Derrida's assumptions about Plato's use of language with those of another contemporary thinker whose view of language came to have much in common with Plato's own. I refer here to Eric Voegelin, and particularly to the slender but majestic final volume of *Order and History.* In that final posthumous volume, entitled *In Search of Order,* Voegelin, whose work was deeply influenced by Plato, discusses what he calls "The Paradox of Consciousness" and "The Complex of Consciousness-Reality-Language," concepts that Louis Orsini, in Chapter 7 of this volume, will find of great relevance for understanding Plato's *Parmenides.*

The paradox of consciousness consists in the fact that consciousness must be understood in both its intentionalist and participatory modes. We say that we are conscious of something, that we remember something, that we think about something. "By its position as an object intended by a consciousness that is bodily located," Voegelin writes, "reality itself acquires a metaphorical touch of external thingness." For those not familiar with Voegelin's work, it might be useful to gloss this sentence before we proceed. We often think of reality as being "out there," as having an objective existence, Voegelin is saying, especially since this reality can be seen as a projection of a consciousness that itself has an objective and concrete locus in the physical body. Hence, the term "reality" is often equated with "objective reality." Indeed, it might be added at this point that many contemporary critiques of allegedly "classical" objective truth exclusively (and wrongly) equate classical philosophizing with precisely this one meaning of "reality." But this is hardly the whole story; indeed, it is a distortion of the classical paradigm. Voegelin continues: "On the other hand, we know the bodily located consciousness also to be real." The language here, in this posthumous work that was not polished by its author for publication, is sometimes rather terse and needs to be explicated. What Voegelin is saying is that the consciousness is "real" in more than the sense that it is an objective fact, an externally verifiable "thing." For there is a "second sense" in which "reality is not an object of consciousness but the something in which consciousness occurs as an event of participation in the community of being."[12]

The word "reality," then, is equivocal. And given the nature of reality, we should not expect anything else. We should not expect—as Derrida implicitly does of Plato's use of the word *pharmakon,* as Cratylus explicitly does of the name Hermogenes—an uncomplicated, one-to-one relation between name and thing. For the word reality covers the experiences both of objects intended by subjects (what we generally mean by the phrase "objective reality" or what Voegelin calls "thing-reality") as well as the comprehending reality in which the consciousness participates (what Voegelin calls the "It-reality," the "It" being the structure referred to "in everyday language in such phrases as 'it rains'"). Hence, "There is no autonomous, nonparadoxic language, ready to be used by man as a system of signs when he wants to refer to the paradoxic structures of reality and consciousness. Words and their meanings are just as much a part of the reality to which they refer as the being things are partners in the comprehending reality; *language participates in [this] paradox.*"[13] (emphasis mine). Language that is truly philosophical, such as Plato's in the *Phaedrus,* would thus openly acknowledge its own paradoxical nature if it is to be true to the paradoxical nature of reality.

Voegelin then goes on to relate this last statement to the very issue that lies at the heart of the *Cratylus* : is language "conventional" or "natural"?

> The conventionalist opinion, today the more fashionable one, is moved by the intentionality of consciousness and the corresponding thing-reality to regard words as phonic signs, more or less arbitrarily chosen to refer to things. The naturalists are moved by a sense that signs must have some sort of reality in common with the things to which they refer, or they would not be intelligible as signs with certain meanings. Both of the opinions are precariously founded because their adherents were not present when language originated, while the men who were present left no record of the event but language itself. As I understand the issue, both groups are right in their motivations, as well as in their attempts to explore the conditions incidental to the origin of language and its meaning; and yet both are wrong inasmuch as they disregard the fact that the epiphany of structures in reality... is a mystery inaccessible to explanation.[14]

Like Socrates in the *Cratylus,* Voegelin wishes to mediate between conventionalists and naturalists. The fact that "the epiphany of structures in reality is"—ultimately—"a mystery inaccessible to explanation" should not result in a scepticism about knowing, *unless we think of knowing only in the intentionalist mode.*

I shall conclude this section with a few speculative questions, all pointing in a similar direction. Is Derrida's scepticism the result, first, of an entirely understandable disenchantment with an intentionalist view of language, a view he wrongly ascribes—by implication—to the Plato of the *Phaedrus* ? And does Derrida, the critic of Saussure's conventionalist linguistic system,[15] having first deconstructed this intentionalist view, then, in response to the results of his deconstruction, perhaps go on to desire—like Cratylus—the natural sign, only to react once again, with an equally understandable scepticism, to this unrealizable desire? Aristotle, in the *Metaphysics* (1010a), attempts to refute the extreme relativism of those Protagoreans who, observing that all of "nature is in motion, and thinking that nothing is true of that which changes, . . . came to the belief that nothing indeed may be truly said of that which changes altogether and in every way." From this belief, Aristotle continues, issued the most extreme forms of scepticism, such as that held by Cratylus, who finally thought that nothing should be spoken but only moved his finger."[16] Would it be too reductive to suggest that Derrida's writings, which so often appear to teeter on the brink of meaning, are our (post)modern equivalent to Cratylus' finger-wagging?

Rhetoric and Truth

The word rhetoric has undergone a remarkable change in our critical vocabulary. When a critic talks of "rhetoricity" today what is usually meant is the figural nature of language. This is what Paul de Man means by rhetoric in his essay "Semiology and Rhetoric":

> Rhetoric radically suspends logic and opens up vertiginous possibilities of referential aberration. And although it would perhaps be somewhat more remote from common usage, I would not hesitate to equate the rhetorical, figural potentiality of language with literature itself.[17]

Tropes and figures, however, are only a small part of what the ancients conceived of as the art of rhetoric. Rhetoric was the art of persuasion. When the history of rhetoric is written, Plato is usually portrayed as its enemy, Aristotle as its champion; we shall note this same pattern in the histories of literary criticism. Plato's *Gorgias* is thus traditionally seen as an attack against rhetoric on behalf of dialectic . In part this is what it is, but—as de Man's criticism constantly points out—"rhetoricity" can never be abandoned. Plato knew this; indeed, that it what the *Gorgias* is in large part about.

In arguing against rhetoric, Socrates should not be taken as believing that one must abandon rhetoric.[18] What he is criticizing in this dialogue, and even more fully and powerfully in the *Phaedrus,* is a notion of rhetoric that is divorced from dialectic. Indeed, Socrates is himself a master rhetorician, as Plato himself acknowleges at one point in the dialogue. After Socrates gives an imaginative and moving account of his love affair with *philosophia,* thus personifying philosophy as a lover, Callicles responds by saying, "Socrates, it seems to me that you run wild in your talk like a true mob orator" (*hôs alêthôs dêmêgoros,* 482c). Again and again as the dialogue proceeds, Socrates uses allegories, fictions, and images in order to try to persuade Callicles of his point. Persuasion, however, is different from coercion. It is Socrates' contention that most rhetoricians enslave their audiences and keep them from engaging in reasoned argument. Socrates is aware that the same charge can be made against his own impassioned arguments, and so Plato therefore has Socrates' interlocutor, Callicles, make such a charge on two occasions (482c, as mentioned above, and 494d), thus anticipating that such charges can and will be made. One notes in Socrates' use of myth in this dialogue a movement from allegory, to image, to a grand myth at the conclusion of the work that presents itself as "true," thus questioning the very notion of what "truth" means.

In his essay "The Rhetoric of Temporality," de Man questions the romantic preference for symbol over allegory. "Whereas the symbol postulates the possibility of an identity or identification, allegory designates primarily a distance in relation to its own origin, and, renouncing the nostalgia and the desire to coincide, it establishes its language in the void of this temporal difference".[19] Allegory may, however, be viewed—in a nonromantic context—as a heuristic device that is a blend of rhetoric (pleasing fiction) and truth (what the allegory means); rhetorical *exempla* offer provisional fictions that may be discarded as one proceeds toward greater dialectical precision. Allegory is no longer, for de Man as it was for Plato, such a heuristic device, a way of moving along a scale of relative degrees from nontruth to truth. In this context, Paul de Man's remark quoted above can be viewed as that of an orator/sophist who is profoundly aware of the separation between rhetoric and truth, but whose scepticism about knowing discourages him for taking the next step. And this scepticism derives from an nominalist/intentionalist view of language[20] that refers to provisional fictions as "mystifications."

De Man's intentionalism is implied in his attempt to reverse, in "The Rhetoric of Temporality," Coleridge's preference for symbol over allegory. Coleridge, in preferring the symbol, argued for a return to a participationist, analogical way of thinking about language. As W. J. Bate has written, in a succinct and readable description of Coleridge's relation to the participationist tradition:

> With his back firmly braced upon the entire classical tradition, and the Hebraic and Christian thinking with which it had combined, he [Coleridge] affirmed at every opportunity that reason—as in the Platonic conception of it (*nous*)—is able, as it transcends the experience and judgments drawn from the concrete world, to touch directly a reality to which it is itself the mental analogue or counterpart.[21]

De Man wishes to discredit (or as he might say, "demystify") participationist thinking—which assumes that "creatures are not Being as such but are 'participations,' that is, finite analogues of Being as such"[22]—and the result is a return to pre-Coleridgean, Enlightenment intentionalism. Where de Man differs from Enlightenment intentionalism is that he is fully aware of its reductiveness and he wishes to unmask its naive claims to transparent referentiality. De Man appears to wish, therefore, to demystify both intentionalism and participationism. But participationist thinking assumes that mystery—in large part because of what Voegelin calls the paradox of consciousness—cannot on principle be overcome. Plato (and Voegelin) accept the necessary relation between mystery and rationality. In Paul Ricoeur's terms, understanding for them involves a hermeneutic of faith; for de Man, understanding involves "demystifying" such a hermeneutic in favor of what Ricoeur calls a hermeneutic of suspicion.[23]

Plato's "Attack" upon Poetry Reconsidered

In histories of literary criticism Aristotle is usually cast as the hero, Plato as the villain. It cannot be denied, of course, that Plato explicitly censures poetry in the *Republic* and that Aristotle in the *Poetics* appears to be responding to Plato's critique. Yet what has not received adequate attention is the fact that Plato in the *Republic* itself answers his own objections. Even so subtle and aware a critic as Harold Bloom literalizes Plato in this regard, for in the preface to the first volume of *The Art of the Critic* he writes, "It is true that Socrates, in *Republic* 10, rejects poetry that is an *imitation,* but nowhere does Plato discourse explicitly as to what the nature of a nonmimetic or visionary poetry might be."[24] Perhaps the key word here is "explicitly," for Plato does articulate what a nonmimetic or visionary poetry might be, but he does so not through the kind of explicit statement we associate with Aristotle, but through poetic exemplification, through the "rhetoricity" of his own discourse.

The famous critique of poetry in *Republic X,* for example, must be read in the context of the work as a whole, and this means reading the *Republic* as itself a work of carefully crafted and symbolically evocative *poesis* that culminates in the Myth of Er. In this myth Plato explicitly evokes in his reader many of the emotions—such as pity, fear, laughter, and astonishment—that he earlier had associated with Homer (the first and greatest of the tragic poets, according to Plato, *Republic* 595b and 607a and

Theaetetus 152e) and had considered as worthy more of being extirpated than elicited. These are those specifically tragic emotions the stirring up of which Aristotle felt compelled to defend in the *Poetics.* Plato's alleged attack on poetry should be viewed, to a large degree, as a critique of flatly naturalistic literature and of those contemporary habits of interpretation that would read even the great mythic poems such as Homer's epics as exciting adventure stories sapped of their philosophical intentions. Plato's critique of Homer, that is, is more a critique of the way Homeric poetry was being understood than of the poetry itself. It is no wonder, then, that the hero of the myth of Er is Odysseus and that in the tale Plato evokes precisely those tragic emotions that he had only just moments earlier castigated. The myth of Er must be read, Plato is suggesting, not as a naturalistic and exciting adventure story—i.e. not literally—but as a symbolically evocative *mythos* that provides an artistically fitting conclusion to the poem that is the *Republic.*[25]

What characterizes Plato's use of myth, in the *Republic* and elsewhere, is his awareness, on the one hand, of myth's shadowy ontological status and, on the other, of his belief that myth can point us in a profitable direction. If there is, in Derrida's terms, a "transcendental signified" to which a particular myth may correspond, Plato—even as early as the *Republic*—is very cautious about stating myth's ability to evoke it. After narrating the famous allegory (Plato actually describes it as an *eikôn,* an "image" or "semblance" 517b) of the cave, for example, Socrates tells Glaucon, "Maybe God knows whether or not it happens to be true; but this, at any rate, is how these appearances appear to me" (*ta d'oun emoi phainoumena houto phainetai,* 517b). There is to be sure in Plato a desire for the center, but even the early Plato recognizes that fictions—while provisional—are necessary, that one never gets quite beyond the realm of "play," albeit, in Paul Friedländer's words, "serious play."[26] Derrida himself writes: "It has been thought that Plato simply condemned play"[27] and then goes on to question this assumption. Indeed, Plato refers favorably to play throughout his works and, as Derrida notes, in his sixth letter he referred to play as "the sister of seriousness" (*hê tês spoudês adelphê*).[28] I would not want, however, to leave the reader with the impression—as does Derrida—that the Platonic dialogues reflect merely the free play of floating signifiers. For Plato, the intuition of the form of a thing (whether it be rhetoric or justice) is what guides the seriously playful intellective process.

In the following section I shall discuss the relation of some examples of feminist criticism to Platonic thought, but is worth commenting, in the present context in which I have just alluded to Plato's famous parable of the cave, upon Luce Irigaray's speculations on Plato's imagery. Irigaray suggests that Plato depicts his cave ("antre") as a womb ("ventre"),[29] and that the prisoners in trying to escape to the light are in fact attempting to leave behind imagery associated with the mother and enter the more abstract and truthful realm of the phallus/father. The prisoners must negotiate the distance

> Entre. . . Entre . . . Entre l'intelligible et le sensible. Entre le bien et le mal. L'Un et le multiple. Entre tout ce que l'on voudra. Oppositions qui supposent toujours le *saut* d'un pire a un mieux. Une ascension, un déplacement (?) vers le haut, une progression le long d'une ligne. Verticale. Phallique?
>
> Between . . . Between . . . Between the intelligible and the sensible. Between good and evil. The One and the many. Between anything you like. All oppositions that assume the *leap* from a worse to a better. An ascent, a displacement (?). Vertical. Phallic even?[30]

There is something to be said for the associations of the cave with the world of becoming and hence of generation and feminity, on the one hand, and the world of Being with light and the father, on the other. Part of the problem with Irigaray's critique, however, is what one might call the generative fallacy, the reduction of the symbolic meaning of mythic images to their (speculative) historical genesis. Symbolic language, it is true, always retains the traces of its own origins. But Plato knows that there is no uncontaminated language lying around somewhere to be used to refer unambiguously to transcendental signifieds. Plato is not Cratylus. He is aware of what Eric Voegelin refers to as the paradox of consciousness and the complex of consciousness-reality-language. Plato did not assume that his own myths were unproblematic. In composing his parable of the cave, he used the language symbols that were available to him in order to explore and illuminate (the metaphor seems irresistible) his own experiences of what it means to be enslaved to opinion as opposed to being open to truth. As Jürgen Gebhardt beautifully remarks in his fine "Epilogue" to Voegelin's *In Search of Order* : "the philosopher's reflective acts of cognition—as Voegelin states. . . , referring once more to the first philosopher Plato—are distinguished by the precarious balance they strike between the finality of the language of truth experienced and articulated historically and the nonfinality determined by the language's position in an ongoing, open-ended process."[31] Irigaray appears to wish to restrict Plato's mythopoesis to the finality of the language of truth experienced and articulated historically. Even if Irigaray were right about the genesis of Plato's metaphorical language, and if she then were to go on to articulate the consequences of her position for a reevaluation of Platonic thought, her argument—in trying to deconstruct Plato from a radically feminist perspective—would paradoxically be enacting the very process of illumination that Plato intended the parable of the cave to represent. For the assumptions of the philosopher—as opposed to what Plato calls the philodoxer ("the lover of opinion," *Republic* 480) and what today we might refer to as the ideologue—are on principle always open to question. One presumes that Plato would have been open to such a critique, that he would have wished to have been led out of the shadows. For Plato was aware that, however much one wishes to ascend to the light, it is precisely in the In-Between—Irigaray's "entre," which she punningly rhymes with "antre" (cave) and "ventre" (womb)—that human beings reside. The point of Irigaray's punning on the words "antre" (cave), "ventre" (womb), and "entre" indeed has its parallel in *Symposium,* in which Plato articulates his notion of the *metaxy* (In-Between), symbolized through a mythic representation that self-consciously combines masculine and feminine qualities, and it is to the *Symposium* that I shall now turn.

The Metaxy ("In-Between"), Philosophy, and the Question of Gender

The *Symposium* is one of Plato's great literary efforts. David Halperin, in his essay in this volume, goes so far as to say that the *Symposium* "remains beyond dispute the finest work of fiction, of prose literature, to survive from the classical period" (*infra,* 69). It is hard to believe that critics can still write about Plato's alleged hostility to art when he has left us so striking a literary masterpiece. The literary quality of the work, moreover, cannot be separated from its philosophical meaning. Indeed, one of Plato's intentions is—as in the *Republic*—to question the very distinction between poetry and philosophy.

Recent critical theory often emphasizes the historicizing of all "discourse" and sets this historicizing against allegedly Platonic transcendentalizing tendencies. We see this in recent reflections on "subject positions"; the disinterested subject is, according to this view, a chimera and the subject is "constructed." Such a view tends to be contrasted with the "transcendentalizing" nature of classical "metaphysics." It may come as something of a surprise to be reminded that Plato, at the beginning of that allegedly otherwordly and transcendentalizing work, *The Symposium,* goes out of his way to cast doubt—with his characteristically subtle irony—on philosophical absolutism. The dialogue that, through Diotima's speech, argues for the ontological primacy of the unitary Beautiful itself, begins by framing that speech with narrators of questionable reliability and a fanatical Socratism that Plato perceives as being rather ludicrous.

Let us look at the beginning of the dialogue, a masterpiece of Platonic narrative art. The dialogue begins with a question from an unidentified enquirer who wants to know what transpired that evening when Socrates and others, at a by now famous banquet, gave speeches on love. Apollodorus responds to this unidentified enquirer: "I believe I am not exactly unpracticed concerning the things you are asking about" (172a). The dialogue that will suggest that the spirit of existential enquiry defines human nature in its most exemplary manifestation itself begins with a question from an enquirer with whom the reader naturally identifies; for is it not the reader's own curiosity that causes him (or her; in the *Republic* Plato argued that women as well as men had the capacity to be philosophical rulers) to learn about the famous symposium at which Socrates and others gave their views on the meaning of love? The enquirer has a question: what happened that day? The only way that we can truly find out is through an eye-witness. Apollodorus tells this enquirer not what happened directly, but of a conversation he had with Glaucon, who had asked the very same question. The dialogue consists of Apollodorus telling this unidentified enquirer what Apollodorus had told Glaucon (who had asked Apollodorus to tell him what someone said that a certain Phoenix, the son of Phillip, had said that he, Apollodorus, knew) that Aristodemus had told him (Apollodorus). To describe a very complicated narrative frame[32] in a somewhat more streamlined manner: the dialogue consists of Apollodorus telling an unidentified enquirer what he (Apollodorus) had told Glaucon that Aristodemus, who was actually at the banquet, had told him (Apollodorus). Do we really know what happened at that banquet at which "Plato" makes explicit his "metaphysics" of love and being? Our chief narrator, Apollodorus, it turns out, was not even there and he heard the story from Aristodemus.

Both our eye-witness Aristodemus and our narrator Apollodorus are, moreover, depicted by Plato as rather foolish, and the nature of their foolishness casts real doubt upon the allegedly "absolutist" cast of Platonic thought. They are both disciples of Socrates, or perhaps Socrates "groupies" would be a more appropriate way to put it. As David Halperin observes in his essay, "for Apollodorus and Aristodemus alike . . . philosophy seems largely to consist in a personal, not to say idolatrous, cult of Socrates" (*infra*, 59). Plato describes Aristodemus, "the little guy who's always barefoot (*smikros, anupodetos aei,* 173b)," as a caricature of Socrates. Our narrator Apollodorus is self-righteous and has the (questionable) conviction of a recent convert to Socratism, as we see in his remarks to Glaucon, as he reports them to the unidentified enquirer. Since he met Socrates, Apollodorus says, he has

> made it my business to know everything he says and does every day. Before that I was running in circles, acting at random, thinking I was accomplishing something though I was unhappier than anyone, no less than you are now, imagining that anything was more necessary than philosophy.[33]

So Apollodorus describes himself to the companion who asked about the banquet. In a priggishly self-righteous manner, Apollodorus says,

> As far as I'm concerned, any sort of philosophical discussion I have or listen to is immensely enjoyable, apart from its practical benefit. It's when I hear other kinds of talk, particularly the sort you have with the rich and with businessmen that I get angry, and pity you and your friends for thinking you're accomplishing something when, in fact, you're not doing a thing! I suppose, in turn, you think I'm unhappy, and I suppose you're right; but for my part it's not that I think it of you, I know it for a certainty (*egô mentoi humas ouk oiomai all' eu oida*). (173c-d)

As with many disciples, Apollodorus here is distorting the master's message. The philosopher is the lover of knowledge, not the one who possesses knowledge; his knowledge is tentative, not certain and beyond argument. Whereas Socrates is depicted in this dialogue as physically the toughest of Athenian soldiers, his disciple Apollodorus is known as "softy" (*to malakos,* 173d5). Can you imagine a committed ideologist, of whatever persuasion, beginning a serious ideological tract with a comic depiction of a ridiculous young convert to that particular ideology? Herein lies one important difference between ideology and philosophy.

Thus Plato believes, with much postmodern theory, that the disinterested subject is a chimera, for Diotima's "metaphysical" account of the ladder of knowledge is purposely presented to us through the eyes of a self-interested disciple of Socrates who is depicted as a somewhat ridiculous character. Plato is as aware as any deconstructionist of the virtual necessity of subjective distortion, although he believes we can move beyond mere impressions towards greater understanding.

I come now once again to the controversial issue of Plato's relation to feminist issues. Women are indeed excluded from the banquet, and they make their appearance either as lowly flute girls or in the disembodied presence of the lofty priestess Diotima. Plato was a brilliant narrative artist with the flair of a novelist, and it should be remarked that one does not recall any female character depicted by Plato with the lively particularity of an Alcibiades. However "essentialist" Plato was in his basic understanding of the differences between the sexes, however, it could be argued that in his depiction, via Diotima, of the philosopher, he wishes to criticize the excesses of "male" rationalism in favor of a blend—in the manner analogous to that described by Sharon Larisch in Chapter 9—of male and female qualities.

Diotima has just told Socrates—in what I take to be the philosophical core of the *Symposium*—that love (*Eros*) exists in between (*metaxy*) the mortal and the immortal (202e). Love's character was determined by the qualities of his mother and father. His father was Resource (*Poros*) and his mother was Need or Poverty (*Penia*). She continues:

> Therefore, as the son of Resource and Poverty, Love finds himself in this situation: first of all, he is always impoverished . . . . Possessing his mother's nature, he is always in need . But, then again, through his father he turns out a schemer (*epiboulos*) for beautiful things and good things, is courageous, bold, and intense, an awesome hunter always devising some machination or other (*aei tinas plekôn mêchanas*), eager for understanding and inventive; he is a lover of wisdom (*philosophôn*) all of his life and an intellectual virtuoso (*sophistês*) . . . . Love is never utterly at a loss nor completely wealthy. He exists in the middle, between ignorance (*amathia*) and wisdom (*sophia*). (203d-e)

Plato does indeed appear to be here anticipating Freudian associations of the feminine with lack and the masculine with fullness. A few observations should be made about this passage, however, before we jump to the conclusion that Plato's articulation of the philosophical experience is marred by the stereotypically "gendered" nature of his symbolic language. For one thing, the scheming quality of the father (*epiboulos*, 203c4) is not quite absent in the mother, whom Diotima says schemed (*epibouleusousa*) to seduce the father of Love. For another, Plato is rejecting the uninhibitedly "male" quality of aggressive self-assertion (embodied in Alcibiades)[34] and desire for mastery by depicting need as being essential to the philosophical experience. Most importantly, the participants in the dialogue reverse (one is tempted to say "deconstruct") the gender roles of the allegory. Plato does not see need or lack as the lesser or dependent "term" in a hierarchical arrangement that would grant greater importance to the experience of fulness. In the allegory, it is the female who is lacking and needs the resourcefulness of the male. *In the narrative itself, however, it is the male Socrates who is in need and the female Diotima who is full.* One way to read this reversal of gender roles is to infer that Plato wishes the listener to understand that the philosophical experience he is describing is a universal one, not limited to men alone, that it is not necessarily gender-specific. It was after all Plato who in Book V of the *Republic* maintained, in a stunningly revolutionary passage, that women as well as men had the capacity to be philosophical rulers and should be trained as such, since the only difference between men and women is "that the female bears and the male begets" (454e). Plato is thus (prophetically) protecting himself against the charge of phallocentrism, for even if his language does generally tend to subordinate the female to the male, by having the narrative reverse the gender roles of the myth of the conception of Eros, Plato is engaging, in brief, in what I described at the beginning of this essay as *prophylactic phallocentrism.*[35]

I do not wish to make the argument that Plato is any more of a feminist—in the modern sense—than he truly was. Even in Book V of the *Republic,* he refers to women as generally the "weaker" sex (456a), although as Gregory Vlastos has argued, Plato's estimate of women's characters could be viewed as the result of empirical observations of contemporary Athenian women whose disadvantaged status would be reversed under

Plato's own educational program.[36] Even if Plato's language does generally tend to subordinate the female to the male and thus may be called "phallocentric" or at least "arsenocentric," it should be said that Platonic philosophy in principle welcomes the critique of all assumptions, including Plato's own on all issues, including the issue of gender. This very openness is itself symbolized, in the *Symposium,* in the myth of the conception of Eros and the subsequent in-between nature of Eros as the symbol of the philosopher. It is of course possible that the language symbols of the philosopher, after they have been articulated historically, may eventually carry so much connotative baggage that the philosopher will be in need of a new vocabulary, a situation we are experiencing today. But does not this very acknowledgement of the need for a new philosophical vocabulary itself confirm the intent of Plato's symbolism of the essentially needy philosopher?

Difference, Sameness, and the In-Between

We have found several of Plato's dialogues, apart from the usual ones taught in courses in critical theory, crucial to an understanding of some postmodern assumptions. I have already argued for the importance of the *Cratylus* and the *Symposium.* It is time to draw attention as well to the *Parmenides* and the *Sophist.* These dialogues are central for gaining a perspective on one of the most famous of Derrida's essays, "Différance."

Let us begin by examining Derrida's assertion that "*différance* is not."[37] One cannot, truly, speak "différance," according to Derrida, because the "word"—coined by Derrida—describes precisely what constantly differs from itself and defers presence. One should recall in this context the goal of the Athenian stranger in Plato's *Sophist.* His goal is to hunt down the sophist, who claims that "what is not" (*to mê on,* 258b) has no existence. Here, paradoxically, the consequences of the positions of the relativistic sophist and the absolutist Parmenides come to the same thing. Parmenides, like Derrida, believes that difference is not. Since only the One (and not the many) has being, and since difference is never in what is the same, then "difference can never be in anything that is" (146e). The sophist in Plato's dialogue of that name can take refuge in the view that falsehoods have no real existence, for if a lie does not exist, then it cannot be refuted. If "*différance* is not," then how can we enter a discussion with Jacques Derrida on this point? With the Athenian stranger as our model, let us try.

We must, first of all, do what Derrida says is taboo, i.e. attempt to break "différance" down into its constituent parts. These two parts are "différance" in the sense 1) of "difference" and 2) of the deferring of presence. We must, with the Athenian stranger, 1) suggest that difference can only exist if it differs from something other than itself. And that something is sameness. If we do not admit the existence of sameness as well as difference, then all discourse is impossible. This is precisely the view of the Athenian stranger, who suggests that

> difference (*to heteron*) by partaking of existence, *is* by virtue of that participation (*methexin*), but on the other hand *is not* that existence of which it partakes, but is different, and since it is different from existence, quite clearly it must be possible that it should *be* a thing that *is not.* (259b)

As if he had been reading Derrida's analysis of Plato's sometimes contradictory uses of the word *pharmakon,* the Athenian stranger, in a passage I quoted earlier, goes on to say:

> Merely to show that in some unspecified way the same is different or the different is the same, the tall short, the like unlike, and to take pleasure in perpetually parading such contradictions in argument—that is not genuine criticism, but may be recognized as the callow offspring of a too recent contact with reality. . . . Yes, my friend, and the attempt to separate everything from everything from every other thing not only strikes a discordant note but amounts to a crude defiance of the philosophical muse. . . . *The isolation of everything from everything else means a complete abolition of all discourse.* (259d-e)

If one accepts the notion that only difference exists, then discourse (*logos*) becomes impossible.

We must now engage in a critical analysis of what Derrida means by 2) the deferral of presence. What does Derrida mean by the term "presence"? Here Derrida draws upon Heidegger's equating "the difference between Being and beings" with "the difference between presence and the present" and he gives a quotation from "The Anaximander Fragment" of Heidegger:

> Oblivion of Being belongs to the self-veiling essence of Being. It belongs so essentially to the destiny of Being that the dawn of this destiny rises as the unveiling of what is present in its presencing. This means that the history of Being begins with the oblivion of Being, since Being—together with its essence, its distinction from beings—keeps to itself.[38]

This proposition provokes the following comments from Derrida:

> Since the trace is not a presence but the simulacrum of a presence that dislocates itself, displaces itself, refers itself, it properly has no site—erasure belongs to its structure. . . . the present becomes the sign of the sign, the trace of the trace. It is no longer what every reference refers to in the last analysis. It becomes a function in a structure of generalized reference. It is a trace, and a trace of the erasure of the trace.[39]

Both Heidegger and Derrida, in these passages, are more Platonic than it might first appear—as long as we do not think of Plato as an absolutist who ascribes reality only to immutable Being.[40] We should remember that the Plato of the *Parmenides* and the *Sophist* rejects the association of reality exclusively with Being rather than—in Heidegger's terms—with "beings." "Being," Heidegger says, "keeps to itself." It is precisely the Parmenidean assertion that essential reality is unknowable that provokes the Platonic/Socratic critique—in favor of the notion of "participation"—of the Eleatic belief that only the One is real.

For Heidegger and Derrida, then, the present is not to be equated with full presence. Here Plato, the prepostmodernist Heidegger and the postmodernist Derrida are at one. Despite Derrida's assertions to the contrary, one often feels that his scepticism is a defensive reaction against a frustrated (and, from a Platonic perspective, unrealistic) expectation of full presence.[41] One recalls here, once again, Abrams' remark that Derrida is an "absolutist without absolutes." Indeed the philosopher who most resembles Derrida in the passage cited above is the great theorizer of the One, Plotinus. Both Plotinus and Derrida state that human beings experience only a "trace" of pure presence, but there is a world of difference between these respective traces of Plotinus ("trace" = *ichnos,* as in, e.g., *Enneads* III. 8. 20) and Derrida. For Plotinus, the trace in the necessarily material world of the divine and immaterial One, regardless of how remote from the One that particular emanation might be, still beckons the seeker to continue the quest for more complete participation in divine being. Pure presence is experienced—as in traditional classical and Christian thought—only as an intense desire, as a movement of the soul towards what has been experienced and then symbolized as the divine source of being. This existential movement is articulated brilliantly by Plotinus, who is consistently on his guard against hypostatizing the One into a proposition, or into what Eric Voegelin refers to as "thing-reality." For Derrida, the trace hints at a pseudodivinity that tantalizes the consciousness with the phantom reality of pure presence, while such presence is in fact consistently retreating from consciousness. Part of Derrida's problem is that he—unlike Plotinus, and unlike Plato—reifies or hypostatizes the One (the ultimate transcendental signified) into a thing the reality-status of which can then be refuted. It is perhaps more accurate, however, to relate the One to what Eric Voegelin calls "It-reality," the comprehending reality in which the consciousness participates. In a real sense, then, what Derrida is critiquing throughout his work is not Platonic philosophy, which argues for the In-Between nature of existence, but a literalized or reified version of the Parmenidean association of truth with Being rather than beings.

Postmodernism is indeed a critique of Western "metaphysics." As Eric Voegelin reminds us, however, the word "metaphysics" is itself a kind of philological mistake. It was originally merely the translation, from the Arabic, of the treatise that appears after the *Physics* in a medieval edition of Aristotle's works and came to refer to a purely propositional exposition of what was originally genuine philosophical experience and its articulation in language symbols.[42] "Metaphysics" itself, that is, is a reduction of philosophy to "thing-reality." Thus we cannot properly speak of Plato as a "metaphysician," since the term "metaphysics" is foreign to Plato's philosophical vocabulary. Plato was interested in exploring reality, not in building metaphysical systems; nor was it his highest priority to achieve terminological consistency. In "Plato's Pharmacy" Derrida has offered a critique—in terms largely of "thing-reality" philosophizing—of a thinker who has articulated his experience of reality in a language that is necessarily paradoxic. I have spent much of this essay discussing similarities between Platonic and postmodern philosophical concerns. But this is a point of perhaps irreconcilable difference.

NOTES

[1]"La Pharmacie de Platon," *La Dissémination* (Paris: Éditions du Seuil, 1972), 172. "Platonism," as Barbara Johnson translates, is "the dominant structure of the history of metaphysics" ("Plato's Pharmacy," *Dissemination* [Chicago: University of Chicago Press, 1982], 149).

[2]In an article entitled "Plato's Critique of Postmodernism," David L. Roochnik similarly argues (282) that "Plato comprehends, and then criticizes, the thoughts that underlie what we would now call postmodernism" (*Philosophy and Literature,* 1987, 282-9). Although Roochnik and I would agree upon what constitutes a quintessentially "postmodern" set of attitudes, our analyses are quite different.

[3]"Modernism," with its apocalyptic sense that it is the final and culminating stage of historical progress, makes the term "postmodernism" both necessary and absurd. On the historical emergence and philosophical connotations of the term "modern," see Tilo Schabert, "Modernity and History," *Diogenes,* No. 123, Fall 1983, 110-124 and "Modernity and History I: What is Modernity?" in Athanasios Moulakis, ed., *The Promise of History: Essays in Political Philosophy* (Berlin and New York: Walter de Gruyter, 1986). For a useful definition of "postmodernism," see Jean-Francois Lyotard, *The Postmodernist Condition* (Minneapolis: University of Minnesota Press, 1984). "I will use the term *modern,*" Lyotard writes, "to designate any science that legitimates itself with reference to a metadiscourse . . . making an appeal to some grand narrative, such as the dialectics of Spirit, . . . the emancipation of the rational or working subject, or the creation of wealth. . . . [S]implifying to the extreme, I define *postmodernism* as incredulity towards metanarratives" (xxiii-xxiv). See also Lyotard's "Answering the Question: What is Postmodernism?" in *Innovation/Renovation* (Madison: University of Wisconsin Press, 1983), 329-41 and, more recently, John McGowan, *Postmodernism and its Critics* (Ithaca and London: Cornell University Press, 1991).

[4]"How to Do Things With Texts," cited from *Critical Theory Since 1965,* ed. Hazard Adams and Leroy Searle (University of Florida Press, 1986), 438. Abrams' essay first appeared in *Partisan Review* in 1979.

[5]Kadir remarks that, in this dialogue, "the dialectic as such is mooted by paradox, a paradoxical entailment that ironically undermines dichotomous discourse and binarist ideation" (infra, 116). For Thomson, in the *Cratylus* Plato suggests that "a moral education proceeds not from fidelity to some radiant, unambiguous ideal but from occupying the position between the natural and conventional views—between the search for ontic certainty and the recursive consciousness of writing."

[6]Trans. B. Jowett in *The Collected Dialogues of Plato,* ed. Edith Hamilton and Huntington Cairns (Princeton: Princeton University Press, 1961), 463. All translations will be cited from this edition, unless otherwise stated. The Greek will be cited from the *Oxford Classical Texts.* I have occasionally made slight variations in the translations cited.

[7]*Adam's Task: Calling Animals by Name* (New York: Knopf, 1986), 192.

[8]*Self-Knowledge in Plato's Phaedrus* (New Haven and London: Yale University Press, 1986), 234.

[9]"La Pharmacie de Platon," 149; trans. Johnson, "Plato's Pharmacy," 130.

[10]"La Pharmacie de Platon," 170; "Plato's Pharmacy, 148.

[11]As Jasper Neel acutely observes, "The possibility that Plato *may* be playing, may in fact be toying with the play of meaning himself, never seems to cross Derrida's mind. Derrida reads *Phaedrus* the way he reads Saussure" (*Plato, Derrida, and Writing* [Carbondale and Edwardsville: Southern Illinois University Press, 1988], 187). The fact that "Plato" never speaks to us directly in his dialogues in order to deliver the Absolute Truth in its unmediated purity further confirms the view that Plato was open, tentative, undogmatic; in brief, Plato was—to employ a not inappropriate pun—not so sure/Saussure.

[12]*Order and History,* vol. 5 (Baton Rouge and London: Louisiana State University Press, 1987), 15. For Voegelin, the "luminosity" of consciousness consists specifically in the awareness of itself as an event in reality as reality becomes luminous for its own apprehension.

[13]*Ibid.,* 17.

[14]*Ibid.*

[15]As Derrida writes in *Of Grammatology*, "Beyond the scruples formulated by Saussure himself, an entire system of intralinguistic criticism can be opposed to the thesis of the 'arbitrariness of the sign' " (trans. G. Spivak, [Baltimore and London: Johns Hopkins University Press, 1974], 326).

[16]Trans. Hippocrates G. Apostle, *Aristotle's Metaphysics* (Bloomington and London: Indiana University Press, 1968), 66-67. Aristotle goes on to say that Cratylus "criticized even Heraclitus for saying that one cannot step into the same river twice, for he himself thought that one could not do so even once" (67). As the translator explains in his commentary, "while speaking about a thing, the thing has changed; but in pointing a finger, one indicates the continuous change which really takes place." And of the reference to Heraclitus the same commentator remarks: "It takes time to step into the river once; but, according to Cratylus, during this time it is not the same river" (291).

[17]*Allegories of Reading: Figural Language in Rousseau, Nietzsche, Rilke, and Proust* (New Haven: Yale University Press, 1979), 10.

[18]For a recent account that emphasizes Plato's positive contributions to the history of rhetoric, see James L. Kastely, "In Defense of Plato's *Gorgias,*" *PMLA,* vol. 106, no. 1, January 1991, 96-109.

[19]*Blindness and Insight: Essays in the Rhetoric of Contemporary Criticism* (Minneapolis: University of Minnesota Press, 1983), 207.

[20]Cf. Fredric Jameson's view of de Man as nominalist in the section entitled "Deconstruction as Nominalism" in *Postmodernism, or the Cultural Logic of Late Capitalism* (Durham, N.C.: Duke University Press, 1991), 217-259: "De Man was an eighteenth-century mechanical materialist, and much that strikes the postcontemporary reader as peculiar and idiosyncratic about his work will be clarified by juxtaposition with the cultural politics of the great Enlightenment philosophes: their horror of religion, their campaign against superstition and error (or 'metaphysics'). In that sense, deconstruction itself . . . can be seen to be an essentially eighteenth-century philosophical strategy. . . . What de Man clearly was was not a nihilist but a *nominalist,* and the scandalized reception that greeted his views on language is comparable to nothing quite so much as the agitation of Thomist clerks confronted unexpectedly with the nominalist enormity" (246, 250). De Man's work, Jameson writes, can be seen "as the place in which a certain experience of nominalism, in the specialized realm of linguistic production itself, was, as it were, lived to the absolute and theorized with a forbidding and rigorous purity" (251). The purity sought by de Man is the state of total demystification. For a critique of de Man's reading of the Coleridgean symbol that is similar to my own, see Thomas McFarland, "Involute and Symbol," *Coleridge, Keats, and the Imagination*, eds. Barth and Mahoney (Columbia and London: University of Missouri Press, 1990), 29-57.

[21]*Coleridge* (New York: Collier Books, 1968), 185.

[22]Cited from Eugene Webb's fine discussion of participationist thought in *Eric Voegelin: Philosopher of History* (Seattle and London: University of Washington Press, 1987), 72-73. In order for Webb's phrase to make sense, one must, of course, resist hypostatizing—in nominalist fashion—the phrase "Being as such" into merely one entity or thing among others.

[23]See Ricoeur's *Freud and Philosophy : An Essay in Interpretation*, trans. Denis Savage (New Haven and London: Yale University Press, 1970), 9.

[24](New York: Chelsea House, 1985), I, xx.

[25]In *Republic* 367a, Adeimantus laments, what justice is "in itself, by its own inherent force, when it is within the soul of the possessor and escapes the eyes of both gods and men, no one has ever adequately set forth in poetry or prose." One implication of this passage is that this theme will find its poet in the Plato of the prose-poem known as the *Republic.* In *Plato's Defence of Poetry* (Albany: State University of New York Press, 1984), Julius A. Elias similarly argues that throughout his works Plato offers a defense of poetry that answers his own objections.

[26]*Plato: An Introduction,* trans. Hans Meyerhoff (Princeton: Princeton University Press, 1973), 123.

[27]Beginning of Chapter 9 ("Play: From the Pharmakon to the Letter and from Blindness to the Supplement") of "Plato's Pharmacy," 156.

[28]Letter VI 323d; cited by Derrida as part of the epigraph to Chapter Nine of "Plato's Pharmacy" (156).

[29]"Des hommes donc—sans spécification de sexe—demeuraient dans un mème lieu. Temps mème, dans un mème lieu. Lieu qui aurait la forme d'un antre, ou ventre." In the translation of Gillian C. Gill: *"As the story goes, then, men—with no specification of sex—are living in one, same, place. A place shaped like a cave or womb" (Speculum de l'autre femme* [Paris: Les Éditions de Minuit], 301; *Speculum of the Other Woman* [Ithaca: Cornell University Press, 1985], 243).

[30]306; 246-7.

[31]*In Search of Order*, 116.

[32]See the beginning of David Halperin's essay, in this volume, for a good discussion of the complicated narrative frame of the *Symposium.*

[33]Trans. Suzy Q Groden, *The Symposium of Plato* (University of Massachusetts Press, 1970), 37-38. English quotations from the *Symposium* will be cited from the Groden translation.

[34]Who, as Plutarch tells us, dreamed that he was dressed in women's clothes the night before he died (*Alcibiades* 39). "In the soul of this proudly aggressive man," Martha Nussbaum interestingly speculates, Alcibiades' dream "expresses the wish for unmixed passivity" (*The Fragility of Goodness: Luck and Ethics in Greek Tragedy and Philosophy* [Cambridge: Cambridge University Press, 1986], 199). Plato symbolizes philosophical *erôs*—of which Alcibiades is finally incapable— as partaking of both activity and passivity. What Alcibiades could not achieve in reality thus expressed its repressed self, with a vengeance, in a dream.

[35]It would not be quite correct to translate this, into common parlance, as "safe sexism." "Prophylactic phallocentrism" might be taken as metonomy for a general Platonic strategy that David Halperin will point out in his essay. Plato, Halperin says, goes about "systematically undermining and subverting the very theories that his philosophical *personae* propound"; as opposed to Derrida, however, Halperin believes that Plato knows what he is doing and that we, as readers, "must come to terms with Plato's . . . determination not to leave his readers with a body of dogma" (infra, 62). Cf. Plato's use of the word *politeia* in the myth of Er, where Plato appears to be subverting the huge edifice of the *Republic.* Er is observing the first person, among a group of pilgrims, who chooses a lot for his next life. This person makes the tragic mistake of impulsively choosing the life of a despot and, when he realizes the horrors this life will bring to fruition, he begins "to beat his breast and bewail his choice." Then we are presented with one of the startling reasons that this person made the poor choice he did. He had, it turns out, spent his previous life "in a well-ordered commonwealth" (*politeia*) and had therefore "become virtuous from habit without pursuing wisdom" (619). Because he lived in a perfect republic (*politeia*)—*politeia* is Plato's word for the city his work sketches out as well as the title which by which his work came to be known—our first protagonist in the drama of choosing a life makes a choice that is tragic. Does this imply, as Derrida might suggest, that the *Republic* has no foundation, that Plato's elaborate construction of the castle of his

Republic in the air with this passage comes tumbling down? Is the *Republic,* in other words, undoing itself? I would rather give Plato the benefit of the doubt and suggest that perhaps he knew what he was doing, or undoing. Plato was interested in articulating, by counter-example, what was profoundly wrong with contemporary Athens. But his construction of a paradigmatic *politeia* was, to a large extent, a metaphor through which he wished to sketch out the contours of the human soul. Those who wish to read the *Republic* as a literalist blueprint for constructing a utopia, therefore, will be profoundly misreading Plato's intention. For if anyone were literally to inhabit such a *politeia,* this person might well, by Plato's own account, paradoxically be ensuring his enslavement to the life of the tyrant in his next life. The *politeia,* therefore, is not necessarily a place in the spatio-temporal world, but refers to the constitution of the soul. Earlier in Book X, Plato specifically differentiates between an actual *politeia* and the *politeia* within each individual's soul (608). I am grateful to Louis Orsini for pointing out to me Plato's charged reference to the *politeia* of the soul at the conclusion of the *Republic.*

[36]"Was Plato a Feminist?" *Times Literary Supplement,* No. 4,485 (March 17-23, 1989), 276-289. For a less positive assessment of Plato's attitude towards women, see Julia Annas, "Plato's *Republic* and Feminism," *Philosophy* 51 (1976), 307-321. On the Platonic "appropriation" of the reproductive images associated with the female body, see the last chapter of Page duBois' *Sowing the Body: Psychoanalysis and Ancient Representations of Women* (Chicago: University of Chicago Press, 1988). DuBois' reading of Plato is marked by the very same tendency we have noted in Irigaray's reading of the cave analogy: duBois' reading, like Irigaray's, tips the balance—in Gebhardt's words—on the side of "the finality of truth experienced and articulated historically" rather than on "the language's position in an ongoing, open-ended process."

[37]Cited from the translation by Alan Bass in *Critical Theory Since 1965,* 122. The essay "Différance" was first published in 1968.

[38]*Ibid.,* 134.

[39]*Ibid.*

[40]The passage in his *oeuvre* that should forever discourage the association of Plato with idealist absolutism is the description of the battle between the materialist giants and the idealist gods who maintain "with all their force that true reality consists in certain intelligible and bodiless forms" (246c). Real being, the Athenian stranger goes on to argue, exists in the "intercourse" (248b) between becoming and absolute being. The importance of this Platonic passage for the history of literary theory is well discussed by Wesley Trimpi in *Muses of One Mind: The Literary Analysis of Experience and its Continuity* (Princeton: Princeton University Press, 1983), 106-116.

[41]Cf. M. Nussbaum, who criticizes the tendency in some recent literary theory "to respond to the putative collapse of unqualified metaphysical realism (the view that we have truth only when we have a completely unmediated and noninterpretative access to the structure of reality as it is in itself) by espousing some form of radical subjectivism, relativism, or skepticism.... The literary world's lack of interest in . . . alternatives [to radical subjectivism, relativism, and skepticism] seems to betray an excessive attachment to metaphysical realism itself" (*Love's Knowledge: Essays on Philosophy and Literature* [New York and Oxford: Oxford University Press, 1990], 229). See also Jasper Neel, who suggests that "Derrida suffers from a radically

oversimplified, even nostalgic, conception of what Plato, and other thinkers since his time, considered truth to be" (*Plato, Derrida, and Writing,* 197).

[42]Voegelin suggests that the science of "metaphysics" is an example of the deformation of philosophical experiences and their symbolization into doctrines, and he reflects as follows on the philological origin of the word: "the term *metaphysics* is not a Greek term but an Arabic deformation of the Greek title of Aristotle's *meta ta physica;* ... [I]t had been taken over from the Arabs by Thomas and for the first time used in a Western language in the introduction to his commentary on Aristotle's *Metaphysics;* and ... ever since there existed an odd science that was called metaphysics.... [T]he cliché 'metaphysics' has become the magic word by which one can cast a shadow on all philosophical analysis in the Classic sense" (*Autobiographical Reflections* [Baton Rouge and London: Louisiana State University Press, 1989], 79-80).

by Eugene Webb

Socrates, Modernity, and the Problem of a Genuine Postmodernism

The term "postmodernism" is used in so many ways in such a variety of realms—philosophical, literary, artistic, and social—that it is difficult to know what the word is supposed to mean, except that it must refer to something not modern that comes after and presumably makes an advance upon modernism. This, however, is a start, and it suggests a challenging problem: to understand what "modernism" is (or was) in such a way as to see how one might go beyond it without lapsing from it, i.e., without falling back from it into what it was itself in some ways an advance upon. Phrased in this way, this seems a challenge that cannot help but call to mind Kierkegaard's description of the challenge that faced him in the *Philosophical Fragments*: to make an advance upon Socrates and yet say essentially the same things as he, only not nearly so well.

Before proceeding directly to the bearing of Socrates' and Plato's thought on a possible critique and transcendence of modernism, however, I would like to cite as two seminal texts for this discussion a statement by one of the major figures of modernism, Ludwig Wittgenstein, and another not by but about another major modern figure who is also frequently invoked as at least an incipient postmodern, Martin Heidegger.

Friedrich Waismann reports that, in response to Moritz Schlick's suggestion that the idea that good is grounded in God's nature is more profound than the idea that it proceeds from divine command, Wittgenstein argued that this would imply the fallacy that value could be rationally analyzed; to end the discussion he said finally, "Gut ist was Gott befiehlt" (Good is whatever God commands).[1] Wittgenstein remained faithful throughout his career, and despite the radical changes his thought underwent in the shift from the *Tractatus* to the *Philosophical Investigations*, to the belief that fact and value constitute two different realms, the latter of which lies beyond the analytic capabilities of reason and language.[2]

The statement about Heidegger is by Jean-François Lyotard, himself one of the leading voices of "postmodernism," in his recent book, Heidegger et "les juifs."[3] Lyotard uses the term "the Jews" to stand not for just any people of Jewish descent but specifically for those who are committed to the Jewish sense of a divine calling to take seriously questions of right and wrong. He says that whereas Heidegger spoke of a "forgetfulness of being" in the Western philosophical tradition descending from the Greeks, there has also existed alongside it all the while the "other" tradition of the Jews, a non-Western people in the midst of the West, that has served to remind us of our forgetfulness not of Being but of "the Law." That, he says, is the really significant point of the question about Heidegger's association with the Nazis: "that Nazism tried to make us forget once and for all the idea of something owed, of the difference between good and evil" (135).

The question of right and wrong, in the tradition of the Jews, can be fully meaningful only if it includes a consideration of one's relation to God and to one's neighbor—that is, if it takes seriously the question of "the other." This, however, raises a point Lyotard does not bring up but one that is essential to the question he does raise about Heidegger's relation to "the Jews" and one that penetrates, I think, to the heart of the problematic character of Heidegger's thought: the ambiguous status in it of the "other" as such. Heidegger talks at length of the "call" of conscience, but what that is a call to is strictly a relation to oneself, that is, to authentic consciousness of one's "ownmost" possibility, which is primarily the possibility of choosing to face with open eyes one's own mortality. Not only is there no real place in Heidegger's thought for the alterity of a genuinely "other" person, but when he does speak of others it is either as potential sources of temptation to inauthenticity ("the *they*") or else as models to be used as instruments in one's own quest for authenticity. Even when he speaks explicitly of "otherness," it has nothing to do with the possibility of a relation to a personal other, a "thou"; it is only that which he says one can discover when "an experience of Being as sometimes *other* than everything that *is* comes to us in dread,"[4] i.e., the otherness of death, and his discussion of a possible "authentic being with others" is only a fellowship in the confrontation with death. Heidegger's is a philosophy with an "I" and an "it" but no real "thou," either human or divine, and no place for a theory of obligation involving a relation to a personal other. It is also a call to heroism without a theory of value that could explain what is good about heroism as such or why one hero might serve as a better model than another.

The call to face resolutely one's death sounds bracing, and one can understand the appeal it has had. There are, however, some things one cannot help but wonder about when one hears it. One is whether there might not be more to existential fullness than just resoluteness in the face of death, whether there might not be some more positive plenitude intrinsically worth seeking. Another is whether Heidegger's notion of heroism is not also rather limited. Both issues have to do ultimately with matters of value, a topic that—despite what seem value-charged connotations to such terms as "authentic" and "inauthentic," "resoluteness" and "hero"—Heidegger explicitly sets aside in favor of what he intends as a purely descriptive, non-evaluative phenomenology of Dasein. One may well ask, however, whether there is not some deep evasiveness, perhaps even "inauthenticity," involved in the attempt to formulate a conception of existential heroism without addressing the question of the good. In fact one cannot help but wonder in this connection, whether Plato's idea of the Agathon might not be worth thinking about more carefully if the alternative to it is something as restricted as Heidegger's "authenticity," and also ultimately as arbitrary—just as the "good" commanded by Wittgenstein's God may be said to have been arbitrary.

These two texts, then, point, I think, to a central problem of modernism that a genuine postmodernism, if such a thing should ever come into being, will have to deal with. As Lyotard's comment, as well as what might be speculated about in the as yet unwritten critique, "Paul de Man et *les juifs,*" might suggest, this is a problem that currently haunts like a guilty conscience both modernism and what usually passes for "postmodernism."

In his commitment to the phenomenological bracketing of the question of the good, Heidegger seems a characteristically modern thinker, but he is also frequently cited as one of the originators of the postmodern movement. This dual status of Heidegger's thought is also indicated by the ambiguity of his relation to Socrates. Like Nietzsche, and probably following his lead, Heidegger made Socrates something of a whipping boy for the ills of modern thought. Nietzsche seems to have blamed Socrates both for the imprisonment of western philosophical thought in metaphysics and for his own guilty Christian conscience, which he hoped his Overman would break free from for the sake of the Will to Power. Heidegger blamed Socrates and Plato and all their heritage for imposing on western thought the shackles of the metaphysics of being, and he made his own project the Destruktion of the western philosophical tradition, which he hoped to accomplish by a return to pre-Socratic thinking.[5] In attempting to do this, he was, of course, acting in a quintessentially modern manner, declaring an epochal break in history and exalting an earlier, supposedly purer tradition in order to extirpate from his mind the traces of his own despised ancestors. To accomplish this, however, he had to try to perform with regard to the thinking he opposed the kind of dialectical critique of which Plato's Socrates was the West's premier teacher. In doing so, he imitated willy-nilly the historical Socrates as one who had tried to sort out what could be known concretely from what was merely abstract verbiage. In this effort too Heidegger was following, perhaps unwittingly, a longstanding modern tradition that at one time had looked to Socrates for its inspiration as it tried to make an epochal break with its predecessors.

Socrates was, in fact, something of a patron saint of modernity in its first stirrings. He was invoked by the humanists of the renaissance as a model of rationality and one who might help them to deliver themselves from the superstitions of what they were beginning to call the "middle age" in contrast to Socrates's "ancient" and their own "modern" ages.[6] Modernity as they conceived it had to involve first of all a recovery of the wisdom of the ancients in order that standing on their shoulders they might see further than they had. Perhaps Socrates may also eventually serve to point the way toward a genuine postmodernity.

One of the the most basic ways of understanding modernity was, of course, that just mentioned: as the point of an epochal break with the past, the idea that the modern is what is radically different from and better than what came before it. That claim has been made by so many, however, and in such a variety of ways that it is not always clear what exactly the newness of modernism is supposed to have been.

One analyst of modernism has asserted "an equivalence between modernity and the kind of consciousness called in philosophy *critical,*" by which he explicitly said he meant Kantianism.[7] There is a point to this, as we will see in a moment. A good case can be made, however, for tracing modernism back considerably further, especially since Kant himself can be said to have been rooted in the previous modernisms of figures like Hume, who Kant said awoke him from his dogmatic slumbers, and Descartes, who first formulated as an explicit program the rejection of all earlier thought and its replacement by such truths as could be known with mathematical certainty using his own up to date methods of radical doubt and reasoning of the sort exemplified preeminently by his own new science of analytic geometry. Or one could follow Hans Blumenberg[8] in tracing the roots of modernism back still further, well before Descartes, to the nominalism of William of Ockham in the fourteenth century, which came to be known even in the late Middle Ages as the *via moderna*, in contrast to the *via antiqua* of the main medieval tradition of thought.[9]

To identify the defining feature of modernist thought seems at first a bit simpler than pinning down its origin, since all the thinkers just mentioned share one major assumption: that whereas people of the past tended to be deficient in their grasp of the powers of rationality, the "moderns" know how to think rationally and are determined to do so, giving credence to no other truth-claims than those they can establish themselves by their own reasoning processes. This, however, is only one aspect of modernism, and perhaps not the one that is most important.

Anthony J. Cascardi has argued recently that the truly central feature of modernism is not its conception of itself as "the age in which reason definitively prevailed," but rather its belief in "the mutual exclusion of reason and activities with value-dependent goals," the idea commonly known as the fact-value dichotomy: "the model of reason as mathematical representation," says Cascardi, "is only one side of a coin which also projects a vision of desires and of the will as beyond all rational control."[10]

To speak of desire and will brings us to a central point of Socratic thought that contrasts sharply with modernism: the idea that will and desire are distinguished by the fact that will is rational and desire is not, that the purpose of the philosophical calling is not speculative knowledge but the care of the soul and the cultivation of genuine will through the control of desire and its subordination to reason.

The question of the relation between desire and will is also a point at which we can see the relevance of Wittgenstein's comment regarding the idea that the good is whatever God commands. In his discussion with Schlick, which echoed a controversy of the thirteenth and fourteenth centuries, Wittgenstein was taking the position of Ockham and the *via moderna* against Schlick's, uncharacteristic and perhaps unwitting, advocacy of that of the *via antiqua* as represented by such figures as Dante, Aquinas, and Bonaventure, with roots going back to Socrates' claim that virtue is knowledge of the good and that no person willingly does evil.

Aquinas, to cite the most systematic of the thinkers in the *via antiqua*, had argued in essence that God necessarily wills the good because he wills his own being and because being and good are identical. The Socratic roots of these positions can be seen from the arguments Aquinas gives for them. Regarding the latter point he said, for example:

> Good and being are really the same.... The essence of good consists in this, that it is in some way desirable. Hence the Philosopher [i.e., Aristotle] says "The good is what all desire." Now it is clear that a thing is desirable only in so far as it is perfect; for all desire their own perfection. But everything is perfect so far as it is in act. Therefore it is clear that a thing is good so far as it is being; for it is being [that] is the actuality of all things.[11]

Regarding the corollary idea that God wills the good necessarily, Aquinas said: "For the divine will has a necessary relation to the divine goodness [i.e., His own perfection of being], since that is its proper object. Hence God wills His own goodness necessarily, even as we will our own happiness."[12]

Although it was Aristotle Aquinas cited as a philosophical source, it was from Plato and Socrates before him that Aristotle had learned to think of the good as that which all desire when they properly understand their desires, and it was also from them that he learned to think of happiness as the ultimate goal of all human action, whether or not that goal is clearly understood.

What Ockham argued, on the other hand, was that any necessity governing God's will would be a restriction of His freedom and a diminution of his sovereign majesty. Consequently he held that the good was not identical with being but was whatever God arbitrarily declared it to be by an act of his absolute power.

To return to more recent thinking and to someone set aside temporarily a few moments ago, another figure that probably lay behind Wittgenstein's position, as he lies behind almost everything else in modern continental thought, is Immanuel Kant. Kant took over the fact-value dichotomy from David Hume and worked out his own solution to it, but one that left the dichotomy itself intact. The good for Kant was what could be known through logical reasoning as a systematic, universal imperative. Interestingly, the structure of Kant's thought here parallels that of Aquinas in a certain respect, in that his categorical imperative has as its ultimate justification that it makes for action that accords with the nature of a rational man, as Aquinas's God had willed the good because it was in accord with his nature to do so. The important difference, however, is that with Kant the good is conceived, somewhat in Ockham's manner, as the object of an imperative rather than of appetite. Aquinas had said that both God and His rational creatures necessarily act in accord with their nature to pursue their happiness, insofar as they understand it. One of the basic features of Kant's thought, on the other hand, was that it separated the question of the good entirely from considerations of happiness. Even an objectively good act that might bring with it some intrinsic satisfaction could not be considered a moral act for Kant unless it was done for the sake of duty rather than enjoyment. And even apart from the question of the moral status of the act, knowledge of the good would not in itself lead to good action.

This is as about far as one can get from Socrates, for whom knowledge and virtue went hand in hand and for whom the whole purpose of philosophy was not the development of abstract notions of right and wrong but the development of the soul's capacity to love concretely its own good, which is to say, its possibility of fullness of life. It has become a truism of the tradition deriving from Kant to say that Socrates and Plato were simple-minded in thinking the way they did, since it is taken as obvious that wicked people know quite well that they are acting wickedly and do so anyway, but to say this is really to miss Plato's point. Werner Jaeger stated the issue well when he said that "[f]or Socrates, it is no contradiction of the statement *virtue is knowledge* to say that in the experience of most men knowing good is not the same as doing it. That experience merely shows that real knowledge is rare."[13]

Where, then, did the modern separation of fact from value and desire from the good come from? Although there is scarcely time here to do justice to the subject, I will suggest that it comes, at least in part, from a genuine advance in the differentiation of consciousness of which the early modern thinkers became acutely aware—even if they may have exaggerated their own role as its originators.

The development of which I am speaking is the differentiation, both theoretical and experiential, of the full range of intentional operations by which it becomes possible to operate distinctly in attending first to the data of experience, then second to the act of interpreting those data by construing them in intelligible configurations, and third to critical reflection and judgment regarding the adequacy of such construings, then finally fourth to questions about how to act in the context of the reality that can be known through the careful performance of the first three levels of operation.

It is essential to a proper understanding of this analysis to bear in mind that all of these operations are driven by what might be described as an *eros* of consciousness, a fundamental dynamism of questioning that moves one to reach beyond mere experience to seek intelligible patterns in the data of experience (real or imaginative), and then further to reach beyond mere ideas to a grasp of reality through critical reflection on the adequacy of ideas to real experience and of courses of action to real situations. It was this dynamism Aristotle was referring to when he said at the beginning of his *Metaphysics* (980a), "All men desire to know," and then went on to speak of the delight we take in the exercise of our senses (i.e., the first level of intentional operation) and of how wonder about "the *why*" of things moves us on toward the pursuit of wisdom through understanding and knowledge (the second and third levels of operation).[14] In the *Nicomachean Ethics* he describes how the capacity for good decision (the fourth level of operation) is developed. Aristotle assumes that this presupposes a successful performance on the first three levels because, as he puts it, "each man judges well the things he knows, and of these he is a good judge" (1094b29).[15]

Viewed in the light of this schema,[16] it is easy to understand that fact and value are known by distinct but interrelated operations, the first three levels of operation in the case of fact, and in that of value, the fourth. That this need imply no problem of a dichotomy is clear from the facts that (1) the *eros* that drives the operations on all four levels is a reaching toward the specific satisfactions (i.e., values) to be gained in and by their successful performance, and (2) all of the higher level operations are cumulative—that is, they are founded upon the successful performance of each of the lower levels of operation. Just as reality, the world of fact, is known by careful acts of attention, interpretation, and critical reflection and judgment, so value can only be known adequately by the cumulative performance of all four levels of operation. The true good differs from apparent good precisely in that apparent good is what appeals only to the data of experience on the first level, that is, pleasurable sensation, whereas, true value is the good not merely of sense but of the rational person living with genuine understanding in the full context of reality. This, of course, is precisely what Socrates was driving at when he talked about the difference between desire and will and said that "real will," to cite Jaeger's paraphrase, "exists only when based on true knowledge of the good at which it is directed" whereas "mere desire is an effort aimed towards apparent goods."[17]

It was fascination with the powers that might come from a differentiated capacity for critical reflection and judgment that gave rise to the early modern hope of a complete cognitive and practical mastery of the material world, but it was also the incompleteness of that very process of cognitive and ethical self-appropriation that caused that hope to take the form of the characteristically modern effort of rationalistic system building. The entire tradition of philosophical idealism from Descartes through Leibniz to Hegel and beyond may be interpreted as an effort to elide the second and third levels and eclipse the fourth, that is, to know both reality and the good purely through the analysis of ideas—as is evidenced by the tendency of so many of the thinkers of that tradition to speak of geometry as the paradigmatic form of true knowledge in all domains.

In this, of course, they were following the lead of Plato himself, who seems also to have fallen under the enchantment of geometry and of the possibilities of certainty and completeness implicit in the theory of forms. To separate out the thought of Socrates from that of the Plato through whom we mainly know him is a notorious crux of philosophical history, but one thing that seems to stand out about the Socrates described in all sources is that he was unusually sensitive to the kind of critical question that makes system builders uncomfortable. Various commentators have suggested that the reason Plato had to replace Socrates with the Athenian Stranger in his last, fundamentally didactic (even if outwardly dialogical) writing, the *Laws*, is that the kind of direct exposition of Platonic doctrine there presented would so obviously have been out of character in the mouth of the ever probing, self-questioning Socrates. Alasdair MacIntyre even speaks of the *Laws* as turning Socrates from a hero into a potential victim, whose fidelity to the promptings of doubt would have marked him for elimination by the Nocturnal Council described in Book 12: "His prosecutors would have had an even easier task in Magnesia than they had in Athens."[18] Socrates, our perennial "other," has had an ambiguous history in the mind of the West from the start. In his life and trial in Athens, in the dialogues of Plato, for the Renaissance humanists, for Nietzsche, and now perhaps also for ourselves again, he vacillates in our perceptions between ally and enemy, savior and outcast.

It seems that his time to be an ally is returning. When one speaks now of "postmodernism," one of the things it usually is taken to include is a radical critique and "deconstruction" of the "beautiful totalities" the system builders of modern philosophical idealism were trying to construct and of which the shade of Socrates continues to be the remorseless gadfly. Let us hope he can also escape his usual fate as a victim this time around. The postmodernism that may give him a new lease on life is itself a sufficiently new and ambiguous phenomenon that one cannot be sure where it will lead. In some respects it seems, despite the irrationalism that sometimes appears on its fringe, a further advance in the development of the critically reflective capacity in thought of which he has always been a symbol. And in its emphasis on the erotic dimension of experience it sometimes seems to be reaching beyond mere hedonism toward the possibility, at least, of a renewed, more critically grounded eudaimonistic ethic. And yet something else one cannot help but notice in it also, despite its air of defiant cheerfulness, is a note of nostalgia and disappointment, perhaps even of bitterness—as if the failure to attain the System with a capital "S," as Kierkegaard liked to call it, had become a matter of such chagrin to the generation that realized its impossibility that irrationalism and hedonism seem tempting alternatives. In this respect the thinking that goes by the name of "postmodernism" often seems rather a despairing version of late modernism than a real breakthrough beyond it—even if, as Kierkegaard phrased it, this can take the form of a despair that "in a kind of innocence does not even know that it is despair."[19]

Jean-François Lyotard, in fact, in his essay, "Answering the Question: What is Post-Modernism?" suggests it is really part and parcel of modernism itself—"Il fait assurément partie du moderne"—and that "a work cannot become modern except by being already postmodern" ("une oeuvre ne peut devenir moderne que si elle est d'abord postmoderne").[20] With a characteristically modern epochalism, the postmodern, he goes on to say, places under suspicion everything received from the past, even if from only yesterday, but with an "astonishing acceleration" so that the generations hurtle one after another into the wastebin of history. At the end, however, in what seems an appeal for a more genuinely postmodern postmodernism, he urges us to renounce our "modern" nostalgia for the whole and the one, for a totality of imaginative vision and understanding, lest we lapse back into the "terrorism" of a modernism that has not yet accepted its own inevitable frustration.[21]

Now this does seem to represent an advance of a sort, and one that Socrates himself might well have applauded. For modernism to renounce the terrorism by which, in its drive to possess once and for all a full and absolute system of truth, it has repeatedly excluded as virtually subhuman all of its predecessors except the few it considers harbingers of itself would at least make modernity more humane—both less bloody and more historically just. If we could give up our unfortunate habit of trying to excommunicate everyone who thought before us every time we begin to think we have finally understood something, we might not only extricate ourselves from an implicitly patricidal and fratricidal relation to our forebears and any other people who do not share our special "modern" experience, including an entire world of peoples outside the modern West, but we would also, perhaps, through respect for the universal humanity our "others" have shared with us, place ourselves in a position to gain access to the perspectives of their experience that might deliver us from the incestuous prison of our peculiar, distinctly limited rationality—perspectives that might contain what could become for us, too, the seeds of a neglected wisdom.

NOTES

[1] *Wittgenstein und der Wiener Kreis: Aus dem Nachlass*, ed. B. F. McGuiness. Oxford: Basil Blackwell, 1967, 115.

[2] Cf. Allan Janik and Stephen Toulmin, *Wittgenstein's Vienna* (New York: Simon and Schuster, 1973), 235-36.

[3] Paris: Galilée, 1988.

[4] "What is Metaphysics," trans. R. F. C. Hull and Alan Crick, in *Existence and Being* (London: Vision Press, 1949) 354.

[5] Luc Ferry and Alain Renaut, in *Heidegger and Modernity*, describe Heidegger as divided between seeing Nazism as on the one hand "a postmodern actualization of modernity, and on the other hand, the antimodern activity of a humanity linking up, against the decline of Europe, with the great Greek past" (quoted in "Bookmarks," *Philosophy and Literature* 14 [1990]: 450).

[6] Cf. Werner Jaeger, *Paideia: The Ideals of Greek Culture, 2: In Search of the Divine Centre*, trans. Gilbert Highet (New York: Oxford University Press, 1943), 13, 77. See also Tilo Schabert, "Modernity and History I: What is Modernity?" in Athanasios Moulakis, ed., *The Promise of History: Essays in Political Philosophy*, (Berlin and New York: Walter de Gruyter, 1986), 22-32. Schabert traces the origin of the symbol of "modernity" back to Cassiodorus in the sixth century A.D.

[7] Donald Marshall, in his preface to Stephen W. Melville's *Philosophy Beside Itself: On Deconstruction and Modernism* (Minneapolis: University of Minnesota Press, 1986), xii.

[8] *The Legitimacy of the Modern Age*, trans. Robert M. Wallace (Cambridge: MIT Press, 1983).

[9] Frederick C. Copleston, *A History of Philosophy, 3: Late Medieval and Renaissance Philosophy*, Part 1: *Ockham to the Speculative Mystics* (Garden City, New York: Image Books, 1963), 21.

[10] "Genealogies of Modernism," *Philosophy and Literature*, 11 (1987): 212 and 209. See also Alasdair Mac Intyre, *After Virtue* (Notre Dame, Indiana: Notre Dame University Press, 1982) and *Whose Justice, Which Rationality* (Notre Dame, Indiana: Notre Dame University Press, 1988).

[11] *Summa Theologica*, trans. Fathers of the English Dominican Province, I, q. 5, a. 1.

[12] *Summa Theologica*, I, q. 19, a. 3.

[13] *Paideia: The Ideals of Greek Culture* (New York: Oxford University Press, 1939-1944), 2: 65

[14] Richard McKeon, ed. *The Basic Works of Aristotle* (New York: Random House, 1941), 689-91.

[15] McKeon, 936.

[16] Aristotle's description of these levels of operation and their interrelations was, of course, only a beginning that has required a great deal of further analysis. See Bernard Lonergan, *Insight: A Study of Human Understanding*, 3rd ed. (New York: Philosophical Library, 1970), and

Eugene Webb, *Philosophers of Consciousness: Polanyi, Longergan, Voegelin, Ricoeur, Girard, Kierkegaard* (Seattle and London: University of Washington Press, 1988).

[17] *Paideia*, 3: 68.

[18] *A Short History of Ethics* (New York: Macmillan, 1956), 56.

[19] *The Sickness Unto Death*, ed. and trans., Howard V. Hong and Edna H. Hong (Princeton: Princeton University Press, 1980), 42.

[20] "Réponse à la question: qu'est-ce que le postmoderne?" *Critique*, 35, no. 419 (April, 1982): 365.

[21] Ibid., 367.

Part Two:
Dialogues with Postmodernism

by David M. Halperin

Plato and the Erotics of Narrativity

I

One of the most curious and seldom-remarked facts about Plato's dialogues is that many of them are not, in fact, dialogues. By this I do not mean that Plato's Dialogues are not "real" dialogues or "true" conversations (measured against some normative standard of conversational reciprocity): I am not about to lodge against Plato the routine liberal complaint that he fails to portray genuinely mutual, freewheeling discussions—choosing to represent, instead, a series of highly asymmetrical exchanges between Socrates (or some other Platonic mouthpiece), who does most of the talking, and various other, more or less coöperative, interlocutors, who (with the refreshing exceptions of Callicles in the *Gorgias* and Thrasymachus in the first book of the *Republic*) are largely "yes-men."[1] What I mean, rather, is that a number of Plato's so-called dialogues are not dialogues at all in the formal sense: their characteristic mode of representation is not dramatic but narrative.[2]

The formal, theoretical or conceptual, distinction between dramatic and narrative literature is not one that is likely to have been lost on Plato. For that very distinction originated with Plato himself.[3] In the third book of the *Republic*, Socrates divides literature into three kinds, according to whether it employs as its representational medium "simple narration" (*haplê diêgêsis*),[4] "imitation" (*mimêsis*), or a combination of the two (392d-394c). "Simple narration" is defined as that mode of representation in which the author does not conceal himself (393c11) but speaks to the audience in his own person (394c2-3) "without imitation" (393d1, 394a7-b1)—that is, without citing the direct speech of his characters and thereby impersonating or "imitating" them. "Simple narration" can be found mostly in dithyrambs, Socrates tells us (394c3); the late antique grammarian Servius added didactic poetry, as exemplified by the first three books of Virgil's *Georgics*, to the same category.[5] "Imitation" is originally introduced by Socrates in the *Republic* as an alternative to "simple narration": it is defined as narration that is effected through imitation, and it refers, in the first instance, to those passages in epic poetry in which the poet's characters speak *in propria persona* (392d5-6, 393c8-9); it is later defined more starkly, however, as "the opposite" to simple narration (394b3), and it comes to refer to the exchange of direct speeches between characters, such as occurs in tragedy and comedy (394b6-c2). A third representational mode, combining simple narration and imitation, is exemplified by epic poetry, and by many other (unmentioned) forms of literature (394c4-5).

Several of Plato's dialogues belong, interestingly enough, to this third mode, which later grammarians often called by the name of "mixed" narrative. It is a literary form that does not achieve anything like the purity, the freedom from "imitation," that characterizes the sort of "simple narration" that Socrates devises in the *Republic* by converting the exchange of speeches between Agamemnon and Chryses in the *Iliad's* opening episode into indirect discourse (393c11-394b1): on the contrary, it requires of the (vocalizing) reader very nearly the same histrionic antics as does drama. Moreover, Plato's "mixed" narratives are not narrated, after the manner of Homer or the historians, in anything approaching what we now call a third-person omniscient mode. Instead, Socratic conversations are *reported* in the first person without any preliminary introduction (as if they were addressed directly to the reader or to some silent interlocutor who never comes forward to claim the addressee's role) by a fictional, if historically grounded, character. That character usually turns out to be Socrates himself, as in the case of the *Charmides* (which begins, "We got back on the previous evening from Potidaea . . ."), the *Lysis* ("I was making my way from the Academy straight to the Lyceum . . ."), and, most notoriously, the *Republic* ("I went down yesterday to the Peiraeus with Glaucon . . ."); the bizarre exception is the *Parmenides*, which turns out to be narrated by Cephalus ("When we reached Athens from our home in Clazomenae . . ."), who recounts a Socratic dialogue as it was reported to him by Antiphon the elder, Plato's half-brother, who had himself heard it from Pythodorus.[6]

Even more intriguing are those dialogues which seem at first to have the form of drama—to consist of a conversation directly represented without the mediation of a narrative frame—but which quickly abandon that dramatic mode in favor of a "mixed" narrative by making one of the initial interlocutors into the uninterrupted narrator[7] of another entire conversation. Some of these dialogues are narrated by Socrates himself after a few preliminary, and rather desultory, exchanges with a member of his circle (as in the case of the *Protagoras* and the *Euthydemus*), but others consist of a Socratic conversation related by a third party to an entirely different audience in response to some brief, introductory request for a story. This latter type is exemplified by the *Phaedo* and by the *Symposium*.[8] Phaedo is prompted by the questions of Echecrates to embark on a lengthy account of Socrates' valedictory conversation with his friends; Apollodorus repeats, for the second time in three days, the story of what was said and done at Agathon's private victory celebration—this time, to a group of nameless acquaintances whose importunities actually *precede* the spirited exchange with which the text of the *Symposium* opens. Moreover, in all of these cases, except for the *Euthydemus*, the dramatic dialogue that introduces the narrative is not resumed at the end of it (although in the *Phaedo* the dramatic situation is at least alluded to in the final words of the dialogue), thereby leaving the dramatic frame—if that is what it can properly be called—incomplete and asymmetrical. Why does Plato adopt such a peculiar narrative strategy?

II

I should say right now that I don't propose to answer this question. I intend to pursue it, however, by examining the dialogue whose narrative structure Plato most fully thematizes: namely, the *Symposium*. That work also possesses—not coincidentally, we may assume—what is probably the most intricate compositional form of any of the dialogues. The *Symposium* begins with an exchange of remarks, in dramatic (or "true" dialogue) form, between Apollodorus, a devoted follower of Socrates, and some unnamed acquaintances. Apollodorus has just been asked, apparently, to tell the story of Agathon's victory party—a story he had related, he says, to another acquaintance, named Glaucon, two days before—and after some further banter with his friends he accedes to their request. His narrative occupies the remainder of Plato's text, which concludes when Apollodorus comes to what is presumably the end of his story: we never learn what response, if any, his auditors make to it. Apollodorus, however, did not himself attend Agathon's party, which in fact took place many years before the conversation that he is currently engaged in; he can only recapitulate the narrative handed down to him by Aristodemus, an earlier and equally devoted admirer of Socrates, who did attend. The centerpiece of Aristodemus' narrative is a speech about the nature of *erôs* made by Socrates to Agathon and his assembled guests; that speech itself contains a lengthy narrative describing another conversation on the same subject between Socrates and one Diotima, a Mantineian prophetess, and that conversation in turn culminates in yet another speech by Diotima, also about the nature of *erôs*, which is reported by Socrates virtually without concluding comment.

The formal literary structure of the *Symposium*, then, is that of a dialogue which contains within it a series of inset narratives, each of them containing another dialogue and each of them taking the reader further away in time from the dramatic date of the conversation between Apollodorus and his acquaintances. Each framing narrative recedes to disclose another nested inside it, one containing the next like a set of lacquered Chinese boxes. Nor does Plato attempt to make this series of insets transparent to the reader by dissolving the sequence of narrative frames through an illusion of dramatic immediacy, of the reader's direct access to the events narrated. On the contrary: with the chief exception of Diotima's speech, which for a few pages occupies the entire foreground of the narrative, Plato constantly reminds the reader of the many narrators that intervene between the reader and the transmitted story—he emphasizes the *reported* character of the account—by sprinkling throughout Apollodorus' narrative such phrases as "he said that he said" (*ephê phanai* or, simply, *phanai*), phrases often omitted in translation through a wish to avoid unnecessary awkwardness but so copious in the original as to make the text of the *Symposium* an ideal object lesson in the use of indirect discourse in Attic Greek.[9] Thus, the earliest event depicted, Diotima's refutation of Socrates, reaches us by an elaborate, lengthy, and rather devious process of transmission. Indeed, that process of transmission (as it is described in the opening pages of the dialogue) is even more complicated than this preliminary summary has indicated; if one were to represent the descent by oral tradition of Diotima's discourse in the form customarily reserved for conveying the transmission of written texts in a manuscript tradition, the stemma would look something like this:

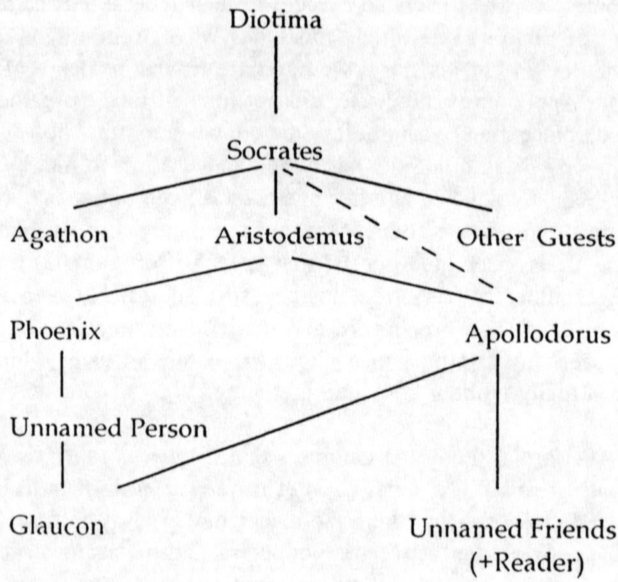

(Unbroken lines indicate direct descent; the broken line indicates "contamination.")

Moreover, the opening of the *Symposium* emphasizes, by means of the very language Apollodorus uses in speaking to his friends, that what is about to follow will be a report, a narrative (*diêgêsis*), not a dialogue of the sort that is currently taking place between Apollodorus and the assembled company. Glaucon tells Apollodorus (in the latter's recounting of their conversation) that someone who had heard the story of Agathon's party from Phoenix *narrated* it to him, Glaucon, though ineptly; he then asks Apollodorus to *narrate* it to him in turn; Apollodorus remarks that Glaucon's *narrator* had evidently not *narrated* the story clearly; who *narrated* the story to you?, Glaucon inquires; Socrates' account agreed with what Aristodemus *narrated*, Apollodorus assures us; well, then, *narrate* it to me now, Glaucon urges; if I have to *narrate* it to you as well, Apollodorus tells his unnamed interlocutors, I'll try to *narrate* it to you from the beginning as he *narrated* it to me (172b3-174a2). I have, of course, been over-translating for the sake of emphasis: Plato's usage, far from sounding so odd as my rendering would suggest, is (as always) in perfectly good Greek style, which seeks rather then eschews redundancy and employs *diêgêsis* for the recounting of a story. Nonetheless, Plato's insistence is remarkable and significant: if any doubts remain on that score, one need only compare the opening of the *Theaetetus*. There Plato, for reasons of his own, takes a pointedly opposite tack, underscoring his preference for the dramatic over the narrative mode of representation. Euclides has heard from Socrates a *narrative* (142d1) of the latter's earlier *dialogue* (142c7, c8-d1) with Theaetetus, has taken notes at the time, written it all out later, checked it repeatedly with Socrates, and now possesses a complete written transcript of it; when asked specifically for the *narrative* (142d5), however, Euclides explains that his account is written in *dialogue* form (143b7), not in *narrative* form (143b6-7: each term occurs twice, for the sake of emphasis), because, he says, "I wanted to avoid in the written account the tiresome effect of bits of *narrative* interrupting the speeches, such as 'and I said' or 'and I remarked' wherever Socrates was speaking himself, and 'he assented' or 'he did not agree,' where he reported the answer. So I left out everything of that sort, and wrote it as a *dialogue* between the actual speakers" (143b8-c5; trans. Cornford, with modifications). The procedure described by Euclides exactly reverses what Plato has done in the case of the *Symposium*. Plato's deliberate avoidance in the *Theaetetus*, then, of both oral transmission (in the work's dramatic register) and of narrative structure (in its formal register) must be programmatic for that dialogue and is doubtless intended to contrast with the representational strategy chosen by Plato for the *Symposium*.

The elaborate and bizarrely complex compositional form of the *Symposium* can be accounted for in at least two ways that do not refer directly to the philosophical doctrines enunciated in the dialogue. First, Plato's choice of historical setting and his spacing of the various conversations at temporal removes from one another create a retrospective irony: by granting the reader more knowledge about what life has in store for the interlocutors than any one of them possesses at any given moment, Plato imparts to their words a significance of which they themselves are unaware. He thereby puts the reader in a position to judge "how the mettle of their characters, the value of their aspirations—their loves—have withstood the test of time."[10] Their lives and loves can now be measured against their words and convictions, which lie under the posthumous judgment of history and fate. Plato invites his reader, in short, to subject the symposiasts' respective notions of *erôs* to "biographical criticism." Second, Plato projects the speeches about *erôs* backwards to a period when Athenian power was at its height and all of the speakers were enjoying great personal prosperity.[11] The exuberance of Agathon and his guests, the brilliance of their conversation, and their supreme sense of self-confidence express not only a certain personal vitality but also the cultural energy of Athens at the moment of its hollow triumph in the first phase of the Peloponnesian War. All the persons depicted in the *Symposium*, moreover, with the possible exceptions of Aristophanes and Socrates (depending on how much of a Platonist you are), are poised on the brink of disastrous personal and political careers. By glancing back to a moment in time when the consequences of these men's convictions and choices had not yet unfolded, by retracing the stages of their precipitous decline to its imagined inception, Plato seems to locate a cause for the fall of Athens and for the ruin of its leading citizens in a failure of love, in the vicissitudes of a misguided *erôs*.

III

The receding narrative frames accomplish another purpose, however, in which the erotic theory adumbrated in the *Symposium* appears to be directly implicated. The complex structure of Apollodorus' narrative serves to illustrate that theory. For it manifests the workings of desire.

Erôs, according to Diotima, is a principle of self-perpetuation in mortal natures: it springs from a sense of lack, of limitation, pursues a fullness of being that forever eludes it, and in the course of that ongoing struggle establishes a tenuous hold on existence, on presence. As a great daemon, *erôs* mediates between the divine world of being and the mortal world of becoming (202e3-203a1); as the offspring of *Penia* and *Poros*, of Poverty and Means, *erôs* is neither mortal nor immortal: rather, it oscillates continually between being and non-being, between presence and absence, by turns thriving and dying and coming back to life on the very same day (203d8-e3). These fluctuations reflect more than the periodic waxing and waning of sexual appetite. They describe the dialectic of presence and absence—of possession and loss, gratification and frustration, pleasure and pain—that structures the phenomenology of desire and informs the relation of the erotic soul to its objects. For it is the nature of beauty, and of all the objects we most passionately desire, everlastingly to renew the desire they defeat, at once ministering to our sense of lack and deepening it—like Shakespeare's Cleopatra in Enobarbus' famous description, who "makes hungry / Where most she satisfies." In such a precarious fashion *erôs* maintains identity through time: it represents an element of fixity amid the endless cycles of change; it is the source of whatever (illusory) permanence or continuity obtains in the realm of mortal affairs.

Erôs achieves its ends by means of procreation—by the continual production of something new or young to replace what is old and dying (207d2-3, 208b1-2). Among the beasts (207a7-d3, 208a7-b5), and among those human beings who resemble them insofar as their erotic desire expresses itself in a bodily fashion (208e1-5), procreation is a physical process of giving birth (*genesis*): one member of a species produces another to replace it and the race as a whole endures over time (207d2-208b6; cf. *Laws* 721bc). But procreation is not confined to the replacement of one individual by another in a species: it also takes place *within* each individual and secures a kind of identity for that person through time. Just as our hair and flesh and bones and blood and all our body is constantly dying and being renewed, so are our habits, character, opinions, appetites, enjoyments, pains, and fears all subject to fluctuation: the self is destroyed and reborn from one moment to the next (207d2-e5). The mind itself is not exempt from our mortal condition (in Diotima's view [207e5-208b4], if not according to the Socrates of the *Phaedo*).[12] The *tropos* (208a7) or *mêchanê* (208b2), the procreative manner or mechanism internal to the human individual that is responsible for implanting permanence in the flux of thought, thereby enabling us to retain knowledge, is not *genesis*, or giving birth, however, but *meletê*: "care," "study," or "practice" (208a3-7). Practice preserves knowledge by recreating it anew and preventing it from being lost through forgetfulness.

The compositional form of the *Symposium* appears, in the first instance at least, to corroborate Diotima's erotic doctrine. The sequence of inset narratives effects the recovery of some historical incidents and some intellectual insights that might otherwise have been lost; it rescues them from human forgetfulness, enabling them (in Diotima's phrase) to partake of immortality (208b3). Indeed, on a pious reading of the *Symposium*, the continual renewal and successful preservation of Diotima's discourse by means of the self-regenerating narrative represented in the dialogue may furnish a clue to the sublime wisdom and beauty, perhaps even to the divinity, of her erotic doctrine. In any case, the series of receding narratives has the effect of making present to the reader a number of moments in the past, plucking them from the eternal flow of time and preserving them, stabilizing their identity without, however, denying their transience. The attempt to recapture lost time is marked by Plato (no less than by Proust) as an expression of desire: the successive narrators and enduring narrative of the *Symposium* enact the very processes of loss and renewal, of emptying and filling, with which Plato's dialogue as a whole is concerned.[13] Such processes are familiar and characteristic effects of *erôs*. Desire makes itself felt in the impulse of each narrator to leave behind him another narrative to replace the one he had heard, which would otherwise have consumed itself in the course of its delivery and disappeared without a trace. Apollodorus' series of nested narratives exemplifies, then, the procreative labor of *meletê*: only by means of that ongoing oral tradition has the knowledge of what was said and done at Agathon's victory party been preserved—been captured and held fast in a force-field of desire—and thus been saved from dissolution in the endless cycles of becoming.

The opening clause of the *Symposium* explicitly identifies the preservation of the story as a product of *meletê*: *dokô moi peri hôn pynthanesthe ouk ameletêtos einai*, Apollodorus declares (172a1), and he repeats his words, for additional emphasis, at the close of his introductory speech (*hôste, hoper archomenos eipon, ouk ameletêtôs echô*: 173c1). The expression has given Plato's translators some difficulty,[14] but its significance is unmistakable: Apollodorus' language both anticipates and confirms Diotima's understanding of *meletê* as the procreative mechanism that rescues knowledge from oblivion by renewing it, by transmitting it from the old to the young—in this case, through an unbroken (albeit tangled) chain of oral narrative. Apollodorus effectively, if inadvertently, represents his account of Agathon's party as the product of a self-regenerating tradition of storytelling animated by the dialectic of desire. The *Symposium* is not only about *erôs*, then: rather, its complex narrative structure is itself designed to manifest and to dramatize the workings of *erôs*.

Narrative is the transmission of a *logos*—of a unitary discourse, a speech or story that is designed to be told. Narrative is thus the process or activity by which one *logos* gives birth to another. *Logos* is a vehicle of knowledge. The retention of knowledge over time is a product of *meletê*. *Meletê* represents an instance of the procreative impulse which achieves a certain stability and permanence in the boundless sea of becoming by replacing what is lost with a new version of itself. Procreation is the immediate aim of *erôs*. Therefore, the ultimate cause of narrative is desire.

But narrative can also be the object, as well as the manifestation, of desire—especially if it is a good narrative. The epic narratives of the archaic poets are a case in point. Both those poems themselves and the heroic deeds that inspired them are products of *erôs*, according to Diotima, insofar as they express a mortal creature's desire to perpetuate itself in the eternal memory of mankind. Lovers who are spiritually pregnant give birth not to mortal children but to *aretê*, to "virtue" or "excellence"—precisely those heroic qualities of word and deed that achieve fame (*kleos*) and that make heroic accomplishments memorable across the generations (208c4-209e4). The goodness of the actions of Alcestis or Achilles arouses in us a desire to preserve the memory of such actions and of the persons who performed them, to possess them perpetually. The poet ministers to this desire and is himself its most eloquent instrument: his desire manifests itself by prompting him to conceive a virtuous offspring, an epic poem, which fixes the glorious deeds of the heroes for all time by enshrining them in a self-regenerating narrative—that is, in a narrative which is itself, by virtue of both the excellence contained within it and its own excellence as a narrative, an object of desire, something we wish to possess forever. The narrative is preserved by being told, by being handed down in an oral tradition like the one responsible for preserving the story of Agathon's victory celebration. All such narratives, as well as the actions that inspire them, are "images of excellence" (*eidôla aretês*), declares Diotima, reserving the phrase "true excellence" for what is generated by the man who ascends by means of contemplation to the vision of "the beautiful itself" (212a2-7).

Further details in this sketch of the erotics of narrativity can be filled in by glancing at Socrates' critique of writing in the *Phaedrus*. Although earlier in that dialogue Socrates had declared that there is nothing disgraceful in the mere writing of speeches (258d1-2), in the myth of Theuth he attacks the art of writing on the ground that it will promote forgetfulness in the souls of those who learn it by allowing the memory to fall out of "practice" (*mnêmês ameletêsiai*: 275a2-3). Writing will therefore destroy knowledge. For knowledge must not be conceived as something that can be captured by a written formula. Rather, it is a dynamic, self-regenerating possession of a living soul, dependent upon *meletê*; it is a continuing capacity to understand, and so it cannot be reduced to a set of mere propositions: it cannot be fixed in any static form. Writing can only remind us of what we already know (275d1-2). The only sort of writing that can actually impart knowledge is writing that is inscribed upon the soul of the learner by means of dialectic—that is, by an art of living speech (276a5-9) which takes into account the nature of its subject and the nature of the specific audience to whom it is addressed (270b1-272b2). Only such discourses as are engraved upon the soul deserve to be called "legitimate children" (278a6): these refer primarily to the *logoi* one has conceived within one's own soul (278a6-7), presumably as a response to the procreative stimulus afforded by an erotic encounter (cf. *Symp.* 208e1-209e4, 210a7-8, c1-3, d4-6), and secondarily to whatever "sons and brothers" (*ekgonoi te kai adelphoi*) one's own *logoi* may have engendered and properly raised up in the souls of others (*Phdr.* 278a7-b2).

When these arguments are carried over to the context of the *Symposium*, they suggest that the discourse of Socrates—and, to varying degrees, of the other speakers at Agathon's dinner party—was "a living and animate speech by one who knows" (*Phdr*. 276a8), a progeny conceived and produced (in his case, at least) by a philosophical *erôs* for being and truth (cf. *Rep*. 485a10-b3, 490a8-b7, 501d1-2) and/or by a more personal *erôs* for the beauty of Diotima's soul. It was itself a beautiful child, an image of excellence in both its content (Diotima's wisdom) and its form (which was superbly adapted to the needs of the audience), and it aroused in others the desire to acquire it, to retain it, and to make it their own. Thus, it engendered an entire family ("sons and brothers") of *logoi*, of reported speeches, any one of which is capable of awakening in a listener the same desire as the original—for the very reason that each is the living possession of its speaker, whose own *erôs*, expressed in the exercise of *meletê*, fixes the essential features of the *logos* (its message, rather than the specific verbal medium in which it is expressed) in the memory and thereby preserves its identity over time.[15] In the *Symposium* it is Alcibiades who makes this point. Turning to Socrates, he says, "At any rate, whenever we hear other *logoi* from some other speaker—even a very good orator—virtually no one cares anything about them; but when anyone, whether a woman or a man or a little boy, hears you speak or hears your *logoi* from another speaker, even if the speaker is a very poor one, we are seized and swept away by them" (215d1-6).

Here, then, is Plato's official explanation of his representational strategy in the *Symposium*. I call it "official" because it seems to agree almost perfectly with the precise terms of Diotima's erotic theory. Alcibiades' remark, taken in the context of the *Symposium* as a whole, would appear to authorize something like the following set of inferences. Socrates' sayings, even when they reach us by second- or third-hand accounts, impress themselves in our memory by their beauty or excellence and thereby arouse in us a desire to retain the wisdom encapsulated in them; the *erôs* they awaken sets in motion the mental faculty called *meletê*, our capacity for attentiveness, care, or alertness, and we exercise that capacity in order to hold Socrates' discourses in our minds and memories, preserving the gist of what he said or what we heard. This highly charged erotic process is what gives rise to the elaborate and labyrinthine tradition of oral narrative which Plato portrays at the beginning of the *Symposium*.

The anti-type to Socratic dialectic is Lysianic rhetoric. Phaedrus is obliged to carry a written copy of Lysias' speech about with him: he is unable to retain it, because its glittering sophistries will not take root in the soul; he was struck by Lysias' declamation of it (*Phdr*. 227a1-c5), evidently, and it is only this enduring enthusiasm which reanimates, however feebly, the speech in his own delivery of it

(234d1-6). But not even Phaedrus' charming delivery is sufficient to make Socrates remember Lysias' speech, and when he and Phaedrus wish to criticize it they are obliged to pore over the written text.[16]

IV

The *Symposium*'s apparently perfunctory dialogic opening plays a crucial role in Plato's larger argument for the erotics of narrativity. For it testifies in a direct and unmediated fashion to the allure of narrative; it presents narrative as an object of intense desire. The amazing strength of the longing precipitated in the listener by the excellence of Socrates' narrated words, of his reported speech, is dramatized in the dialogic preamble to the narrative in the *Symposium* by the eager insistence of Apollodorus' nameless interlocutors. Their determined request, voiced (apparently) before our text begins, reminds Apollodorus of the similarly pressing entreaties of Glaucon, only two days before, who—not content with an incoherent account originating with Aristodemus and passed on to him via *two* intermediaries—called after Apollodorus and said such things as "I've just been looking for you," "so tell me the story yourself," "don't make fun of me—tell me when the party took place," and "so tell me the story, won't you?" (172a6-173b7). A similar urgency drives Apollodorus' acquaintances to express annoyance with his protracted anecdote about Glaucon and to betray their lack of interest in Apollodorus himself (they dismiss his remarks as old news: he's "always" the same, they say—the word *aei*, applied to Apollodorus, occurs three times in six lines to underscore their impatience with him—and they've heard everything *he* may have to say many times before: 173d4-10); they have no use for him except as a *conduit* for the narrative, which they have resolved to hear: "Just do what we asked of you—tell us the story of who said what" (173e5-6).

To be sure, Apollodorus' interlocutors are not seekers after truth. They are wealthy businessmen (173c6), *hommes d'affaires*, and—if we are to believe Apollodorus, an admittedly hostile witness—they are motivated not by philosophical *erôs* but by vulgar curiosity. Hence, Plato's dramatization of their desire in the dialogic opening of the *Symposium* has the effect of marking Apollodorus' narrative as an instance of gossip, a piquant and mildly scandalous tale repeated by one inquisitive neighbor to another. But to say that is not to join Apollodorus in denigrating the motives of his companions (or those of the other intervening narrators) as being different in kind from his own. For gossip itself reflects the operation of *erôs*. Plato, our supreme poet of the mixed motive, has devised in the form of Diotima's teaching a totalizing theory designed to explain the moral psychology of everyone—even, or especially, of those who repudiate or ignore it. "Vulgar curiosity" expresses the same desire to obtain and retain noteworthy deeds, and reflects the same appeal exerted by Socrates' reported speech, as the reverent attentiveness of Apollodorus. Gossip, then, is a low-level form of philosophical discourse, and philosophy—whatever *else* it may be—is at the very least a high-class kind of gossip. Diotima's account of *meletê*, after all, was not intended to describe the mental equipment of the philosopher but to define the procedure by which we all preserve whatever knowledge we possess. If the story of Socrates' speech and conduct at Agathon's party is passed on from one person to another in the form of gossip, that is just another testimony to the reflected excellence of Socrates' words and deeds which inspire in others such a desire to retain them that they are told and retold until they achieve a perpetual hold on the collective memory. Or so the "official" doctrine of the *Symposium* would have it.

Plato's combined use of dialogue and narrative in the compositional form of the *Symposium* may be understood in this light. Plato uses the dramatic frame of the *Symposium* to stage the erotics of narrativity, to reveal narrative as both an expression and an object of desire—a means of gratifying the desire it incites and of renewing the desire it gratifies. Narrative itself is erotic insofar as the illusion of dramatic immediacy it provides typically serves to collapse the distance between the occurring and the recounting of an event, or between the characters in a tale and its audience, while the very fact of narrative serves to consolidate that distance, to institutionalize and perpetuate it. For narrative itself is a sign of a gap that has opened up between the "now" of a telling and the "then" of a happening, a gap that demands to be continually crossed and recrossed, if we are to succeed at reconstituting in imagination, however fleetingly, the lost presence of a past that is forever slipping away from us. By endlessly abolishing the distance it interposes and interposing the distance it abolishes, by making the past present without actually bringing it back, narrative at once satisfies and (re)generates desire: that is why we are both eager and sorry to come to the end of a good narrative. That is also why we never tire of retelling the same old stories (*Symp.* 173c2-5). The erotics of narrativity display the same dialectic of presence and absence, of loss and renewal, that informs the erotics of sexual passion.

The *Symposium*'s dramatic frame also enables Plato to insert the reader into the erotic circuit that connects those who transmit and those who receive a narrative. By placing the reader outside the charmed circle of Socrates' personal acquaintance, by making the reader a stranger to Socrates as well as to those for whom his words were originally intended and thus withholding from the reader—initially, at least—unmediated access to Socrates' charismatic presence, Plato identifies us with Glaucon and with Apollodorus' other, nameless, interlocutors and he offers their desires as a model for our own. Their eagerness, their lively anticipation serve to boost the value of what we are about to hear, making us especially keen to hear it; like the laugh-track accompanying a televised situation comedy, their repeated requests for the story advertise its appeal and construct our own responses.

V

But it is precisely at this point that we can no longer avoid confronting a significant problem for what I have been calling the "official" doctrine of the *Symposium*. For although Plato locates us, his readers, squarely within the oral tradition of Socratic narrative (in which he often must have found himself), he also removes us, as the readers of a *written* text, from that tradition. *We* do not need to exercise the kind of care or practice required to hold words of wisdom in our memories, nor will *we* be expected to transmit them to others by means of oral narrative, for we possess a finished transcript, and when in doubt we can always refer to the text. We share with Apollodorus' interlocutors only the experience of receptivity, of being the incidental and unintended audience of a narrative, those into whose hands it has fallen of its own accord. Otherwise, our relation to the narrative is a different one, an entirely *literary* one, and all the work to be performed by *meletê* has been transferred, in our case, to the sphere of interpretation.

At the conclusion of this essay I shall have something to say about the erotics of interpretation. For the moment, however, I want to linger over the multiple ironies occasioned by Plato's use of the *written* medium to celebrate the erotics of *oral* narrativity. These ironies proliferate beyond the simple *mise-en-abîme* effect, familiar from the *Phaedrus*, produced by any criticism *of* writing *in* writing; they go beyond the mere paradox that Socratic orality is the offspring of Platonic inscription,[17] that the logocentric world apparently glorified in the *Symposium* turns out, on closer inspection, to be an entirely logographic effect. They even go beyond the fact that Plato's "official" justification of his representational strategy in the *Symposium*, a justification that revolves around the erotics of oral narrativity, is accessible only to a careful *reader* of the *Symposium*'s *text*—inasmuch as that justification can be arrived at solely by means of the kind of intense, minute scrutiny and comparison of individual passages that a written text alone makes possible—and would not be accessible, I believe, to even an orally trained auditor of a vocalized performance. Rather, the ironies I speak of strike at the heart of the "official" explanation of the relation between the compositional form of the *Symposium* and the erotic doctrine contained in it. Indeed, they even call into question whether Plato's *Symposium* contains *any* erotic doctrine that can confidently be ascribed to Plato himself, whether the very notion of an erotic *doctrine* is not in Platonic terms a self-cancelling, self-refuting one.

Let us turn, then, to what might be called the "unofficial" story about the erotics of narrativity that Plato has to tell us. The first thing to notice is that even in the dramatic register of the *Symposium* the theory of narrativity officially promoted by the Dialogue breaks down. According to that theory, the beauty or excellence of Socrates' discourses—even when they are conveyed by "a very poor speaker" (*Symp.* 215d4)—is supposed to focus the attention of the hearer and to impress the gist of those discourses indelibly on the hearer's memory, thereby facilitating the preservation of Socratic wisdom through oral transmission. The compositional form of the *Symposium* is supposed to testify to the triumphant power of this erotic dynamic, but Apollodorus' opening narrative of his recent conversation with Glaucon testifies instead to its failure. For, as Apollodorus tells his companions, Glaucon had been unable to obtain a clear account of Agathon's party from the person who had told him about it (172b3-5), despite the fact that Phoenix, who had informed this nameless intermediary, had gotten the story directly from Aristodemus, just as Apollodorus himself had done (173b1-4). The person who told the story to Glaucon, then, is no farther removed in order of descent from "the true account" than is Apollodorus' own audience—or the reader of Plato's text. And yet, Glaucon's informant " 'couldn't say anything clear' " about it (172b4-5). Indeed, he even left Glaucon under the impression that Agathon's party had taken place relatively recently, whereas in fact it took place more than a dozen years before, " 'when we were still children,' " as Apollodorus represents himself as telling Glaucon (172b6-173a8). In short, the *Symposium*'s dialogic opening dramatizes the *loss* of Diotima's *logos* as much as it signals its retention (see, also, 178a1-7, 180c2: even Aristodemus and Apollodorus can't remember it all).[18] Far from rescuing the memory of what was said and done at Agathon's from forgetfulness, far from securing the preservation of Diotima's precious teaching, the process of narrative transmission is evidently just as liable to dissipate as it is to save valuable knowledge.

The clearest signal of despair, the most eloquent confession on Plato's part of his own lack of confidence in the *Symposium*'s official doctrine of the erotics of narrativity occurs when Apollodorus acknowledges that, not content to have gotten the story of Agathon's drinking-party from Aristodemus, an eye-witness, he checked "a number of things" (*enia*) directly with Socrates, who confirmed the accuracy of Aristodemus' narrative "with respect to each particular" (*kathaper*) contained in it (173b4-6). Rather than trust to reports, to the all-too-obviously fallible vicissitudes of oral transmission, that is, Apollodorus goes straight to the source, blithely vaulting over the mediating narrator and collapsing the intervening narrative frame. What seems most disturbing about this procedure in the context of the *Symposium*'s erotic theory is not that Apollodorus' decision to check Aristodemus' testimony against a more reliable source bespeaks an essentially *documentary* anxiety, one more appropriate to the correction and recension of a written transcript than to the verification of an oral history: the comparison of verbal eye-witness accounts, after all, is a standard element in Greek historiography (e.g., Thucydides, 1.22.2-3). Instead, the truly discordant effect produced by Apollodorus' scientific collation of verbal texts—by this Platonic fiction of authentication, this dramatic illusion of historical accuracy—is that it ultimately serves to authorize one particular inscription: it privileges the version of events and speeches set down in the written document we happen to be reading at the moment; the accreditation it provides helps to underwrite the dramatic "truth" of the individual narrative inscribed in the text of Plato's *Symposium*. Far from vouching for the efficacy of oral transmission and thereby vindicating the erotics of narrativity, Apollodorus' scruples merely establish the pedigree and authenticate the veracity of the story contained in a single text—a story whose precise features have at last been stabilized, fixed for all time, and conveyed into our hands by means of Platonic inscription. In this way, the conversation between Apollodorus and his friends that opens the *Symposium* does at least as much to privilege logographic inscription as it does to dramatize the erotics of narrativity.[19]

Furthermore, Plato calls into doubt the extent to which any narrative that actually succeeds in reproducing itself, as Aristodemus' narrative at least occasionally manages to do, can escape Socrates' critique of writing in the *Phaedrus* and qualify as a genuine instance of dialectical speech. In what way, after all, does Apollodorus' narrative distinguish itself from those stories that disintegrate in the process of transmission (such as the story of Agathon's party that reached Glaucon via Phoenix)? Does it not distinguish itself in being relatively stable and fixed in its features (not to say canned)—a recital that may require practice but that, once committed to memory, can be produced at any moment for the asking? Is there any indication that Apollodorus' narrative *is* in fact adapted to the needs of his specific audience, as true dialectical speech is said to be (*Phdr*. 270b ff.)? The evidence, such as it is, tends to point in the opposite direction. Apollodorus seems to be reciting, without much discernible regard for the intervening change of audience, the very story that he had recited to Glaucon only a day or two before. Indeed, he promises his nameless companions that he will "attempt to narrate" the story to them "from the beginning, [just] as [Aristodemus had] narrated it" originally to him (173e7-174a2): being "well-practised" appears to signify to Apollodorus nothing more than the ability to reproduce exactly what Aristodemus had recounted to him. He never refers or even alludes to his auditors in the course of his recital, nor does he seem to take account of their personal attachments or predilections in the actual framing of his tale (except, perhaps, for his inclusion of money-making, along with gymnastics and philosophy, among the human pursuits that spring from an erotic impulse: 205d3-5), so it is hard to know in what sense the story he tells is geared specifically to the persons he is ostensibly addressing. In fact, Plato implies that Apollodorus' story is *not* so geared: when Apollodorus gets to the end of it, he simply shuts off, like a phonograph record that has finished its play.

In this respect Apollodorus' narrative represents an instance of the kind of oratory that Plato likens to writing.[20] In the *Protagoras*, Socrates complains that "if you should ask an orator a question, *they are like books*—unable to make any reply or to ask any question themselves; even if you inquire about something they said, however trivial it may be, they are just like a bronze gong that has been struck and that goes on noisily ringing unless someone takes hold of it—so these orators, in response to the slightest inquiry, spin out a long speech" (329a2-b1). The inability to answer questions and the tendency to go on saying the same thing forever—which seem to be characteristic of Apollodorus and to account, at least in part, for his success at preserving and transmitting Socratic *logoi*—are cardinal features of writing, in Plato's eyes. He comes back to the topic[21] in a famous passage of the *Phaedrus*, where Socrates compares writing to painting and complains once again that written words "seem to talk to you as though they were intelligent, but if you ask them anything about what they say, from a desire to be instructed, they go on signifying the same one thing forever" (*Phdr*. 275d4-9 [trans. Hackforth, adapted]). Apollodorus' narrative, then, does not so much resemble dialectical speech as it does a written text. Instead of championing the erotics of oral narrativity, the dramatic frame of the *Symposium* would seem to promote a rhetoric of textual inscription.

A similar conclusion can be drawn from a glance at the philosophical pretensions of Plato's narrators. Apollodorus and Aristodemus claim to be living a life devoted to intellectual inquiry and (in that sense if in no other) to be Socratic philosophers. Apollodorus constantly rebukes his acquaintances for failing to follow his, or rather Socrates', example and for considering anything else to be of value besides philosophy (173a1-3, c2-d1). He represents himself, via Glaucon, as a "companion" of Socrates (172b6) and he prides himself on the fact that for almost three years now he has been consorting with Socrates and making it his business to know, each and every day, everything that Socrates says and does (172c4-6). He believes everyone to be wretched, save only Socrates, and although he does not except himself from the general human condition, he merely *supposes* himself to be in a bad way, whereas he *knows* this to be true of non-philosophers (173d1-e3)—a sly rhetorical move that seems to caricature the Socratic style of formulating knowledge claims.[22] Similarly, Aristodemus figures (in Apollodorus' characterization) as "the greatest lover of Socrates among the men of that era" (173b3-4). But his devotion seems to express itself most visibly in an exaggerated aping of Socrates' personal mannerisms: like Socrates, Aristodemus is "always barefoot," for example (173b2; cf. 203d1, 220b6)—though Socrates himself dons footwear on special occasions (174a4). For Apollodorus and Aristodemus alike, then, philosophy seems largely to consist in a personal, not to say idolatrous, cult of Socrates.[23] Instead of engaging in Socratic inquiry, they tell stories about Socrates.[24] They don't give birth to discourses themselves, despite Apollodorus' claim to the contrary at 173c3-4; they memorize and recite the discourses conceived by others. (If Aristodemus actually did deliver a speech about *erôs* at Agathon's party, he [or Apollodorus] seems to have forgotten it—a fact that is neatly obscured, in one of Plato's most inspired bits of dramaturgy, by Aristophanes' critically-timed disruption of the original order of the speakers at the symposium.) Plato never represents either of his narrators *doing* philosophy: we never see either of them advancing or examining philosophical claims; we only see them recapitulating uncritically the philosophical claims made by others, most of all by Socrates. Far from being true philosophers, Apollodorus and Aristodemus appear to function entirely as sites of Socratic inscription.

In short, Plato would seem to have used the *Symposium*'s dialogic opening to dramatize both the defeat and the excessive triumph of the erotic doctrine officially sanctioned by the dialogue. On the one hand, the doctrine proves to be unsuccessful insofar as narrative is shown not to work as well as it might have been supposed to do: even a living tradition of oral narrative is insufficient, evidently, to capture, hold, and preserve precious knowledge. On the other hand, the official doctrine proves to be too successful insofar as narrative is shown to work better than it ought to do: when narrative does manage to contain and to transmit wisdom, to reproduce itself repeatedly and accurately, it reduces human storytellers to mere sites of textual inscription.

This combination of failure and over-achievement makes it possible to pinpoint elements in the *Symposium*'s official doctrine that ought to have aroused suspicion on first encounter. Let us look again, for example, at Alcibiades' testimony to the excellence of Socratic speech—the passage that is supposed to provide the key to understanding the bizarre compositional form of the *Symposium*. According to Alcibiades, "whenever we hear other *logoi* from some other speaker—even a very good orator—virtually no one cares anything about them; but when anyone, whether a woman or a man or a little boy, hears you [Socrates] speak or hears your *logoi* from another speaker, even if the speaker is a very poor one, we are seized and swept away by them" (215d1-6). This statement, if descriptively accurate (as the *Symposium*'s "official" erotic doctrine implies), would bear witness to a quite remarkable, and highly unlikely, phenomenon. It would indicate that Socrates' discourses are so excellent that they transcend their specific verbal medium: they effectively trump any rhetorical strategy used to convey them and overcome any rhetorical ineptitude on the part of the speaker, acting as a kind of universal solvent on the words in which they are transmitted. A report of Socrates' *logoi* is therefore bound to be a sure-fire, fail-safe hit, because its value is supposedly independent of the form of its utterance. But is this in fact the case? Not only is Alcibiades' assertion suspiciously grandiose; not only is it belied as much as it is confirmed by the *Symposium*'s dramatic opening; not only would it, if true, render Plato's dialogues indistinguishable in their effects from the writings of Xenophon and other Socratics: it also makes a mockery of the claims advanced on behalf of dialectical speech in the *Phaedrus*. Socrates' sayings, on Alcibiades' view, are intrinsically well-adapted to the needs of *any* audience, no matter how deficient (woman, man or boy). They do not have to be inscribed on the soul of each hearer by an art of living speech that takes into account the nature of its subject and of the specific audience to whom it is addressed. The speech of Socrates is allegedly universal speech, equally suited to any audience.

Now there is a kind of speech that *is* designed to be passed around indiscriminately among everyone and to work its effects indifferently on any audience it may reach. Socrates describes it in the *Phaedrus*: "Once a *logos* is put into *writing*, it drifts all over the place, getting into the hands not only of those who understand it, but equally of those who have no business with it" (275d9-e2 [trans. Hackforth, adapted]). Alcibiades' claim, which sounded suspiciously grandiose when taken to refer to the speech of Socrates, becomes much more plausible when applied to the writings of the Socratics, especially to Plato's dialogues (even though the Socrates of Plato's *Phaedrus* would be the first to repudiate such an application of that claim). A *written* speech by Socrates, after all, will be just as good on every reading as it was on the first reading, and it is guaranteed not to suffer in transmission. Socrates' oral disquisition on *erôs* at Agathon's party might qualify, within the dramatic terms of Plato's fiction, as a true instance of dialectical speech and might claim to owe its preservation, within the fictional world of Plato's dialogue, to being superbly well-adapted to the needs of its original audience, but it is the written version of that disquisition, the version recorded in the text of Plato's *Symposium*, that would seem to have been designed to suit the needs of any audience, "whether a woman or a man or a little boy." In short, Alcibiades' praise ultimately redounds less to the virtue of Socratic speech than to the power of Platonic writing.[25]

Inscription is a trope of identity. It figures the repetition and reproduction, the maintenance and the preservation, of the same. As such, it can function as an image for the central and defining activity of *erôs* in Diotima's view, namely procreation. Diotima had described *erôs*, after all, as a principle of fixity in the realm of mortal affairs, a source of permanence or continuity amid the endless cycles of change. Like *erôs*, inscription also maintains identity over time, ensuring the transmission of the same: as Socrates repeatedly says, written discourse goes on saying the same thing forever. But there turns out to be something highly questionable about the use of inscription to figure the procreative operations of *erôs*. For inscription maintains identity in a slightly but importantly different fashion from desire: it works by eliminating change, whereas erotic procreation works by means of change, by continually producing something new to replace what is being lost. Significant consequences result from this difference between inscription and procreation. Offspring are formally but not numerically identical to their parents, for example, whereas a text is numerically identical to itself in all of its inscriptions. Similarly, good sons (on the Greek view) resemble their fathers—but not to the extent of being identical to them, or mere simulacra of them, which is how a written copy or a transcript resembles its original. Procreation is not replication: the process of substitution, replacement, and renewal can never be perfect; if it could, *erôs* would enable us to achieve immortality in our own persons instead of only a pale semblance of immortality through our offspring.

Socrates demonstrates some recognition of this in the *Phaedrus*. Although he includes writing with sowing and begetting among the activities that figure dialectical speech and that by so doing serve to distinguish it, ostensibly at least, from rhetoric, he also describes the *logoi* that one's own *logoi* engender in others as "sons and brothers" (*ekgonoi te kai adelphoi*) of the original *logoi*—as merely *related* to the original *logoi*, then, rather than as perfect copies of them (278a7-b2).[26] Still, Socrates' figurative use of writing alongside his metaphors of sowing and begetting has the effect of blurring the distinction between procreation and replication, making insemination (whether sexual or agricultural) into a trope for the reproduction of identity while making inscription into a natural mode of reproduction. As Harry Berger puts it, "the emphasis is on the reproduction of the same, the suppression of otherness, and the more secure transmission guaranteed by the automatism of natural process."[27] The result is to represent philosophical instruction from the student's perspective as an act of intellectual insemination by the teacher and to represent it from the teacher's perspective as an exercise in male parthenogenesis, an attempt to reproduce himself and his doctrines in the student. In this Socratic fantasy, philosophy is ultimately figured as homotextuality.

VI

What I have been trying to suggest is that the *Symposium*, like the *Phaedrus* in its own way,[28] while seeming to privilege the erotics of narrativity, actually privileges writing over dialectical speech. Or, rather, it privileges dialectical speech in certain passages and privileges inscription in others. The dialogue's "official" position is balanced against, and undercut by, an "unofficial" critique of that position, and the praise we might have expected to be reserved for narrativity is in fact displaced onto—or, at least, shared with—textuality. Like Alcibiades, who arrives at the victory celebration intending to crown Agathon but who crowns Socrates instead of, or in addition to, him (213d8-e6), the *Symposium*'s purpose is deflected from its ostensible goal and redirected towards an unanticipated result. Despite its lack of a concluding logical or definitional impasse, then, the *Symposium* can still be reckoned an aporetic dialogue, insofar as it calls into question the positive doctrine it seems to put forward.

Like Berger (and Stanley Rosen),[29] then, I read Plato in opposition to Derrida not as a metaphysical dogmatist but as a kind of deconstructionist *avant la lettre*, a cunning writer fully alive to the doubleness of his rhetoric who embraces *différance* and who actively courts in his writing an effect of undecidability.[30] The *Symposium* exhibits a series of alternating doctrinal and counter-doctrinal pressures, and interpreters of the dialogue need to remain sensitive to each set of pressures. It would be wrong to conclude from my reading of the work that it contains no positive doctrine, that it lacks any genuinely Platonic philosophical content, or that it merely spoofs the notion of an erotics of narrativity, being wholly ironical in purpose and designed simply to demonstrate the futility of philosophical inquiry or to satirize the quest for a true doctrine. Such a conclusion would ignore the very real and considerable intellectual energy that Plato puts into the construction of theory and the formulation of doctrine. It would mistake the enormous seriousness with which Plato approaches the philosophical enterprise and it would fail to acknowledge the extent to which the erotic theory propounded in the *Symposium* actually succeeds in attaining to a high degree of both logical rigor and experientially descriptive power.[31] But without denying the positive philosophical thrust of the *Symposium* and the other dialogues, we must also learn to come to terms with Plato's equally serious determination not to leave his readers with a body of dogma.[32] If my reading of the *Symposium* is justified, it would seem that Plato—in this one dialogue, at least—systematically goes about undermining and subverting the very theories that his philosophical *personae* propound and that many elements of the dialogue systematically combine to promote.

Plato's *Symposium*, then, leaves both its philosophical and its literary critics with a series of pressing questions which they will be hard put to answer positively and decisively. For example: is Plato proposing a theory of the erotics of narrativity or is he criticizing such a theory? Does the literary form of the *Symposium* reflect or contradict the dialogue's philosophical content? Does Platonic writing sustain or subvert the themes of Socratic speech? Does Plato do what Socrates says or does

Socrates say one thing while Plato does another? If in fact there do not seem to be satisfactory answers to these questions, that is because both halves of the disjunctions they present accurately describe the textual strategies of the *Symposium*; it is because Plato has gone out of his way to withhold from his readers the means of sacrificing in good conscience one of the alternatives to the other.[33] The result, which the contemporary field of Platonic studies dramatically exemplifies, is to leave Platonic interpreters in a state of restless and urgent desire.[34]

And therein lies the clue, some readers will say, to solving the unresolvable contradictions in the *Symposium*'s theory and practice. The way to devise a new unified or synthetic reading of the *Symposium*, on this account, is not to attempt to reconcile its various internal contradictions but rather to transcend them by moving to a higher level of interpretation—to what might be called either a meta-philosophical or a meta-dramatic level of interpretation (it's not immediately clear which term would be more appropriate, for reasons that are significant and that will be explored below). Instead of attempting to discover the philosophical and dramatic unity of Plato's *Symposium*, to specify in exact terms its thematic and formal coherence, it might be possible to recuperate a unified, systematic interpretation of the dialogue as a whole if one were to seek it at the level of the work's textual strategy which, after all, is such an erotic one. This appearance-saving project should appeal to philosophers and to literary critics alike, inasmuch as both subscribe to principles that recommend it—to the principle of charity, in the case of philosophers, and to the Jamesian precept of granting the artist his (or her) *donnée*, in the case of literary critics. At all events, the enterprise is not particularly strenuous: in order to salvage the unity and coherence of Plato's *Symposium* from its self-cancelling textual practices, one need only emphasize the erotic dimensions and consequences of its overall textual strategy.

Here is how such an interpretation would run. Plato's various doctrinal and counter-doctrinal gestures, his deliberate alternation of positive and negative moments, of theoretical construction and critique, produce in readers of the *Symposium* continual cycles of comprehension and incomprehension, constantly shifting proportions of blindness and insight. The perpetual loss and renewal of understanding on the part of the interpreter, to which such a procedure gives rise, reflects a familiar erotic operation, namely the dialectic of presence and absence that structures the phenomenology of desire—in this case, the phenomenology of hermeneutic desire.[35] True to its own theory, the *Symposium* lures us to interpret it and frustrates our efforts to interpret it, and the doctrine embedded in it seems forever to dissolve in our hands just when we thought we had finally grasped it. More truly an *erôtikos anêr* than the speaking Socrates whom his writing constructs as an irrecoverable and perpetually recovered philosophical presence, Plato artfully withdraws from us in the very act of appearing to surrender himself and his "doctrines." If, in short, the *Symposium*'s erotic theory ultimately fails to justify the compositional form of that dialogue, at least it succeeds in describing and accounting for the dialectical alternation of comprehension and incomprehension that the *Symposium* generates in its interpreters.

VII

There are difficulties with this appearance-saving move, not the least of which is the uncritical fetishizing of such values as "unity," but it would seem at first to be well grounded in the text of the *Symposium*. For Diotima treats interpretation itself as an erotic enterprise. One of the daemonic functions of *erôs*, she informs Socrates, is to serve as an interpreter between gods and men, filling and bridging the gap between beings who otherwise would never meet (202e3-203a4).[36] Hence, the whole art of prophetic interpretation (*hê mantikê*) depends on *erôs* (202e7-203a1); in the *Phaedrus*, Socrates teaches that *mantikê* and *erôs* are akin to one another insofar as they are both forms of beneficial madness (244a-245c, 265b2-5).[37] But *mantikê* also has a role to play in the inner life of the human individual: it is needed to decode the prophetic language of the soul and to mediate between the levels of the psyche. Prophetic interpretation is therefore required in order to give human beings access to themselves, to negotiate the gap between the surfaces and depths of human motivation. Nothing so palpably breaches an opening in the soul, disclosing undreamt-of chasms within it—and, thus, nothing so urgently calls for an art of prophetic interpretation to reveal human beings to themselves—as the experience of erotic passion.[38]

It is a consequence of Plato's theory of desire, and of the transcendental ontology connected with it, that the lover's conscious wishes, the content of his or her mental representations, do not make manifest the objective structure of his or her intentionality: as Plato's Aristophanes establishes by means of his famous myth in the *Symposium*, the ultimate aim of erotic desire may remain engimatic even to the most experienced lovers.[39] Those who spend their entire lives together "could not say what they wish to gain from one another," according to Aristophanes. "No one would think it was sexual intercourse, or that for the sake of sex each partner so earnestly enjoys his union with the other. But it is clear that the soul of each lover wants something else, which it is not able to say, but it divines (*manteuesthai*) what it wants and hints at it" (192cd).[40] Similarly, when Diotima announces to Socrates that the aim of desire is procreation, he remarks that it would take the art of divination (*manteia*) to figure out what she means (206b9): Socrates, in other words, stands just as much in need of an art of prophetic interpretation to decode the enigma of the erotic aim, when Diotima articulates it, as do the most experienced lovers, when their own souls obscurely grope for a way of representing it.

Without successful interpretation, without the benefit of a glimpse into the deep structures of his or her motivation,[41] every lover would remain ignorant of the reason and purpose behind his or her own *erôs*—what Aristophanes and Diotima alike call its *aition* (192e9; 207e7; cf. 207b7, c7). The same model might be applied to reading, which resembles *erôs* insofar as it often seems to consist of apprehending something meaningful about a work without being aware of exactly what that something is. Only an art of interpretation can make the levels of literary meaning transparent to a reader, on this account, just as prophecy is necessary to render legible the depths of the human psyche. In love as in literature, human beings evidently require a Platonic analysis, of the sort Diotima performs on Socrates, in order to learn how to interpret the cryptic, prophetic messages that their souls are continually sending them.

Erôs breaches an opening in the soul only to close it; its prophetic utterance at once voices its meaning and necessitates an art of prophetic interpretation, an erotic hermeneutics,[42] to decode it. Interpretation, like desire, like narrativity, is both the solution to its own problem and the problem posited by that solution. For interpretation arises, on Diotima's view, only in response to a perceived loss of understanding;[43] it is only when meaning eludes an interpreter, when it starts to slip away from her, that she marshalls the arts of interpretation in order to recapture it. Just as *meletê* manifests itself to the exact degree that knowledge is constantly departing from the knower, according to Diotima (208a3-7), so hermeneutic *erôs* comes into being neither when meaning is fully present (and there is no need for interpretation to recover it) nor when it is entirely absent (and its presence is never missed) but only when it ostentatiously withdraws, leaving a trail of telltale traces behind it. At the same time as interpreters set out to regain lost meaning, however, their very activity is a sign of the distance that has intervened between the objects of their investigation and their own understanding of those objects, for interpretation effectively posits a lack of understanding as the condition of its own activity.

It is no accident, then, that Diotima, the personage who stands at the end of the hall of narrative mirrors that constitutes Apollodorus' tale in Plato's *Symposium*, is herself a prophetess—a professional interpreter. For Diotima is a figure of *différance*: she is a woman in a man's world whose characteristic gesture is one of deferral, of postponement or delay (staving off the plague), a mantic performance that mimics the work of the interpreter who, by her recuperative activity, both announces and, for the moment, prevents the advent of understanding:

she signifies that its arrival—fatal to the ongoing practice of philosophy and literary criticism alike—is imminent but not yet upon us.

VIII

The unitary reading of the *Symposium* just proposed ultimately rests on the common element that Plato seems to find in desire, in narrativity, and in interpretation. Good narratives and cunning texts are like beautiful bodies, according to Plato: they excite desire and provide certain kinds of temporary, local gratification, without however yielding up the secret of their fascination. Rather, they renew desire even as they gratify it because the quality in them that awakens it in the first place tends to recede as one approaches it, transcending as it does the particulars that instantiate it. Just as *erôs*, in Diotima's myth, mediates between being and non-being, constantly perishing and reanimating itself, so narrativity mediates between the past and the present, at once articulating and traversing the distance between them, and interpretation mediates between interpreters and the objects of interpretation, simultaneously advancing our understanding and deferring it. Chief among Plato's many achievements in the *Symposium*, on this reading of it, would be to have established an analogy between sexual desire, narrativity, and interpretation in erotic terms and, at the same time, to have figured that analogy in his text. What Plato would seem to have done in the *Symposium*, then, is to construct a reflexive relation between the representation of *erôs* and the erotics of representation.

A similar strategy, carried out by quite different means, might also be discerned in the thematic disposition of the *Phaedrus*, in its joint meditation upon *erôs* and rhetoric. Although each topic is treated separately from the other, in its own half of the dialogue, Plato seems to establish a dialectical interdependence between them by the mutually referential treatment he accords them. For in the *Phaedrus*, unlike in the *Symposium*, Plato does not depict people in the actual throes of erotic passion—he does not, that is, directly represent the experience of *erôs*. Instead, he stages erotic *fictions*: he has his characters make *speeches* in which they represent themselves as the subjects of hypothetical passions and he has them compete with one another in composing rhetorical simulations of *erôs*. Conversely, when the topic of the dialogue turns from *erôs* to rhetoric, Phaedrus and Socrates do not merely discuss literary techniques in the abstract. Rather, they evaluate different kinds of compositions about *erôs* and they judge different methods of literary technique, at least in part, by their relative degrees of efficacy at seducing the mind (*psychagôgein*) of the reader or listener. It is this very fusion of erotic and literary themes, this intimate association between the rhetoric of *erôs* and the erotics of rhetoric, that since antiquity has baffled those interpreters of the *Phaedrus* who insist on discovering the dialogue's unitary theme, its "one true subject";[44] only recently, as Derrida reminds us, have commentators ceased to complain that the *Phaedrus* is badly composed.[45]

It is profoundly ironic, and potentially quite instructive, that the Platonic dialogue responsible for introducing into the arsenal of literary-critical analysis the criterion of "organic unity" (264c2-5) should itself have been most persistently vulnerable to the charge of artistic disunity; it is similarly ironic that the Platonic dialogue most centrally and explicitly concerned with questions of compositional form—of "logographic necessity" (264b7)—and, hence (one has every reason to believe), most deliberate and self-conscious in its textual strategies should itself have been most severely and protractedly criticized for its alleged compositional flaws, most thoroughly interrogated about its own structural coherence (that is, its own *anankê logographikê*). What all these ironies suggest is that some relation of reflexivity between the representation of *erôs* and the erotics of representation obtains not only in the thematic structure of the *Phaedrus*, spanning and uniting the discussions of desire and rhetoric, but also in the interpretative situation that the dialogue establishes with its readers, implanting in them a mingling of critical suspicion and hermeneutic desire that exactly mirrors the play of oppositions and correspondences between erotic desire and rhetorical technique in the thematic field of the dialogue.

That Plato's interpreters should have scrutinized the *Phaedrus* in exactly the same terms in which the *Phaedrus* represents its interlocutors as scrutinizing literary texts indicates, among many other things, something of the extent to which Plato's texts mimetically construct the desires of their readers, engaging them in a hermeneutic activity that imitates the philosophical activity of the interlocutors represented in the dialogues. (Plato's texts read us, evidently, as much as we read them, even if they also seem to write, to *prescribe*, our own responses to them.) A similar claim might be made about the *Symposium*: Plato engenders in his readers a hermeneutic desire that prompts them to make speeches to one another about *erôs*, to discuss and theorize it in ways that mirror the philosophical activity of the interlocutors in the dialogue. Insofar as Plato can be said to have devised a reflexive relation between the interpretation of his erotic texts and the erotics of textual interpretation, and insofar as he can be seen to have dramatized that relation by means of the hermeneutic situations in which both the *Phaedrus* and the *Symposium* mimetically place their readers, Plato would seem to have secured the formal and thematic unity of those dialogues. If in the case of the *Symposium*, then, the unity of form and theme had earlier broken down when the theory of the erotics of narrativity, on which it had been founded, collapsed, that unity can now be recovered—not at the level of philosophy or drama, to be sure, but at the level of interpretation.

IX

But is *interpretation* what Plato wants us principally to do with his dialogues? Do we read Plato rightly when we take his works as texts to be endlessly interpreted, thereby treating them in effect as works of literature? And to the extent that our hermeneutic activity mirrors the philosophical activity of the interlocutors in the *Symposium*, will it be vulnerable to the same deconstructive critique? These questions bring us to our final topic, which is Plato's philosophy of writing—or, it might be better to say, his erotics of reading. In an earlier essay, I once argued that Plato's use of dramatic dialogue "represents an attempt to recapture the original and authentic erotic context of philosophy—the exchange of questions and answers from which emerges, dialectically, an image of excellence: the lover's beautiful speeches. By its very form, then, the Platonic dialogue aspires to engage the reader . . . to awaken *erôs* in the reader—to arouse, in particular, his [*sic*] hermeneutic *erôs*, 'the desire of the text.'"[46] But what is the *aim* of this textual desire, this hermeneutic *erôs* that Plato arouses in his readers? More specifically, does the reader of a Platonic text feel inspired to interpret the text, to reflect on the philosophical issues addressed in it, or to set about deconstructing the distinction between philosophy and literature? The facile assumption of much current academic work in the field of ancient philosophy has been that there is little practical difference between the literary and philosophical approaches, that in order to interpret a Platonic text one has to philosophize and that in order to understand and criticize Plato's philosophy one has to know how to interpret his texts. Accordingly, my earlier formulation silently elided the distinction between literary interpretation and philosophy by emphasizing the erotic element shared by each and by invoking a hermeneutic *erôs* that supposedly spans both literary-critical and philosophical activity. It is now time to confront more squarely the difference between these two responses to Plato and to ask which of them answers more exactly to the desire that a Platonic text evokes in its reader.

The question proves, characteristically enough, to be undecidable. For Plato's philosophical representatives repeatedly assail the value of the very kind of literary interpretation which their creator repeatedly demands of his readers.[47] In the *Ion*, for example, Socrates scathingly characterizes all those who interpret the poets as "interpreters of interpreters" (535a9). In the *Protagoras* he goes further and mounts an attack on the seriousness of all criticism of poetry: "some say a poet means one thing, others say something different, all of them engaged in discussing [*dialegomenoi*] a matter that they are unable to resolve [*exelegxai*]" (347e5-7). Socrates recommends that the assembled company turn its attention to philosophy instead, and the result—though identically inconclusive—proves to be more valuable. For now the irresolvable disagreement arises not between several interpreters but within a single philosopher, namely Socrates, who finds himself both affirming and denying the proposition that virtue can be taught, thereby discovering his own ignorance and acquiring fresh impetus for further inquiry.[48]

In the *Symposium,* what Socrates and Diotima say is pointedly at odds with what Plato does. The dramatic action of the dialogue, especially the interaction between Aristophanes, Agathon, and Socrates, establishes the latter's erotic, intellectual, and even Dionysiac triumph over his rivals among the poets; in the terms of Plato's allegory, Socrates' ascendancy plainly represents the ascendancy of the life of philosophy over that of poetry.[49] Furthermore, Diotima's failure to include literary texts (or other works of art) among the objects specified in her erotic curriculum implies that literature is not a worthy object of desire in its own right and that the study of it represents a dead end for the lover who aspires ultimately to apprehend "the beautiful itself." To fix one's gaze on a literary object, on the offspring of someone else's erotic activity, is a perversion of correct desire. And to interpret a Platonic dialogue is in some measure to duplicate the idolatry of Aristodemus and Apollodorus, who confuse the vehicle of philosophy with its tenor and who canonize for others what they should be reinventing for themselves. For all that, and despite its own undeniable philosophical ambitions, the *Symposium* itself remains beyond dispute the finest work of fiction, of prose literature, to survive from the Classical Period—as well as one of the all-time trickiest texts to interpret.[50] If Plato didn't want us to interpret it, why did he write it, and why did he write it that way?[51]

This question leads rapidly and directly to another impasse, to a final crux of Platonic undecidability. To those readers of Plato who may be worried that they are about to receive the sort of ultimate answer that will extinguish their desire and put an end to the dialectical play of erotic alternatives sustaining their tenuous existence, I am happy to report that this crux is an absolutely insoluble one. For in order to determine why Plato writes the way he does, whether he wants his reader to philosophize about the subject of a dialogue or to take that dialogue as an object of interpretation in its own right, it is necessary finally to determine whether Plato intends his dialogues to be read as works of philosophy or as works of literature. And that question is notoriously unanswerable,[52] because—in the case of the *Symposium* at least—Plato says one thing and does another.

When it comes to taking sides, then, in what Socrates calls "the ancient quarrel between philosophy and poetry" (*Rep.* 607b5-6), Plato turns out to be a double agent—and to be such an extraordinarily skillful and devious one that it may ultimately prove impossible to determine where his primary loyalties lie. Plato's readers may try to remove the difficulty, to discover their author's allegiance, but in so doing will they be engaging in philosophy or in literary criticism? Plato exacts a high price, in short, from those who would presume to set a limit to the erotic play of his dialectic: he obliges them to recapitulate that dialectic in their own lives, to inscribe in their own activity the very dialectic they had hoped to abolish, and thus to become undecidable enigmas to themselves. So while we await the moment—if it should ever arrive—when we are catapulted out of uncertainty, out of the joy and agony of desire, into a realm of pure transcendence, the best that we can hope for is to work productively within and among the contradictions Plato has devised for us, not to put an end to the dialectic by resolving it in favor of one alternative or another and thereby closing down the circuit through which our desire circulates but to keep it moving so as to prolong the erotic tension that animates our existence as readers and lovers of Plato's texts. Platonic questions demand answers from us but at the same time they ask us to recognize, as we set about trying to answer them, that our task is one in which—to borrow the words of a favorite contemporary philosopher—there's no success like failure, and failure's no success at all.

NOTES

This paper has previously appeared, under the same title, in *Methods of Interpreting Plato and His Dialogues*, ed. James C. Klagge and Nicholas D. Smith = *Oxford Studies in Ancient Philosophy*, Supplement 2 (1992), 93-129, and in *Innovations of Antiquity*, ed. Daniel Selden and Ralph Hexter (New York: Routledge, 1992), 95-126.

An early version was presented at a meeting of the Cambridge Humanities Seminar, in Cambridge, Massachusetts, in the spring of 1982. I wish to thank Alvin C. Kibel, for inviting me to participate in the Seminar, as well as the members of the Seminar, for their interest and advice. The revision of that paper was generously supported by a sabbatical leave from M.I.T. and by a Fellowship, funded by the Andrew W. Mellon Foundation, from the Stanford Humanities Center. I am particularly grateful to Madeleine H. Kahn and to John Kleiner, my colleagues at the Center, for discussing with me some of the issues addressed in this paper and for the inspiration of their intellectual example. I also wish to thank James C. Klagge and Nicholas D. Smith for inviting me to speak at the Virginia Polytechnic Institute and State University, where I presented an intermediate version of this paper at a conference on "Methodological Approaches to Plato and His Dialogues." I owe a great deal to Helen Bacon for her timely encouragement and sound advice, as well as to Harry Berger, Jr., David Konstan, Mark L. McPherran, Nicholas D. Smith, and Emery J. Snyder for detailed and incisive critiques of the revised version. Finally, I wish to thank Martha Nussbaum, who presented a formal commentary on this paper at Blacksburg, for her friendly, helpful, and provocative response. I hope no one will feel disgraced by the result.

[1] For the application of this term, see Gregory Vlastos, "The Socratic Elenchus," *Oxford Studies in Ancient Philosophy*, 1 (1983), 27-58, esp. 57.

[2]Noted in antiquity, quite nonchalantly, by a character in Plutarch's *Table-Talk*, 7.8.1 (= *Moralia* 711bc): commentary by Michael W. Haslam, "Plato, Sophron, and the Dramatic Dialogue," *BICS*, 19 (1972), 17-38, esp. 21.

[3]For further details about the history of this distinction, see Haslam, 20-21.

[4]This phrase is rendered as "simple rehearsal" by Eric A. Havelock, *Preface to Plato* (Cambridge: Harvard University Press, 1963), 21.

[5]See Servius' introduction to his commentary on Virgil's Third Eclogue, and cf. the Third Book of the *Ars grammatica* by Servius' near contemporary, Diomedes. On the revival of the Platonic categories by the Latin grammarians of late antiquity, see Peter Steinmetz, "Gattungen und Epochen der griechischen Literatur in der Sicht Quintilians," *Hermes*, 92 (1964), 454-66, esp. 459-63; generally, Carlo Gallavotti, "Sulle classificazioni dei generi letterari nell' estetica antica," *Athenaeum*, n.s. 6 (1928), 356-66; E. R. Curtius, *European Literature and the Latin Middle Ages*, trans. Willard R. Trask, Bollingen Series, 36 (New York: Harper Torchbooks, 1953), 436-43.

[6]Cf. Kenneth Dover, ed., *Plato: SYMPOSIUM*, Cambridge Greek and Latin Classics (Cambridge: Cambridge University Press, 1980), 8-9, comparing the compositional form of the *Parmenides* to that of the *Symposium*: "Plato's reasons for adopting this technique in a minority of his works are not known; in some others, Socrates himself is the narrator, and the majority are cast in purely dramatic form throughout. Conceivably Plato wished to give authority to his portrayal of Socrates by implicitly inviting us to check it against an independent tradition. On the other hand, he may have intended an oblique suggestion that his portrayal should be judged—like myths or moralising anecdotes—more on its intrinsic merits and the lessons to be learned from it than on its truth to fact."

[7]Only in the *Euthydemus* does the forgotten interlocutor suddenly pop up to interrupt the narrative in the middle and carry on a short conversation with the narrator (that dialogue is also exceptional in that it closes with a resumption of the conversation that had originally opened it).

[8]The *Phaedo* and *Symposium* form a Platonic "diptych," as Charles Kahn remarks ("Drama and Dialectic in Plato's *Gorgias*," *Oxford Studies in Ancient Philosophy*, 1 [1983], 75-121, esp. 119); they should be read as a pair. See John A. Brentlinger, "The Cycle of Becoming in the *Symposium*," in Suzy Q. Groden, trans., *The Symposium of Plato* (Amherst: University of Massachusetts Press, 1970), 1-31, esp. 2; Bruce Rosenstock, "Socrates' New Music: The *Symposium* and the *Phaedo*" (unpublished mss.).

[9]See Roger Hornsby, "Significant Action in the *Symposium*," *Classical Journal*, 52 (1956/57), 37-40, followed by Helen H. Bacon, "Socrates Crowned," *Virginia Quarterly Review*, 35 (1959), 415-30, esp. 418-19: "the reader is forced by the structure of the language itself to participate in two dialogues at once." For a detailed and careful summary of Plato's use of the various constructions of reported speech, see Dover, 80-81.

[10]Brentlinger, 5.

[11]For much of what follows I am indebted to Brentlinger, 5-6.

[12]See R. Hackforth, "Immortality in Plato's *Symposium*," *Classical Review*, 64 (1950), 43-45, and cf. J. V. Luce, "Immortality in Plato's *Symposium*: A Reply," *Classical Review*, n.s. 2 (1952), 137-41.

[13]On the imagery of emptying and filling in the *Symposium*, see Steven Lowenstam, "Paradoxes in Plato's *Symposium*," *Ramus*, 14 (1985), 85-104, esp. 88-97; also, Rosenstock, who argues that "The narrative frame of the *Symposium* . . . represents the life-giving power of philosophic speech."

[14]Shelley renders it, "I think that the subject of your enquiries is still fresh in my memory"; Jowett, "Concerning the things about which you ask to be informed I believe that I am not ill-prepared with an answer"; Michael Joyce, "Oh, if that's what you want to know, it isn't long since I had occasion to refresh my memory"; Walter Hamilton, "I think I may say that I have already rehearsed the scene which you ask me to describe"; Nehamas and Woodruff, "In fact, your question does not find me unprepared." Closest of all to Plato's Greek is Bruce Rosenstock (in "Socrates' New Music"), "I believe I am not out of practice in what you are asking me about."

[15]The distinction between message and medium can be illustrated by the process of retelling a joke. A good joke retains the same power and punch, as well as much of the same propositional content, each time it is told, but each person who tells it changes somewhat the particular words in which it is expressed in order to adapt the joke to his or her own personality, to the character of the audience, and to the context of its telling.

[16]Ultimately, however, Socratic dialectic proves no more immune to human forgetfulness, no more successful at achieving its own retention, than Lysianic writing. For more on the "unofficial" doctrine of the *Phaedrus*, see note 18, below.

[17]Jacques Derrida, "La pharmacie de Platon," *La dissémination* (Paris: Éditions du Seuil, 1972), 69-197. For a brilliant and wide-ranging exploration of this paradox, see the writings of Harry Berger, Jr. In what follows I have been especially influenced by his "*Phaedrus* and the Politics of Inscription" (unpublished mss.), a somewhat garbled version of which has appeared in *Textual Fidelity and Textual Disregard*, ed. Bernard P. Dauenhauer, American University Studies, ser. 3, Comparative Literature, 33 (New York, 1990), 81-103. A revised version appears in this volume.

[18]Plato undoes the "official" doctrine of the *Phaedrus* in a similar fashion, except that the subversive gesture occurs at the end of that dialogue, rather than at its beginning. Socrates' living, dialectical exchange with Phaedrus climaxes in the working out of a rigorous distinction between rhetoric and dialectic, which Socrates arrives at by means of a laborious procedure calculated to exemplify the dialectical operations of division and collection. When the task is completed, Socrates triumphantly concludes, "Now I think we have pretty well cleared up [*dedêlôsthai*] the question of art." To which Phaedrus replies, "Yes, we did think so, but please remind me [*hypomnêson*] how we did it" (277b2-4 [trans. Hackforth]). So much for the vaunted ability of Socratic dialectic to arouse the hearer's attentiveness, to reproduce the content of its wisdom in the soul of the learner, and thereby to preserve itself from oblivion! Cf. G. R. F. Ferrari, *Listening to the Cicadas: A Study of Plato's PHAEDRUS* (Cambridge: Cambridge University Press, 1987), 207-08, who notes Plato's earlier, and pointed, use of *hypomnêsai* at 275a5, d1, 276d3, 278a1, but who concludes merely that Phaedrus "risks dealing with the spoken word as if it were written"; Derrida, "La pharmacie," emphasizes Plato's use of *hypomnêsai* and its derivatives without noting Phaedrus' terminal request for a reminder.

[19]The *Theaetetus* once again offers a point of comparison, inasmuch as the text of that dialogue is an inscription that portrays a live, *viva voce* reading of the written transcript of a live conversation. "So the Platonic dialogues seem to constitute both a reified displacement and a preservative 'emplacement' of Socratic dialectic," comments Michael McKeon, *The Origins of the English Novel, 1600-1740* (Baltimore: Johns Hopkins University Press, 1987), 31.

[20]A number of the contributors to Charles L. Griswold, Jr., ed., *Platonic Writings, Platonic Readings* (New York: Routledge, 1988), emphasize that Plato's criticisms of writing extend to spoken discourse as well: see, in particular, Kenneth M. Sayre, "Plato's Dialogues in the Light of the *Seventh Letter*," and Rosemary Desjardins, "Why Dialogues? Plato's Serious Play," 93-109 and 110-125, esp. 110-111, respectively; so, also, Ferrari, 204-16.

[21]Cf. Derrida, "La pharmacie," 156, who connects the two passages.

[22]Cf. Gregory Vlastos, "Socrates' Disavowal of Knowledge," *Philosophical Quarterly*, 35 (1985), 1-31.

[23]For this, and for what immediately follows, I am indebted to Martha Nussbaum's formal commentary on the original draft of this paper.

[24]In this (as Nussbaum observes) they resemble Alcibiades, who similarly substitutes for an original discourse in praise of *erôs* a series of personal anecdotes in praise of Socrates and who, more than any other character in the *Symposium*, embodies the disastrous consequences of such a misdirected narrative desire.

[25]Cf. Charles L. Griswold, Jr., *Self-Knowledge in Plato's PHAEDRUS* (New Haven: Yale University Press, 1986), 224: "Thus Plato's written dialogues are also better suited to creating that 'immortal' [*Phdr*. 277a2] chain of philosophers than is Socrates' spoken dialectic."

[26]See, also, *Phdr*. 276e6-277a4, in which the notion of achieving immortality through procreation recurs in language reminiscent of *Symp*. 212a5-7.

[27]Harry Berger, Jr., "*Phaedrus* and the Politics of Inscription."

[28]See Derrida, "La pharmacie," 171-72.

[29]In "Platonic Hermeneutics: On the Interpretation of a Platonic Dialogue," in *Proceedings of the Boston Area Colloquium in Ancient Philosophy: Volume I (1985)*, ed. John J. Cleary (Lanham, Maryland: University Press of America, 1986), 271-88, Rosen similarly defends Plato from Derrida's critique, though on somewhat different grounds.

[30]Jacques Derrida, "La différance," in [Ouvrage collectif], *Théorie d'ensemble* (Paris: Éditions du Seuil, 1968), 41-66. Heraclitus had earlier pursued in his writings a similar effect, according to Harold Cherniss, "Ancient Forms of Philosophic Discourse," *Selected Papers*, ed. Leonardo Tarán (Leiden: Brill, 1977), 14-35, esp. 16-18.

[31]Within these methodological limits, then, I continue to stand behind the account of Plato's erotic theory which I offered in "Platonic *Erôs* and What Men Call Love," *Ancient Philosophy*, 5 (1985), 161-204.

[32]I am grateful to Helen Bacon for emphasizing this point to me.

[33] Cf. Ferrari, 210, on the question of the authenticity of the speech attributed to Lysias in the *Phaedrus*: Plato "would have known . . . that he was seeding his text with a question that was likely to prove unanswerable."

[34] Most recently dramatized by the essays collected in Griswold, ed., *Platonic Writings, Platonic Readings.*

[35] Cf. Hans-Georg Gadamer, *Truth and Method* (New York: Seabury Press, 1975), 329-32.

[36] On the mediating function of *erôs*, see Jerry Stannard, "Socratic Eros and Platonic Dialectic," *Phronesis*, 4 (1959), 120-34. On interpretation as a power of *erôs*, see Rosen, 271, 283. On the connection between Plato's metaphysical theory of beauty and the metaphysical assumptions of modern hermeneutics, see Gadamer, 434-44.

[37] But cf. *Tim.* 70b-72d, where Plato appears to retreat from this sanguine view of mantic enthusiasm.

[38] Nothing, perhaps, except Socratic dialectic: for the correspondences between Socratic dialectic and Platonic *erôs*, see Stannard.

[39] I have argued for the interpretation summarized in this paragraph in "Platonic *Erôs* and What Men Call Love," 168-69, 183-84, and in *One Hundred Years of Homosexuality and other essays on Greek Love* (New York: Routledge, 1990), 125-27.

[40] In the *Republic*, Socrates uses language similar to that employed by Aristophanes in the *Symposium* in order to describe our difficulty in apprehending the nature of the good: it is "what every soul pursues, that for the sake of which it does everything, something whose existence it divines (*apomanteuesthai*)," but cannot seize upon; rather, the soul remains "at a loss and unable to grasp adequately what it is" (505de).

[41] For Plato as a "depth psychologist," see the eloquent and persuasive discussion by David K. Glidden, "The *Lysis* on Loving One's Own," *Classical Quarterly*, 31 (1981), 39-59, esp. 46-53, and cf. E. R. Dodds, *The Greeks and the Irrational*, Sather Classical Lectures, 25 (Berkeley: University of California Press, 1951), 218.

[42] This is Rosen's phrase.

[43] Cf. Gadamer, 301, 345-49, 429.

[44] See R. Hackforth, trans., *Plato's PHAEDRUS* (Cambridge: Cambridge University Press, 1952), 8-9, for a survey of the ancient critical controversy.

[45] Derrida, "La pharmacie," 74-75.

[46] Halperin, "Plato and Erotic Reciprocity," *Classical Antiquity*, 5 (1986), 60-80, esp. 78-79.

[47] For a discussion of various ancient attempts to reconcile Socrates' denunciation of *mimêsis* in the *Republic* with Platonic practice, see Haslam, 23-24.

[48] I wish to thank Nicholas D. Smith for this reading of the *Protagoras*.

[49]See Bacon; Brentlinger; and Diskin Clay, "The Tragic and Comic Poet of the *Symposium*," in *Essays in Ancient Greek Philosophy: Volume Two*, ed. John P. Anton and Anthony Preus (Albany: State University of New York Press, 1983), 186-202.

[50]In his essay on the *Phaedrus*, Harry Berger makes a similar point about the contradiction between what Socrates says and what Plato does in that dialogue: "It's a fine irony that the Platonic text whose aporetic play solicits the conflict of interpretations should represent speakers who propose the notion of a writing that is not something to be read, questioned, and interpreted but is, on the contrary, an ideal of psychic programming that would eliminate the danger and power of interpretive or interrogatory reading."

[51]Perhaps Plato wished to demonstrate to his readers the futility of interpretation, but—if so—the lesson he wished to teach us is one we can only learn by failing. Like Alcibiades, who had to fall in love with Socrates in order to discover (if he ever did) how misguided it is to love Socrates as an individual, we can only realize how futile it is to interpret a Platonic text by trying to interpret it. Plato, on this view, doesn't want us to fall in love with his texts and so he invites us to fall in love with his texts so as to cure us homeopathically, as it were, of our folly. Even on this interpretation, then, interpretation is both disease and cure, and the only solution to interpretation is more interpretation.

[52]As Paul de Man, *Allegories of Reading: Figural Language in Rousseau, Nietzsche, Rilke, and Proust* (New Haven: Yale University Press, 1979, 103), observes, Plato is one of those figures "whose work straddles the two activities of the human intellect that are both closest and the most impenetrable to each other—literature and philosophy" (the other figures in de Man's reckoning include Augustine, Montaigne, Rousseau, and Nietzsche).

by Harry Berger, Jr.

Phaedrus and the Politics of Inscription

Strange things start to happen under the spreading Plato tree when Socrates swings into his Phaedrian song and dance about the trouble with writing.[1] After he complains at some length of the inferiority of the written word to the best kind of speech, he goes on to speak of the good discourse as "another sort of writing" in which the dialectical speaker directly inscribes his auditor's soul. Derrida was not the first to pick up on the weirdness of this move, but he made more of it than others when he scattered or smeared it over the rich field of Western culture and metaphysics. Socrates, he writes, treats the good *logos* "not merely as a knowing, living, animate discourse, but as an *inscription* of truth in the soul." And Derrida finds it remarkable that "the so-called living discourse should suddenly be described by a 'metaphor' borrowed from the order of the very thing one is trying to exclude from it"; remarkable that the bad writing—a false brother, a bastard, a traitor, an infidel—should serve as the copy, which is to say, as the model, if not the paradigm, of the good.[2]

I find it remarkable too, but for reasons which, although related to Derrida's, run in a different direction. It is different because my interest in themes that would now be labelled Derridean springs from a reading of Plato fundamentally at odds with his. Derrida ascribes to the author of Plato's dialogues a commitment to the metaphysics of presence that leads him (the author) to close down on, stop the play of, the contradictions inherent in his text; contradictions that arise from the writing Plato condemns, the writing he "never comes to grips with," the writing whose structural basis in the law of difference he "never thematized as such" (159). The bad influence of this commitment and closure dominates the long tradition that Derrida, following Heidegger, calls onto-theology. For the sake of convenience, but also to emphasize the tendency to blame onto-theology, Western philosophy, and other things on Plato, I shall call this tradition Platonism, and at this point, I merely assert, without arguing, that the closure and commitment Derrida deconstructs should be ascribed to Platonism but not to Plato; that the metaphysics of presence is reflected back into the text as Plato's both by Platonism and by its rivals or critics (including Derrida).

Derrida has put into play a finely tuned set of moves with which to question Platonism's view of Plato. But because he assimilates Plato to Platonism, because he converts a Platonistic reading of the text to Platonic intentions, he hasn't done that himself. Far from challenging the Platonistic interpretation, he assumes it, uses it, confirms it. Were he to challenge it I think he would find inscribed in the dialogues a critique of Platonism very similar to his own. In this essay I shall try to track down some of the features of this critique—a critique of the metaphysics of presence—by focusing on the theme of inscription.

To begin with, the representation of inscription in the dialogues makes contact with several aspects of the theme currently known as *the discourse of the other*. Taken in its most general sense, this phrase denotes the citational character of any performed discourse, that is, the alienation of its source from the intentional presence of the performer. The author/other is usually classified as a collective or structural agency: *différance*, for example, or the unconscious, or the unconscious as language, or heteroglossia, or language-games, or the collective discourses shaped by a society's cultural and institutional practices. But in Plato's text, and in the Athens it represents, the role of author/other may also be filled by the class of intentional agents. This includes the gods who are said to possess a speaker in the experience of enthusiasm. It includes poets, dramatists, and writers of dialogues as well as speechwriters who don't deliver their own speeches. In a more restricted but complex way, it includes those acts of impersonation, role-taking, and hypocrisy that constitute the actor as a double or duplicitous person who represents himself as another, and who may impose this representation on himself as well as on others. Finally, a unique and signal form of the discourse of the other is suggested by the principle of dialogical or maieutic modesty Socrates expresses in the *Theaetetus* when he says that the *logoi* never come from him but from the person with whom he speaks.[3] Superficially this means that his procedure is not to dogmatize but to help his interlocutors unpack—or to unpack for them—the arguments, motives, interests, fears, desires, flaws, and contradictions embedded in the opinions they state. But at a deeper level this benign purpose involves him in a peculiar difficulty, which is that his own *logos* is continually blocked and displaced by the discourse of the others with whom he speaks.

It is in the context of these various forms of the discourse of the other that I want to explore Plato's treatment of the theme of inscription. To set the stage for this exploration I shall run quickly through the section of the *Phaedrus* that culminates in Socrates's statement of the ideal of psychic inscription, and as I start I remind you that the specific thesis to be questioned is the thesis that in this passage Plato endorses that ideal. At 275d Socrates tells Phaedrus that the trouble with writing is just like the trouble with painting: the graphic imitation of spoken words is as silent as that of the living creature: it always says "only one and the same thing, and everything that's written rolls or is tossed about alike among those who understand and those to whom it isn't akin, and since it can't defend itself when ill-treated or unjustly abused, it always needs its father to come to the rescue."[4] Socrates then describes this bastard's legitimate brother and, with Phaedrus' help, unpacks the famous figure of the good writing, which consists of "things said for the sake of teaching and learning about the just and also about the beautiful and the good, and really written in a soul" (278a). During this passage he moves beyond the concern with educational writing to condemn all writing, and as he repeats and varies the accounts of soul-writing he gradually increases his emphasis on oral teaching, and on the father whose legitimate word is begotten first in his own soul and then in the souls of others, where it defends not only itself but also its father. The good *logos* is first said to be begotten, then to be written in the learner's soul, then to be sown as by a farmer, finally to be spoken by a teacher whose ethical discourse and didactic intent constitute real soul-writing (276a, 276b, 276e-277a, 278a-b).

This passage gets more puzzling the more closely you look at it, but even in my rapid summary several obvious problems stand out. First, why should Plato represent Socrates as criticizing the medium in which that representation takes place? Or, putting it the other way round, if Plato agrees that writing makes the *logos* vulnerable, alienates it from its father's control, why is he so perverse as to commit—or to condemn—Socrates and his *logoi* to writing? Some have suspected foul play and cried parricide, but that begs the question of who is the father of whose *logoi*: is Plato Socrates's scribe or is Socrates Plato's mouthpiece?[5]

Second, when Socrates says that the legitimate brother can defend itself, he suggests that it doesn't need its father. Why then does he later worry about the father, saying that the epistemic *logoi* sown in a like-minded soul can defend not only themselves but also the farmer or father? Isn't the father present in the psychic inscription? And why would the *logos* need to defend itself (granted that it could) if sown, begotten, or written in a proper soul? Against what or whom should it defend itself? Against the learner, even if he is like-minded?

Third, why should Plato have Socrates promote a form of oral discourse that works by—or like—inscription? This is Derrida's money question, but my motive in asking it differs from his. For him the question is, why should Plato have modelled the good writing on the bad so that—whatever he (Plato) intends—the good is contaminated by the logic of the bad? My interest is in the contradiction between the inscriptive ideal and what I referred to above as the principle of dialogical modesty. Gregory Vlastos has emphasized the counter-inscriptive character of Socratic discourse in explaining the complex irony of the disavowals of knowledge and teaching: "In the conventional sense, where to 'teach' is simply to transfer knowledge from the teacher to the learner's mind, Socrates means what he says: that sort of 'teaching' he does not want to do and cannot do. But in the sense in which *he* would give to 'teaching'—engaging would-be learners in elenctic argument to make them aware of their own ignorance and give them opportunity to discover for themselves the truth the teacher held back—in that sense of 'teaching' Socrates would want to say that he is a teacher, the best of teachers in his time, the only true teacher."[6] With one reservation, which I shall get to eventually, I agree with this, and therefore find Socrates's account of soul-writing suspect: if it is meant to articulate a Socratic ideal or aspiration, it isn't in tune with the counter-inscriptive principle described by Vlastos.

Fourth, there is a problem, at least for me, in the way Socrates uses the honorific terms that have become the trademark of his ethic: the just, the beautiful, the good. Those are the terms over which, he often says, people fight and can't come to a satisfactory agreement because the conflict is not one that can be resolved, as technical disagreements are resolved, by appealing to criteria of number, measure, and weight. The terms are ambiguous enough to serve as blank checks, and Socrates sometimes uses them casually, without discussing them, so that it is up to us to decide what construction to put upon his usage. This occurs in the *Phaedrus* passage. We know from occasional discussions in the *Republic* and elsewhere what meaning Socrates himself attaches to the terms, and they accord with our simplest, most obvious ethical intuitions. But if you take the maieutic principle seriously, it is dangerous to assume that every time Socrates mentions these terms he speaks for himself rather than for his interlocutor. That assumption has to be submitted to contextual interpretation. But this much, at least, may be suggested about the idea that the just, good, and beautiful can be inscribed in a soul: if you do take the principle seriously as a practice grounded in an ethical belief about the best way to teach, then it follows that anything that can be directly written in a soul can't be good, just, or beautiful as Socrates understands those terms.

Finally, when Socrates refers to inscription he introduces a disturbance in the normal communication scheme, the scheme in which a sender mediates a message through a contact or channel to a receiver. Since you can probably guess what this disturbance is, I won't insult your intelligence until later. For the present, a clue will have to suffice. At 276b-d Socrates compares literal writing to sowing seeds in a garden of Adonis; sowing them, as he says, in ink through a *kalamos*, a reed-pen. In this analogy the unfit garden soil presumably stands for a material carrier or receptacle, such as a writing tablet or a scroll. The serious and thoughtful farmer will eschew this receptacle and sow his seeds in proper soil, which turns out to be a proper soul. The soul, then, is the alternative to the scroll. And that is the clue.

The implications of these different metaphors of teaching—fathering, sowing, writing—are diverse but they converge on the theme of the learner's passivity. Plant husbandry is the most benign and idyllic figure. Its focus is on three aspects of transmission: the soul as passive receptacle, the automatism of natural process, and the reproduction of the same, that is, the idea that words are programmed to bear certain kinds of fruit the way seeds are, and will, if sown in the right soil, become plants that are identical with those they came from. This should be reassuring to the farmer/teacher however hard he has to work to put in his crop. Fathering is less benign. The mixed metaphor of sowing seeds through a reed-pen packs a barely concealed phallic punch that's unloaded in the shift from farmer to father. This brings two disturbing ideas into play: first, teaching as phallic penetration becomes comparable to the sexual domination of the passive partner by the active partner, and second, teaching is assimilated to the fantasy of male parthenogenesis, a fantasy whose immediate force is directed not so much against woman *per se* as against any sort of otherness that will reduce the resemblance of the offspring to their father.

Given the restless figural metamorphosis of the passage, and granted that the father is the teacher, it is not always easy to identify the occupant of the filial position: is it the learner and his soul, or the *logos* he receives? Nor is it easy to distinguish the position of *pais*, the son, from that of *paidika*, the pederastic partner. The *Phaedrus*, like the *Symposium*, gives a lot of attention to the abuses of pederasty, to its positive social and educational function, and to the slanderous way its ideology is deployed (in the speeches of Pausanias and Lysias) to justify or conceal the abuses. The dialogues focus on the narcissistic motives behind the ideal of pederastic inscription. *Pais* and *paidika* name the instrument as well as the product by which mortal fathers strive to reproduce and perpetuate themselves. As an institutional alternative and political supplement to the adult male's sexual and paternal role in the household, pederasty enables the desire of phallic penetration to converge with that of paternal self-reproduction.

The major premise of the pederastic ideology depicted in the dialogues is that the father can't replicate himself and his *logos* as perfectly in his biological children (because woman interferes) as in his intelligible children. Socrates sometimes compares fathers to lovers, poets, and legislators because all are makers of images—imitators—whose production is motivated by the desire not merely to memorialize themselves or their *logoi* but to have power over the future. This is harder to achieve with human children than with laws and poems, and even the pederast has to be clever enough to overcome the resistance of the potentially intractable partner he wishes to inseminate with his *logos*. You have only to probe a little way beneath the surface of suave speechmaking in the *Symposium* to find the flood of apprehensions that shakes its basis: the desire of lovers to throw off the yoke of fathers, parents, and the patriarchal *oikos*; the attempt to overthrow the myth celebrating woman's—Aphrodite's—power over male desire by distinguishing a higher, Uranian, Aphrodite who presides over all-male attachments; the fears implicit in that attempt, which registers the Hesiodic association of Aphrodite with the nightmare of terrible fathers hating, burying, swallowing their sons, of the son mutilating the father, of the paternal phallus begetting the archetypal seductress who will enact his revenge by her ability to disempower and emasculate his sons. The dialogues present pederasty and patriarchy not only as competing sources of *paideia*, the name given to the institution for socializing the young, but also as forms of generational and factional warfare. *Paideia* provides the obvious context for exploring the role of collective practices of inscription in Athenian culture, and the accounts given in the *Republic* and *Protagoras* bring out its strategic contributions to this warfare. But before discussing those accounts, let me say a word about a key word I have already used several times, and this happens to be the word "word," or *logos*.

Logos has the range and diffuseness of our term "discourse." In the dialogues its range of denotation includes particular arguments or processes of arguing; words, the meanings they signify, or the things they refer to; conversations, speeches, stories, and sayings (an epigram or proverb can be a *logos*). In the most general sense, a person's *logos* or argument can be equivalent to what we sometimes call a value system, as when it is said that a father hands his *logos* down to his son. What I think is historically important and specific about the term is the assimilation of its cognitive and semantic dimensions to its communicative and performative sense. That is, the concept *logos* reflects in its multivalence a situation in which forms of thought, argument, and public communication were carried on primarily through the oral channel, and were conformed to the structure of that channel. I use the word "logocentric" to denote this situation. "Logocentric" specifies the speech-centered character of a society's culture and institutions, and the effect of this character on collective patterns of thought, belief, motivation, interaction, and public practices. "Logocentrism," thus understood, overlaps with, but is broader than, "phonocentrism," and it excludes a notion sometimes associated with it, a commitment to the alphabetic transcription of speech.

* * *

The accounts given in the *Republic* and *Protagoras* both focus on that stage of *paideia* known as music (or *mousikê*), which covers instruction not only in harmony, rhythm, and song, but also in the traditional morality transmitted chiefly by the poets. There are, however, significant differences in the two accounts. Protagoras claims to be describing the actual practices of Athenian education, whereas Socrates and his interlocutors elaborate a reformed version of this *paideia* as part of their fantasy of the guardian polis. Protagoras tells how boys learn to read and write so that they may memorize the works of good poets and imitate the good men of the past the poets write about (325e-326a). But in Socrates's discussion of *mousikê* there is no mention of reading and writing. The proposed indoctrination of guardians appears to be channeled strictly through the oral/aural medium. The exclusion is rendered conspicuous by three strategically placed passages in which Socrates uses reading and inscription in purely metaphoric expressions (368c-d, 402a-c, 501a-d).

The political significance of this exclusion may be suggested by a glance at the following passage:

> Every group entrusts to bodily automatisms those principles most basic to it and most indispensable to its conservation. In societies which lack any other recording and objectifying instrument, inherited knowledge can survive only in its embodied state. Among other consequences, it follows that it is never detached from the body which bears it and which—as Plato noted—can deliver it only at the price of a sort of gymnastics intended to evoke it: *mimesis*. The body is thus continuously mingled with all the knowledge it reproduces, which can never have the objectivity and distance stemming from objectification in writing.[7]

Reversing Bourdieu's emphasis will bring out the point of the exclusion of writing in the *paideia* of guardians: it is to make sure that inherited knowledge will never be detached from the body that bears it, so that it will not be abstractable from the authorized channel and therefore will not be obtainable through any other channel. To inscribe *directly* in the body is to naturalize what has been inscribed and conceal its socially constructed character. To inscribe in the body, not in any more objective or distanced medium, is to inhibit the possibility of reading, which is to say, the possibility of interpretation. If one's aim is to prevent interpretation, one tries to keep inherited knowledge from being detached from the body.

The educational practices Bourdieu alludes to have been thoroughly explored in Eric Havelock's now classic studies of the musical and mnemotechnical mechanisms of oral culture. Havelock reconstructed the means by which the "Homeric encyclopedia" was "imprinted upon the brain of the community," as he puts it, as if it were "a body of invisible writing."[8] I find the details of his reconstruction compelling and imaginative, but I have doubts about the political assumptions that inform it. Havelock rightly recognizes that the Homeric epics were unlike the oral poetry of the Balkan peasants they had been compared to by Parry and Lord, in that they were the poetry of the "governing class" and were used in Athenian *paideia* to educate "for leadership and social management" (93-94).

Nevertheless, he persistently attributes the process to "the community" as a whole, "oral society" as a whole, and to the technical features of its mimetic practices. This is a structuralist explanation, and it ignores the motivating force exerted on *paideia* by factional and ideological conflict. What Plato's Socrates and Protagoras describe is less a structural *tendency* than a sociopolitical *strategy*. In the *Republic*, which I'll consider first, the aim is to reestablish a warrior aristocracy, while in the *Protagoras* the sophist depicts *paideia* as an instrument by which wealthy oligarchs and aristocrats can gain, regain, or keep control of democratic institutions.

The *Republic* represents the *paideia* for guardians as a particularly devious form of ideological inscription. First, its moral content is determined in advance of the institution of the polis by Socrates and his interlocutors, who are playing at being its founders: their *logoi*, their views of right and wrong, their schemes of institutional order and political culture will be transmuted to the truth, law, and nature unquestioningly embraced by all citizens. Even the rulers will be programmed: their form of reasoning is not *logos* but *logismos* or *logistikê*; not dialogical argument about ends or values but calculation, computation, instrumental reasoning about means. As we learn when Glaucon assents to Socrates's remarkable invention of the philosopher dog, philosophy in the guardian polis is to be reduced to animal conditioning. Second, the founders are to disappear behind the smokescreen of the famous noble or well-born lie which, if it is accepted as truth, will make them the hidden gods and voyeuristic masters of a polis putatively instituted by nature. Third, not only this but also other lies will be instilled through *paideia* so that, for their own good, the citizens will unknowingly live and transmit the lies as truth. Socrates's interlocutors agree with his repeated assertion that what counts in the stories told the young is not whether they are false or true but whether they are *kalos* (fine, beautiful) or bad. The representations made by poets and painters are to be judged fine or bad only in terms of the pre-established standards of guardian morality; these are to be dissociated from, and to prevail over, all other criteria of truth. But for Socrates to insist on calling them lies is to remind us that there *are* other criteria and that they are being suppressed. This reminder encourages us to read the account of the inscription of lies through music with deep suspicion.

Socrates blithely admits that the tales to be told children "are, as a whole, false." This is because we who tell them are ignorant of "the truth about ancient things" (since our only evidence for the existence and behavior of gods and heroes comes from the tales we are now criticizing). But, he continues, just as lying is occasionally justified "against enemies" and as a *pharmakon* to prevent "so-called friends" from doing "something bad," so fine lies are *always* justified in educating children (382c-d) because "the beginning is the most important part of every work"; then, when it's young and tender, "it's best molded and takes whatever impression one wishes to stamp on it"; the opinions thus imprinted tend "to become hard to eradicate," and so, "with respect to virtue," children must be told "the finest . . . tales for them to hear" (378a-d).[9] The properly trained child would intuitively "praise the fine things" and "blame and hate the ugly . . . before he's able to grasp ["reasonable speech," Bloom; "the reason," Jowett, Shorey, Lee], and when the *logos* comes, he would take most delight in it . . . because of his nurture" (401d-402a). That is, whatever *logos* accords with the doctrine stamped in by *mousikê* is to be defined as reasonable by virtue of that harmony.

The language of artistic production is repeated later, when Socrates describes the conditions set by philosophers as the price of their participation in the polis. They would not agree to take a city or individual in hand unless it had already been purged or they themselves could clean it up. This they would do by treating the city and human dispositions as one treats a *pinax*, a wooden writing or drawing tablet: they would first "wipe it clean"—no easy task—and then inscribe (either by writing or drawing) the better laws and dispositions, erasing and revising until they had produced the fairest possible *graphê* (501a-c). As artists and imitators aiming to produce a city of obedient androids, the philosophers' desire reflects that of the founders. We learn in Book VIII that this dream, this nightmare, of inscription is bound to fail, but the real question is, why was the project undertaken in the first place? By whom and for whom was it undertaken? Do the arguments for the guardian polis come from Socrates? Do they come from Plato? Or someone else? There is a clue to a possible answer near the end of the discussion of *paideia.*

At 401d, after going through the proposals for the reform of poetry, and after stating that poets and all other craftsmen must be compelled to inscribe the founders' values on the guardians' environment, Socrates explains that musical *paideia* is "most powerful"—*kyriôtatê*—because "rhythm and harmony most of all insinuate themselves into the inmost part of the soul and most vigorously lay hold of it in bringing grace [*euschêmosynên*] with them; and they make one graceful if he is correctly reared; if not, the opposite" (401d-e). The combined suggestions of sneakiness, violence, and political mastery give this description an uneasy edge—as if the soul has to be assaulted and infiltrated—and call for a closer look at the word Jowett, Shorey, and Bloom translate as "grace." *Euschêmosynê* means "having good *schêma*," and *schêma* in various contexts means form, shape, outward appearance, figure, bearing, mien, stateliness, fashion, the constitution or state of a thing, and finally, a figure in dancing. Socrates's usage crystallizes the image of a good dancer, and it connotes not only the outward bearing of a gentleman (*kalos te k'agathos*, 402a) but also the inward formation of certain socially charged esthetic and moral preferences. And since the root meaning of *schêma* is having, holding, possessing, the term also suggests having good having, good holding(s), good possessing; finally, this sense gets its currency from the etymological kinship of *schêma* to *pleonexia*, a key term and problem in the dialogue. *Pleonexia* means not only having more but wanting to have more; wanting to be bigger, better, superior. It means never having enough because you aspire to total and immortal self-sufficiency even if that involves draining the rest of the world of power, wealth, pleasure, and being. But there is also another, more defensive side to *pleonexia* in a society whose members are aware of competing with each other: *pleonexia* involves wanting to take from another before another takes from you.

The pleonectic society described and dramatized in Book I of the *Republic*, and subversively present in the remaining books, is an apprehensive society. It is founded on a misanthropic perception of the social order as a system of relationships motivated primarily by *apprehension*, that is, by the prehensive desire to take and the apprehensive fear of being taken. Socrates's chief interlocutors, Adeimantus and Glaucon, are especially disturbed by the cynicism and *pleonexia* of the city's traditional culture and by its slander of justice. One of the things that troubles them is that they are half-persuaded by the slander, don't know how to come to the rescue of justice, and want Socrates to do it for them. They want him to come to their rescue as well by making better arguments than they can make for what they would like to believe. They want him to persuade them, since they can't persuade themselves, that justice *per se* is good, and is its own reward. This motivational setting is what drives the utopian critique and construction with which Socrates responds to their demand. Every step of that construction is made contingent on their assent. In that respect they are at very least the co-founders of the polis. Socrates's utopian discourse reflects *their* values, projects the unexamined or repressed fears, desires, and contradictions motivating *their* demand for a defense of justice.

The specter of *pleonexia* haunts the account of the guardian polis if only by conspicuous exclusion, that is, by the extraordinary, indeed desperate, lengths the founders go to in order to contain it. It is characteristic of what I would call meta-utopian discourse—the critique of utopianism—that it dramatizes the source of the utopian exorcism of actuality in *ressentiment*, or paranoid apprehensiveness. The more time and ingenuity the utopian spends in describing reforms, the more we feel there is to reform, and the more difficulty we have in believing the reforms will work. Later in the discussion, when Adeimantus comments on the difficulty of preventing lawlessness from spreading like a plague "until it finally subverts everything private and public" (424d-e), we sense that the extremism of the proposed reforms only measures the misanthropic anxieties of the brothers who endorse them.

* * *

Turning now to the *Protagoras*, I shall focus on one section of the sophist's "great speech," as Socrates wryly calls it, the section that purports to describe *mousikê*. The brilliance of both the dialogue and the sophistical performance it represents owes much to the way Protagoras is made subversively to stir up the apprehensiveness of his audience, and appeal to its *pleonexia*. His audience includes such pleonectic malcontents as the radical Alcibiades and the reactionary Critias, men hard pressed by the tendency of a mobile democracy to produce rich upstarts, or *agathoi*.[10] His performance seems intended to stir up the fears for which he alone claims to have the antidote, and this strategy explains why, in his myth of origins, he fastens on the virtues of *aidôs* and *dikê*, reverence and justice, as preconditions of political virtue. Responding to Socrates's statement that the Athenians did not think virtue was teachable, he fabulates as follows: Zeus proclaimed that whoever did not partake of justice and reverence should be put to death; justice and reverence don't come naturally to the human creature and must therefore be taught; all Athenians teach and are taught virtue "from earliest childhood till the last days of their lives"; those who are most powerful and wealthy keep their children in school the longest, and are in the best position to top off their efforts by sending them to Protagoras for advanced instruction. It is in line with this appeal to the wealthy that he revises Zeus's sentence by adding a property qualification: "not merely death, but confiscation of property, and, in a word, the absolute ruin of their estates."

What Protagoras means by *aidôs* is not adequately rendered as "reverence." He insists at one point that there is something all humans believe, namely, that when people know a man is unjust, and when the man himself knows it, he is expected—and should be taught—to lie in public about it. Protagoras thus teaches that everyone teaches that everyone should be taught, not how to be just, but how to escape being punished for injustice. *Aidôs* in this scheme becomes partly a deterrent—fear of public opinion and punishment—and partly the learned ability to persuade the public by clever speaking that one has justice or some other political virtue even if one lacks it.[11] Packed inside this doctrine is another, which is that no one given the ring of Gyges's ancestor would be expected to get high marks for justice. This is an article of Protagoras's more subversive teaching: since virtue comes only "by training," injustice, impiety, greed, and the other vices must be "natural" to human beings. His myth portrays a deprived and helpless Epimethean creature who begins existence with no inherent protective armor and is the potential victim of all species, including his own. This Epimethean basis produces the nasty brutish Promethean reaction: the stolen fire increases the power to do harm and the desire to advance or protect one's own interest. I think it is thus inaccurate to call the anthropology in his speech melioristic, as has often been done, for what Protagoras teaches can best be called *misanthropology*. The course from savagery to civilization is not envisaged as a gradual development in ethical self-awareness. When he distinguishes civilized humanity from savages, he singles out education, courts of justice, and law as forms of necessity compelling civilized individuals to be heedful of virtue. In his account of the human condition, only the sum total of political and rhetorical constraints separates civilized communities from the self-destroying factionalism of life under the regime of Promethean arts, a regime he slyly associates with the competing sophists in his audience.

It is against this background that we can best appreciate the political force of his treatment of *paideia*. Protagoras first describes how the child's elders begin as soon as he can understand speech to badger him with moral instruction. To each word and act they assign a moral value—just or unjust, noble or base, holy or unholy—and they spend every moment teaching, admonishing, and punishing, until he is ready to be packed off to the *grammatistês*, or writing master. They instruct the master to take more trouble over his charges' good behavior than over their letters and harp playing. Accordingly, he teaches them to read by setting "the works of good poets before them on their desks and compelling them to learn them by heart."[12] This is clearly a reference to individual or group recitation rather than to silent reading. Though writing produces a representation of speech that is not only *extended* but also *abstracted* from the more immediate exchanges of oral discourse, in chirographic as opposed to typographic communication the body remains in closer touch with the abstracted medium. And in predominantly oral cultures this control is increased by the practices of dictation and reading aloud, which reincorporate writing into the phonocentric medium. Reincorporation tends to muffle the potential *difference* and nonlinearity of the graphic medium. The poet's written words are treated as images of his voice. The children who recite the written words and impersonate the poet revive the presence of the "good men of old" whose stories and praises he tells.

This hegemonic process of reincorporation is dramatically emphasized in Protagoras's account. First he describes the learning of letters and reincorporates that into the learning of morality. Then he compares the learning of laws (*nomoi*) to writing lessons: "just as writing masters first draw letters in faint outline with the pen for the pupils who are not yet skilled [or clever, *mêpô deinois*], and then give them the copy-book [*grammateion*] and make them write according to the guidance of their lines, so the city sketches out for them the laws devised by good lawgivers of old, and constrains them to rule and be ruled according to these" (326d). But *where* does this second process of "writing" (*hypograpsasa*) occur? Since traditional *nomoi* are unwritten, this phase of learning and socialization is carried out under more informal and pervasive logocentric controls. What the writing analogy suggests is that the *nomoi* are inscribed in the learner's "soul" as a result of socialization, and that he, by continual mimetic practice, deepens and fixes the inscription. The "soul" replaces the *grammateion,* which is probably a wax-coated wooden tablet. The learner "writes" as he is "written on" and makes himself a copy of what he copies. This metaphor was prepared for earlier, when Protagoras said that the blank surface of the human *grammateion* is first straightened out by punishment if it happens to be warped (325d) so that it will receive an undistorted imprint of *paideia.*

In Protagoras's phrase, "the city sketches out the laws," "the city" is a euphemism for the wealthiest, "who are most able" (*hoi malista dynamenoi,* those who are most powerful, 326c). His speech suggests that the Athenian *nomoi* are actually the code observed by and favorable to aristocrats and oligarchs. By representing the learner as a medium of inscription the sophist emphasizes the structure of dominance and deference relations that wealthy aristocrats aspire to transmit through filial mimesis. In doing so, he is making a bid for a share in that structure. His message is that the inscription may be sealed indelibly by resorting to the sophist for the lessons in leadership toward which Protagoras's speech and Athenian education tend as toward their goal. For the learners are not merely to be ruled by the *nomoi*; they are also to rule by them (326d).

I mentioned earlier that the inscription metaphor introduces a disturbance in the normal communication scheme. Protagoras's account shows us what this is: the relation of speaking to hearing is compared not to writing and reading but to writing and being written on. In this jarring displacement, the recipient is neither an auditor nor a reader but the carrier, the servant and support, of the imprinted *logos*. Although the Athens represented by Plato is a predominantly oral society, its intellectuals know writing well enough to appreciate the symbolic implications of its material structure. They borrow the metaphor of inscription, a truncated form of writing, to express a despotic version of the discourse of the other. It is a fine irony that the Platonic text whose aporetic play solicits the conflict of interpretations should represent speakers who propose the notion of a writing that is not something to be read, questioned, and interpreted but is, on the contrary, an ideal of psychic programming that would eliminate the danger and power of interpretive or interrogatory reading. This ideal is to be approximated, the free play of meaning inhibited, by what I referred to as reincorporation, the embedding of written discourse in the forms of oral communication. Reincorporation secures the interlocutory power of those who control the access to the culture's texts, and the transmission of its values. Oddly enough, the very mediation that threatens the logocentric control of meaning—threatens to liberate meaning through what Ricoeur calls the "textual dialectic"—this mediation becomes the model of a technique that perfects logocentric control. The dream of inscription is comparable to the Gorgianic ideal of spellbinding rhetoric, except that it would not only fulfill the aims of persuasion but also render persuasion unnecessary. More than that, it would render all forms of democratic speech unnecessary; would, indeed, cancel their possibility. It would inscribe the "living and breathing word of him who knows"—or who claims he knows—so indelibly that the future would safely be predetermined, tyrannized, by the past.

What motivates the desire of inscription is the general atmosphere of apprehensiveness on which, as I noted earlier, Protagoras capitalizes. And the source of apprehensiveness is the structure of speech-centered institutions prevailing in the Athenian democracy represented by Plato. In the *Phaedrus* this representation focuses on speech-writing, or logography. Socrates's discussion of soul-writing is preceded by a lengthy state-of-the-art account of logography, and especially of the way it contaminates the logocentric interactions of Athenian public life. Speeches are written by one person to be performed by another; manuals are written to show speechwriters how to be effective; speeches already given are recorded in writing to serve as models for new speeches. The Athenian air, the medium of Hellenic sound, is heavy with inscription. Everywhere writers are speaking through speakers, and writing speeches that—as Aristotle showed—create their speakers (rather than the other way round); speeches that create their speakers' *êthos* in the assembly just as dramatists create it in tragic fiction, just as Plato creates it in dialogues. And since the speeches that speak through and construct those speakers are aimed at appealing to the interests, values, and sentiments of the audience, especially to its more influential members, one could say that the speeches are in effect written by the audience, who also authorize the words of wisdom they ascribe to ancient poets, philosophers, and mystagogues, as well as those they hear from sophists and orators.

Socrates concisely characterizes Protagoras's attitude toward inscription, as well as the speech in which it is expressed, when he says that if public speakers like Pericles are questioned, "they are just like books, incapable of either answering you or putting a question of their own."[13] Later in the dialogue he makes a similar comment about the poets: you can't question them "on the sense of what they say" because some interpreters claim they mean this and others that, "and they go on arguing about something they are powerless to put to the test." The implication that if the poets were present to defend their poems, if they weren't dead, they could help us out—this implication is challenged in other passages that suggest the helplessness of the poets themselves to put their poems to the test either by interpretation or by refutation. For the poets are filled with the god, which I interpret to mean that they're moved by the godlike power of whatever or whoever speaks through them. And this is the power of whatever audience or community pipes the music of its desires through the *allotria phônê* (the other or alien voice) of the poet (347c-e) and then receives it from him as the gift, injunction, or wisdom of the gods.

Poet, sophist, logographer, and orator participate in the system of charismatic bondage that makes them resemble books: all have made themselves sites of inscription so that they may in turn successfully inscribe their opinions in the minds of their audience. Doctors and natural philosophers are also in the system, and Socrates often uses the former as a model for the others who, like doctors, are clever at taking the audience pulse, at determining how to gratify its desire for worldly health or, more radically, how to shape that desire to conform with whatever medicine it is in their interest to dispense. Socratic use of the medical analogy in the dialogues is always loaded because it focuses on the following two problematic features, the first adhering to the analogy itself, the second to medical practice. First, the doctor/patient relation differs from the familiar Socratic ideal of the teacher/pupil relation in being nondialogical: the patient is passive, ignorant, helpless, and dependent; the doctor monopolizes knowledge and power, and maintains mastery over the patients who submit their bodies to medicine. Or rather, not to medicine per se but to medical discourse, which leads to the second feature: as practitioners no less than as teachers, doctors must cultivate the art of persuasive speech, and thus they are vulnerable to charges of sophistry. Distrust of doctors is reflected in the following passage from the Hippocratic "Canon":

> Although the art of healing is the most noble of all the arts, yet, because of the ignorance both of its professors and of their rash critics, it has at this time fallen into the least repute of all. The chief cause for this seems to me to be that it is the only science for which states have laid down no penalties for malpractice. Ill-repute is the only punishment and this does little harm to the quacks who are compounded of nothing else. Such men resemble dumb characters on the stage who, bearing the dress and appearance of actors, yet are not so. It is the same with physicians; there are many in name, few in fact.[14]

Perhaps the reference to their being dumb is ill-advised. The charlatans satirized in "The Sacred Disease" conceal their ignorance and failure by "picking their phrases carefully" and by "their patter about divine visitation and possession by devils" (238-39). The author of "Tradition in Medicine" chides "doctors and sophists who maintain that no one can understand the science of medicine unless he knows what man is" and whose discourse "tends to philosophy, as may be seen in the writings of Empedocles and all others who have ever written about Nature" (83). I am reminded by these passages of the connection Socrates draws between Empedocles and Gorgias in the *Meno*, of the medical sophistry of Phaedrus's *erastês*, Eryximachus, and also of other Socratic statements in which Presocratics are enlisted as logographers to supply purveyors of epideictic and deliberative oratory with the kind of bookish doubletalk that credentiates them as *those who know*, lofty-minded philosophers who rise above petty self-interest and understand the nature of things, and whose ethics and expertise are therefore beyond reproach.

Allusions to medical discourse and this Hippocratic context are especially prominent in the *Phaedrus* from 268a through 270.[15] Socrates appeals to the medical expertise of Akoumenos and his son Eryximachus in the course of an *epagôgê* aimed at persuading Phaedrus that the true art of rhetoric transcends the rudimentary skill taught and practised by the most influential sophists, logographers, and manual-writers.[16] He goes on in a vein of Hippocratic irony to associate the true art with the *adoleschias kai meteôrologias physeôs peri* with which Anaxagoras inflated Pericles's natural speaking abilities and *hypsêlonoia* or "loftymindedness" (269e-270a). I consider the statement ironic because, although Jowett and Fowler render the phrase in a straight-faced manner as "discussion and high speculation about nature," this doesn't catch the full flavor of the Greek. *Adoleschias* is flexible enough to yield "garrulity" (Hackforth), while *meteôrologia* denotes a form of speculation whose height is usually determined by the distance of heavenly bodies. This gives us a handle on the value of the *hypsêlonoia* (a nonce-usage) Socrates attributes to the influence of Anaxagoras, and what he thinks of Anaxagoras and his book is pretty well laid out in the *Phaedo* (97b-99e). As I have argued elsewhere, the figures of Anaxagoras, the philosopher king in the *Republic*, and the philosopher described in the *Theaetetus* interlude, as well as the two Eleatic speakers, give a particular meaning to "loftymindedness": *hypsêlonoia* may be defined as the highflying philosopher's apprehension, his *deos* and contempt of the many, his pleonectic desire to escape from local entanglements to mastery of the All.[17] Judging by what Socrates reports he heard a man reading from Anaxagoras's book—that *nous* "orders [*diakosmôn*] and is the cause of all things" (*Phaedo* 97c)—the implication of the *Phaedrus* reference may be that Pericles learned from Anaxagoras how to speak so as to keep the many under his control (*diakosmein* has a military sense, i.e., "to muster").[18] At any rate, the Hippocratic allusion comes out into the open immediately after, when Socrates explains the reference by saying that the "method of the art of healing is much the same as that of rhetoric" because in both cases no one can "adequately understand the nature of the soul [or the body] without understanding the nature of the whole." When Phaedrus attributes this opinion to Hippocrates, one is reminded of the ironic passage from "Tradition in Medicine" cited above.

The pejorative resonance of this allusion vibrates through the account of what has variously been called "true" or "good" or "philosophical" or "dialectical" rhetoric. In my opinion, Socrates's line of argument in this account has been the victim of general misinterpretation. My view of the way he manages the discussion of good and bad rhetoric is very simple. Initially he sets up the expectation that the two arts will be ethically differentiated, the good rhetoric being more just and truthful than the bad. But this expectation is aroused only to be frustrated: ultimately the only differences between the two will be that the good rhetoric is a more artful and effective way than the bad of deceiving and mastering audiences, that the two dialectical procedures of collection and division are no more than techniques instrumental to this end, and therefore that they have little or nothing to do with the "philosophical rhetoric" or dialectical approach to the good which commentators attribute to Plato and/or Socrates.

To run through some of the key passages that support this view, at 259e Socrates asks Phaedrus whether, if things "are to be said well [*eu*] and beautifully [*kalôs*], there mustn't be knowledge in the mind of the speaker of the truth about whatever he intends to say?" Phaedrus understands this as a question about the ethics of speech and replies that he has heard "that one who intends to be an orator doesn't need to know [*manthanein*, have learned or been taught] what is really just but only what seems just to the majority of those who are to pass judgment, and not what is really good or noble but what will seem to be so, because persuasion comes from that and not from the truth." Socrates proposes that they examine this piece of wisdom, and this is the standard opening move in his practice of refutation. But surprisingly his refutation does not engage the ethical issue. At 262a he remarks that "he who is to deceive another, and is not to be deceived himself, must know accurately the similarity and dissimilarity of things." Especially in the case of such unstable and contested—and crucially important—terms as the just and the good and their contraries, the "good" or dialectical rhetorician knows how to make the just or good appear unjust or bad, and vice versa (261c-e, 263a-c). This presupposes his knowing the truth about the things he discusses (262a), since "he cannot become skilled in making people pass from one thing to its opposite by leading them little by little through resemblances, or [skilled] in avoiding the same [deception], unless he knows the reality of each thing" (262b). Thus one who knows what is truly good and just can choose to employ that knowledge wickedly and unjustly; the dialectical art that makes him technically superior may be employed in the service of morally corrupt ends. To know the good is not necessarily to do it.

The goal of this dialectical rhetorician is power, not virtue. It is "to produce conviction" (271a) and influence souls (*psychagôgia* 271d). In order to do this he must know more than the truth of what he is talking about. He must have true knowledge of "the nature of that to which his words are to be addressed, and that is the soul" (270e); knowledge also of the kinds of soul to be addressed, and the kinds of speeches appropriate to the kinds of souls (270c-272b, 273d-e). This is a purely technocratic *telos*, and it is to this end that the two dialectical procedures of collection and division are to be employed.

The moral parity of good and bad rhetoric, their identical purpose, is brought out in Socrates's comments on *ta eikota*, probabilities. At 266e, 267a, and 272d-e, an important feature of incomplete or undialectical rhetoric is said to be its valorizing of probabilities, which "are more to be esteemed than truths" since, according to its practitioners and teachers, "in the courts . . . nobody cares for truth . . . but for the *pithanon*, what is convincing, and that is the probable," and if the truth of what happened is improbable it should not be told. In his response to this opinion Socrates appears to turn the tables on Tisias and the other self-styled experts who profess to teach the shorter easier road to success in the art of rhetoric. Pretending to address Tisias he says, "some time ago, before you came along, we were saying that this notion of the probable was accepted by the many because of its likeness to the true, and we just now explained that the one who knows the truth is always best able to discover likenesses" (273d). Ronna Burger argues that Socrates here "claims Phaedrus's allegiance for the defense of dialectics," and that "in his demand for the principles of dialectics as the necessary foundation of the true art of rhetoric Socrates points to that desired transformation of *erôs* to philosophical *erôs* presupposed by his recantation" (88-89). This reading is not supported by either the passage or its context. For, in the first place, Socrates had not explicitly discussed the probable in connection with his own account of the skill in producing resemblances at which the dialectician would be superior; he had delegated the trade in probabilities to nondialectical rhetoricians; thus his identifying them here tends to collapse the difference between the two and make them resemble each other. In the second place, the passage itself merely reiterates Socrates's earlier statements about the kind of knowledge that will enable the rhetorician to deceive people and avoid being deceived, the knowledge of the truth of things that will enable him to produce the likeness of truth as well as the truth itself—and note that in those statements the question of the rhetorician's concern for ethical truth is conspicuously excluded.

In the third place, Socrates goes on to make two moves that further dissolve any ethical difference between good and bad rhetoric. First, he summarizes the demand he had previously elaborated three times in successively greater detail (270c-d, 271a-b, 271c-272b): the true rhetorician must know the soul and its diverse forms well enough to be able to enumerate the natures among his audiences; he must know, as Socrates said earlier, that "men of a certain sort are easily persuaded by speeches of a certain sort for a certain reason to actions or beliefs of a certain sort, and men of another sort cannot be so persuaded" (271d); the repeated instances of the intensified indefinite adjective, *toiosde*, emphasizes the purely technical and amoral aim of this *technê*. Second, he repeats that the true rhetorician must be able to perform the two dialectical operations, dividing things (*ta onta*) into classes and comprehending—or embracing, or capturing (*perilambanein*)—each thing (*hekaston*) under a single idea (273d-e). It is significant that the more aggressive *perilambanein* replaces the blander term first used to denote the process of collection, *synagôgê*, and that *ta onta* to be divided and *hekaston* to be embraced or captured may well, according to the sequential logic of the statement, include audiences. Hence in this conclusion to his account of the true art of rhetoric, Socrates returns to the idea of inscription.

* * *

All ancient writing, as Socrates presents it, is logographic and political, and oriented toward control of logocentric institutions. It is motivated by the desire of power and the fear of impotence, and this is perhaps the most salient point to emerge from the discussion in the *Phaedrus*, the *locus classicus* on the subject. Logography thus provides a metaphor that expresses the penetration of any speech act, any speaking presence, by some form of the discourse of the other. Plato's Socrätes would not be surprised by such views as those elaborated by Bakhtin and Derrida. Of course, when Socrates disparages the written word he is speaking to Phaedrus, which in the present interpretive framework means—to an extent not always fully determinable—that he is speaking *for* Phaedrus, and the view of writing he develops reflects the constraints of that discourse. He entertains only two alternatives, both of them based on a strict logocentric understanding: total control of the text's meaning by its "father" or else total loss of control. This is the burden of the Egyptian fable. When Theuth claims that his invention of writing is a *pharmakon* of memory and *sophia*, Thamus objects that it will have the opposite effect on those who learn it. They will not exercise their memory "because through trust in writing they will be calling things back to mind by means of alien marks [*allotriôn typôn*] outside them, not from within themselves," and the *sophia* Theuth offers is more apparent than real, "for having become, through you, *hearers of many things without instruction* they will seem to be knowers of many things while for the most part knowing nothing and being hard to get along with" (275a-b).

The crux of the issue lies in the phrase, "hearers of many things without instruction," and especially in the first word of the Greek text: *polyêkooi* which I just rendered as "hearers of many things." Translators have trouble with this word, in part because of its context and in part because it is a rare Platonic coinage.

Jowett's rendering, which I follow, is "they will be hearers of many things," Fowler's, "they will read many things," and Hackforth's, "by telling them of many things." Granted that reading is performed aloud, "hearing," which presupposes "telling," doesn't seem relevant to Thamus's objection. I suspect that the force of the objection centers not on reading vs hearing but on the implications of the remainder of the Greek phrase: "hearers of many things" *aneu didachês*, "without instruction." My suspicion is based on the only other passage in which the term *polyêkoos* appears (these are the only two entries in LSJ). At *Laws* 810e the Athenian sarcastically refers to the many thousands of voices proclaiming that the young should be indiscriminately fed the works of poets in all meters in order to make them, "by means of recitations, lengthy listeners [*polyêkoous*] and large learners, who learn off whole poets by heart."[19] Against this the Athenian genially offers to make himself the effectual god/priest/king of the new city by offering as the criterion for rules of censorship his own discourses in the *Laws*. Teachers should be compelled "to learn these writings, and to praise them, and if any of the teachers fail to approve of them, he must not employ them as colleagues; only those who agree with his praise of the discourses should he employ, and entrust to them the teaching and training of the youth" (811e-812a).

This passage should be set in the context provided by other references to the role of writing in the methods of thought control which Plato represents as the means by which Egypt succeeded in becoming the model of a change-resistant polity. For example, the Athenian praises the Egyptians' ability to prevent innovation or deviation in dance and choric song by posting lists of approved postures and songs in the temples, ascribing them to "a god or someone divine," and preventing poets from being allowed to teach "whatever the poet himself finds pleasing in the rhythm or tune or words of poetry" (*Laws* 656c-657b).[20] The authorized songs, poems, and dances are consecrated to gods and spirits worshipped at specified times according to the annual calendar of festivals in ceremonies regulated by officials who enforce strict conformity to those ancient paradigms. The only poetic writing to be accorded this "divine" status in the neo-Egyptian polity the Athenian and his Dorian interlocutors are founding is the "tragic" discourse entitled *Laws* (817b).

In the *Timaeus* Critias reports Solon's account of the Egyptian priests who create and control the authorized tradition. The aged priest who patronizes Solon and the childlike Greeks because they have "no store of old belief based on long tradition" seems to belong to an order that has not heeded Thamus' warning: "if any event has occurred that is noble and great or in any way conspicuous, whether it be in your country or in ours or in some other place of which we know by hearsay [*akoên*], all such events are recorded from of old and preserved here in our temples"

(23a).[21] The priest praises writing because, in effect, it calls external things to remembrance "by means of alien marks," while Thamus uses the same reason to condemn writing as a crutch that will prevent the *mathêtês* from exercising the kind of mnemonic skill necessary to receive and transmit ancient wisdom.

The apparent inconsistency between these two Egyptian views of writing can be resolved by premising that what the priest in the *Timaeus* refers to is hieroglyphic writing, which is monumental and controlled by an elite. The priest does not share the skepticism of Socrates, who says to Phaedrus of his Egyptian tradition that the ancestors who passed it on "alone know the truth of it" (274c).[22] In Egypt truth is the province of the temple and its ordained living interpreters. When the priest speaks of the ancient writers recording whatever was *kalon* and *mega* or otherwise *diaphoran*—conspicuous mainly for nobility and greatness (i.e., power)—he is describing the heroic *aristoi* of old and their wars, but the phrase could just as well describe the recording medium itself.[23] Ronna Burger has distinguished the pictographic and elitist character of hieroglyphs from alphabetic writing, which represents "oral speech" and "is in principle democratic" (93, 86). She suggests that Thamus is criticizing hieroglyphic writing in the *Phaedrus*, but her own footnotes throw doubt on this because they indicate that the references to Naucratis and the ibis are connected to papyrus and reeds—and therefore to scrolls that can travel about.[24] In the *Philebus* Socrates specifically credits Theuth with the invention of alphabetic writing.[25] The ability of his beneficiaries to record whatever they hear, to do so quickly and economically, using reed pens, portable papyrus, and phonetic writing, and their ability to read these writings to themselves and each other in private places—these abilities will free them to be indiscriminate hearers of many things without authority or supervision. It is that freedom, and not only their failing memories, that will make them *agnômenes*, lacking in the ancient wisdom imprinted on that faculty, and they will therefore be hard to live with; the phrase *chalepoi syneinai* suggests that they don't make good followers or disciples. Thamus hints at a recipe for turning out docile subjects. Proper instruction means hearing not many things but one, the authorized tradition, and hearing it from its embodiment, the priestly instructor who regulates both what the disciples learn and how they learn it. The danger of *polyêkooi* is that it will encourage a kind of writing not easily subject to the control effected by reincorporation in the official logocentric channels; a kind of writing that finds its way, for example, into Plato's dialogues. This danger is avoided, first, by the hieratic authority of the writers and the place of inscription, and second, by the selectivity of the priests.

Theuth claims that his invention will make the Egyptians wiser, but the response of Thamus indicates that the Egyptian power structure has no use for this kind of wisdom. Indeed, the response prompts one to wonder whether the subversive Promethean aspect of Theuth, the threat posed for the established authority by the rebellious inventor of *technai*, doesn't lurk in the background of Socrates's fable. Thamus/Ammon of Thebes is a god and king associated with the hegemony of the priesthood, and the ambiguous formula, "some god or godlike human" (applied to Theuth at *Philebus* 18b—*eite tis theos eite kai theios anthrôpos*—and used at *Laws* 657a, *theou ê theiou tinos an eiê*), suggests the permeability of the boundary that separates mortals from gods in Egypt. In a theocratic polity the gods and their mortal ministers mutually reinforce each other's power and authority, and some mortals succeed in becoming divine. Egyptian politicians are shrewd enough to know how to take advantage of the strong institutional charisma inherent in this system. As the Athenian shows in *Laws* VII, control of the politics has been centralized, and authorized truth emanates from the center into educational practices, religious beliefs, and political statuses. In Athens, on the other hand, control of inscription is decentered and dispersed throughout the circle, which is a site of continuous contestation. The Egyptian model is thus a pleonectic ideal for Athenians who aspire to the *megethos* and *kratos* of god, king, and priest in a *politeia* to which such a ritualized system of roles has become alien, a thing of the past, precisely because Theuth must have peddled his inventions and discoveries to Greece after having been snubbed by Thamus.[26]

* * *

According to Derrida, writing is censured by the King for its "ineffectiveness" and specious appearance of productiveness, "since it can only repeat what in truth is already there" (134). From this assumption Derrida will draw the consequences that Plato's text, Platonism, and Western metaphysics fall prey to the ineffectiveness Thamus criticizes. I submit on the contrary that what Thamus criticizes is the potential effectiveness of writing as subversive of authorized teaching. Alphabetic writing makes possible logography, the art of rhetoric, and the circle or vortex of inscription, and, through them, the continuous alienation of power and meaning. Platonic writing represents that situation, critiques it, and yet, at the same time, partially submits to it. It gambles on the possibility that inscription can be counter-inscriptive. It is congenial to *polyêkooi*, to rolling about "alike among those who understand and those to whom it isn't akin."[27]

The circle goes round and round from audience to speechwriter to speaker to audience. Of any member of the circle it might be said that the arguments never come from him but from those he is speaking with, or to, or for. Whether or not Socrates is represented as being in the same predicament, his disclaimer only articulates the general effect of the circle. "We are," as he puts it in the *Theaetetus*, "bound to one another by the inevitable law of our being, but to nothing else, *not even to ourselves* . . . we are bound to one another; and so if a person says anything is, he must say it is for, or of, or toward something; but he must not say or let others say, that it is, or becomes, just in and by itself' (160b-c).[28] This argument comes not from Socrates but from Protagoras; Socrates is giving voice to the implications of the Protagorean theory of perception. He will go on to refute this theory. But at another level the Protagorean theory of logocentric bondage will be confirmed by the inescapable constraints of Socrates's own practice.

The institution of logography makes explicit, and historically specific, a situation in which the arguments don't come from the speaker, and in which—as Aristotle would demonstrate in the *Rhetoric*—the "I" uttered by the speaker is the product and not necessarily the author of his utterance. The circularity of this institutional process gives rise, in Derrida's words, "to a structure of replacements such that all presences will be supplements substituted for the absent origin" (167). Logography thus proves a metaphor that expresses the penetration of any speech act, any speaking presence, by some form of the discourse of the other. This structural duplicity, in which presence is the effect of representation, can't have been news to any but the most monumentally pious members of the circle. The rest must have been reasonably disenchanted, possibly cynical, conceivably misanthropic. And maybe this was the condition that kept the system going and made it work. That presence was a representation; that one person's speech was another's text; that the first-person subject spoken by a speech was alienated from the first-person subject who uttered it: these things didn't have to be thematized since, as elements of a system of practice, they could be taken for granted and ignored. But even if ignored, they persist in the undertone of distrust and apprehensiveness that marks the social relations directly or indirectly represented in the dialogues. And in the speech of Lysias which Phaedrus reads to Socrates, this undertone takes a new and sinister turn.

* * *

This speech purports to be the attempt of a self-proclaimed nonlover to warn his auditor against the dangers of yielding to men infected by the madness of *erôs*. Contrasting the lover's *pleonexia* and instability to the nonlover's disinterested prudence and self-control, he not only appeals to the auditor's rational self-interest but also plays on his fear, encouraging him to take measures to protect himself from the dangers conventionally ascribed to love. The trick, of course, as Phaedrus admiringly points out (227a), is that the speech is itself an act of seduction: the imaginary lover is disingenuously pressing his suit for sexual favors. Since he's driven by the same *erôs* he condemns, he both contradicts his argument and compounds his explicit slander of the pederastic system by showing that a lover needn't be a raving maniac; even the slave of desire can be a calculating schemer and role-player.[29] Thus the covert lover's dissimulation is an example of the disorder and bad faith he depicts, a stratagem that justifies and would eventually intensify the apprehensiveness he instills in his addressee.

Socrates responds by improvising a Lysian speech that makes this rhetorical situation explicit: his speech will be by a lover pretending to be a nonlover.[30] But where Lysias's speaker promotes his attentions solely on the grounds of the hedonist calculus, Socrates invents a lover who reasons like a dialectician, gives ethical counsel like a moralist, and opposes to the pleasures of sex the benefits of "divine philosophy." Several commentators argue that this speech has a "higher moral tone" than the other (Ferrari 99), but I think that since the speaker uses the familiar terms of Socrates's ethical *logos* as instruments of deception, he thereby discredits them.[31] What's really at stake here is not the use, misuse, and desire of the body but the use, misuse, and desire of discourse; not the sexual desire and seduction imitated by the speeches but the desire and seduction focused on the love of *logoi*, and especially of clever *logoi* used to deceive. The apparently innocuous character of Lysias's writing conceals its own erotic project. A gymnastic exercise turned out at leisure to entertain the writer and his friends—turned out, as Socrates suggests, with such lovers of discourse as Phaedrus in mind—the speech that praises the nonlover's cleverness cleverly solicits praise for its author's cleverness and calls attention to its own seductive power. And as Socrates also suggests more than once, Lysias writes heady speeches that are to be tasted, consumed, and enjoyed like the food or wine at a symposium; speeches that are to be assimilated or reincorporated so that they *become* the auditor and move or guide him from within; speeches that can be memorized and repeated by performer after performer, thereby achieving a sort of immortality and authority. Because such writing is earmarked primarily as the play and display of clever speechmaking rather than as the vehicle of a serious message, it disarms the impulse to interrogate, analyze, or interpret. However insidious the message may be, it is not to be taken seriously but consumed as if the speech were a placebo that didn't contain a *pharmakon*. Yet as Socrates's Lysian parody clearly shows, the speech is a collection of cynical arguments that slander the conventional practices of a system that involves much more than sex. Those arguments derive from and appeal to the culture of *pleonexia*. The speech is therefore all the more dangerous for being playful and gratuitous, for being a seduction aimed not at possession and use of another's body but at possession and use of another's love of discourse.

What is new and sinister about Lysias's speech is suggested later in the dialogue, at 261a-b, when Socrates asks Phaedrus whether he has heard that the art of rhetoric—the art that "leads souls by means of words"—operates "not only in law courts and various other public gatherings but also in private ones as well." Phaedrus, who shows familiarity with the works of rhetoricians (see esp. 266d ff.), replies in the negative: "the art of speaking and writing is exercised chiefly in lawsuits, and that of speaking also in public assemblies, and I have never heard of any further uses." Socrates goes on to insist that the art which characterizes forensic disputation—the art "directed to confounding good and evil, truth and falsehood" (Hackforth 129)—would be "one and the same in all kinds of speaking," "if it is an art at all" (261e); and a similar generalization is applied to speechwriting (earlier, at 257d-258d, and later in the critique of Lysias's speech).

For me, the point of this—and I'm aware that my opinion is eccentric—is the light it throws both on the speech of Lysias and on the conversation between Phaedrus and Socrates. The speech pretends to be mere *epideixis*, or display, but what it imitates is the mode of forensic or deliberative persuasion, the invention of deceptive arguments aimed at persuading an audience to accept a particular verdict or course of action. In other words, it extends a public practice into the sphere of private relations, relations in which it is conventional to "speak from the heart." If logography had a bad name in some circles (257d-e) this is because its premeditated citational performances and hidden agendas have made it a model and symptom of the sophistry, the dissimulation, the distrust, that pervade the face-to-face interactions of public life. Transforming persons to personas, and presences to representations, speechwriting is an inscriptive practice. Its currency increases the apprehensiveness of a pleonectic society by dramatically foregrounding the elements of manipulation, impersonation, and deception that already hollow out political interactions.[32]

Lysias's speech, as privatized logography, offers to insinuate these elements into the personal sphere whose institutions and discourse inform erotic relations between males. The conventions that govern such relations demand friendship, patronage, and tutelage as well as sex, and so, as I said, the imaginary speaker slanders the conventional relation.[33] But the speechmaker plays a similar game. That is, although the speech is assigned to an imaginary seducer, not Lysias, the writer who pretends to be a nonlover is actually a lover—a lover of his own rhetorico-literary skill, of its product, its effect, and the rewards he expects from it. He aims to seduce people to desire written speeches not only for their readymade eloquence, art, and cleverness but also for their value in helping speakers become more persuasive in erotic pursuits. If the model speech betrays a cynical view of the affairs in which he proposes to intervene with readymade performances, that may only reflect his estimate of the moral state of the speechwriter's market, a market he plans to diversify and expand so as to poach on private preserves.

Lysias's speech sets up the conditions and constraints within which the rest of the dialogue unfolds. It is a clear indicator of the values, desires, and motives of the interlocutor with whom Socrates has to contend. I can describe Phaedrus more briefly, because he has been well characterized in several recent commentaries (those, for example, by Ronna Burger, Charles Griswold, and G.R.F. Ferrari). He is, as Ferrari puts it, an intellectual impresario, an indiscriminate lover of "highbrow talk" whom Socrates pretends to find impressive for his "ability to promote discourses, whether delivering them himself or milking them from others" (6). Like the nonlover in the speech, he expresses contempt for the slavish desires of the body (258e) and for the base pleasures of the many (276d-e), but this disdain—factious, aristocratic, self-stroking—conceals and justifies an equally irrational appetite for discourses. Through Socrates's ironic mimicry, the dialogue shows that Phaedrus is a nonlover of the Socratic *logos* pretending to be a lover, or deceiving himself into thinking he wants what Socrates has to offer when in fact what he tries to do is turn Socrates into another Lysias—to make him, as Phaedrus is himself, a site of Lysian inscription.[34]

Griswold has good things to say about the way Socrates brings out Phaedrus's desire and motives by mimicry, but he takes too sanguine a view of this strategy. Socrates, he claims, imitates Phaedrus "in such a way as both to hold the mirror up to Phaedrus and show Phaedrus what he (Phaedrus) should look like"; he enters into this "comedy of imitation and deception . . . in order to lead Phaedrus to self-knowledge" (28-29). But the mimicry only shows what Phaedrus *does* look like, not what he *should* look like. In this dialogue, as in others, self-knowledge is honored in the breach. Socrates's ironic mimicry, or mimetic irony, continues to showcase Phaedrus's defenses against self-knowledge to the end. It marks his obtuseness, or blindness, or whatever it is, as the source of his power. That power consists in his ability to contain, control, and domesticate Socrates through a strategy which I believe Alexander Sesonske was the first to articulate many years ago: the strategy of reducing the Socratic enterprise . . . to the level . . . of a spectacle, an entertainment." Sesonske quotes Polemarchus's words to Socrates at the beginning of the *Republic*, "Could you really persuade [us] . . . if we don't listen?" (327c), and he observes that one of the "many ways in which one may refuse to listen . . . is to allow the words to be spoken, and attend to them, but to treat the whole process as a game, a mode of entertainment, and thus drain the words of all significant meaning."[35]

The idea that Socrates's interlocutors disarm him by reducing his performances to the status of entertainment activates as a presupposition the idea that there is something to disarm—something dangerous or threatening about Socrates. The idea is familiar enough because it smokes the edges of Plato's portrait of him in all the Socratic dialogues. He is not a mere truth-sayer but a self-proclaimed gadfly to the polis (that is an ironic self-deprecation; calling himself a mere gadfly implies that although he can sting and irritate he can't do very much harm); a stingray to Meno; a hybristic sorcerer to Alcibiades. He is also a sophist, a disputatious *antilogikos* skilled in the shifty tactics of eristic warfare, and famed for his ability to put down his opponents. He thus poses a threat at two levels. First, his ethical medicine is bitter to the taste because in asking people to examine themselves critically he threatens their self-interest and self-esteem. Second, his procedure confuses or entraps his interlocutors, makes them look bad, and draws from their utterances meanings they didn't intend. As Sesonske suggests, Socrates's interlocutors control him by occluding the first level—blocking the ethical challenge—and fixing on the second level, which then provides entertainment for auditors, hangers-on, and even opposing verbal pugilists who take pleasure in a good fight.

Whether it derives from his ignorance or from his skill in managing the resources culture makes available for defending against self-knowledge and self-refutation, Phaedrus's power lies in his ability to reduce Socrates to a Lysian entertainer and a Phaedrian lover of good talk—his ability to contain Socrates within the circle of inscription and keep him from breaching his interlocutor's defenses. To some extent, I think, Socrates's palinode is constructed as an interpretive reflection of Phaedrus's motives and desire. The limits of space prevent me from discussing this speech in the manner it deserves, but a few cursory comments will at least suggest the direction a more adequate reading might take. C. J. Rowe argues that the palinode is "a set piece," a *paignion* "Socrates indulges in . . . just because he is aware of the limitations of the form which Phaedrus has forced him to adopt." Pretending to be serious when in fact it isn't, and pretending to be a spontaneous ecstatic outburst when it is actually a citational pastiche, the speech "turns out—once more—to be just like a book."[36] It is a visualized, simplified, detextualized narrative whose background is the latent set of contradictions and complexities conspicuously excluded from the previous speeches and brought to the surface by the subsequent rhetorical analysis that textualizes the myth.

The palinode is a double act of mimicry that brings its two targets into relation with each other. On the one hand, Socrates parodies an archaic and elitist discourse, like that of Timaeus in its *hypsêlonoia*, aristocratic in its values and ideology, hegemonic in its proliferation of ranks and categories that impose hierarchy on its hubristic overview of the cosmos, the gods, and the psyche. On the other hand, the imagery of the palinode is revised to serve as a parody of Lysian logography, a parody of the erotics of discourse in which sexual desire is diffused and sublimated and displaced until it becomes, alive and powerful beneath its disguises, the motive force of the All.[37] Putting its myths in scare quotes, Socrates flags not only the hegemonic appropriation of archaic culture by the old and new *agathoi* but also the mystifying rhetoric by which the whole of culture and cosmos are conscripted in the service of privatized logography as an art of seduction. The palinode thus fans out the range of discourses funneled and compacted into the figure and proper noun of *Phaidros*, one made bright by reflection of a light source, and one who feels the self-lack that might become self-contempt did he not make himself a trap to catch, a screen or tablet to be inscribed with, the brightness of others. *Phaidros*: both mirror and *grammateion.*

Near the end of the palinode Socrates suggests that the only way he could find or constitute a true dialogical partner and beloved would be to create him by narcissistic projection and reflection (252d ff.). There is considerable bitterness behind that idea: his beauty penetrates you as desire and ricochets back to him not as your desire *per se* but as his image idealized by your desire. What you would have to do to draw the beloved toward you is inscribe his idealized reflection on your surface. This is the mirror stage with a vengeance. And I think it throws a lot of light on the puzzling passage about soul-writing with which I began and to which, finally, I now return.

* * *

At 275e Socrates describes the bastard *logos* as tossed about "alike among those who understand and those to whom its contents aren't akin." "Understand" here renders *epaiousin*, which also means "give ear to"; those who understand may therefore be those who are read to, and if this is so, maybe the others are those who read to themselves, that is, those who aren't being controlled by the lecturer in a context of instruction or authoritative interpretation. Socrates's account of the legitimate *logos* that follows at 276a in fact suggests a circumvention of the ear. This *logos*, he says, is better and more powerful in the manner of its begetting because, written with *epistêmê* in the learner's soul, it has the power to defend itself, knowing (*epistêmôn*) to whom it ought to speak and before whom to be silent.

It has been suggested that Socrates is talking here about an intelligible *logos* that pre-exists verbal expression. Is writing a figure for a more abstract, impersonal, or "spiritual" process of learning, one that's somehow secured not only from the promiscuity of bad writing but also from the constraints and uncertainties of face-to-face discourse? This question suggests the possibility that if there is a truth to be communicated, its text may be jeopardized by oral as well as by graphic mediation, that the problem therefore may not be writing *per se* but loss of control over interpretation, a danger inherent in the transmission of messages whenever a contact or medium intervenes between the sender and the receiver (even when sender and receiver are the same person).

At 276e Socrates says that the serious teacher, taking hold of a proper or like-minded soul, uses the art of dialectic to plant and sow epistemic *logoi* that contain "seed from which other *logoi* springing up in other dispositions or characters [*êthesi*] are capable of making this [process] ever undying, and making their possessor happy." The new *logoi* may be "other" in the sense of "different," but the farming metaphor doesn't support this reading. The comparison of insemination and inscription to planting has an effect similar to that produced by other texts in which the reproductive function is imaged in tropes that suggest male parthenogenesis: as I mentioned earlier, the emphasis is on the reproduction of the same, the suppression of otherness, and the secure transmission guaranteed by the automatism of natural process. This emphasis is heightened by the reference to immortality. Hackforth notes that this can suggest the immortality of the possessor as well as of the transmission process, and I think it can also suggest the immortality of the first possessor, the sower and father; if he himself can't live forever, he can at least try to clone himself in an endless series of replicas.[38] Desiring nothing less than this, which is a kind of filicide, he may wonder whether even the so-called legitimate *logos* will be able to defend against misinterpretation, the symbolic parricide that's an appropriate response to symbolic filicide. For the father who wants to perpetuate his *logos*, defending against misinterpretation is the same as defending against interpretation. Anxiety on this score is expressed by the phrase "taking hold of a proper or like-minded soul." The Greek word which, following the translators, I've just blandly rendered as "proper or like-minded," is *prosêkon*. This word also means "akin to," and, more interestingly, "belonging to"—as a child, for example, or a woman, or a slave, or some other member of an adult male's household, may be said to belong to him. The father, let's say, wishes to inscribe his *logos* on what he considers his property. But if the son is akin to the father, and like-minded, he may want to avoid inscription; that is, he may want to father his own *logos*; and this may account for the coercive participle, *labôn*, "taking hold" or "seizing." The father who desires to live forever by reducing souls to receptacles bearing his imprint may well fear that nothing short of violence will do the trick.

The implication of violence may seem to be softened by the mention of dialectic in the phrase I just discussed, but I don't think it is. Socrates had earlier (265d-266c) described dialectic as an art comprised of two processes, collection and division. The first, he mentions in passing, was illustrated by his second speech. But here, in speaking of rhetoric, he only illustrates the other method, division, or *diaeresis*. (This is the art promoted and carried to an outlandish extreme by the Eleatic Stranger who is, as I've argued elsewhere, represented by Plato as a despotic enemy and devious appropriator of the Socratic *logos*.)[39] The rhetorician is dialectical, Socrates says, if he can analyze the different classes of soul and the different speech-classes, can discern these classes in actual affairs, and can match the right kind of speech with its proper soul-type. At 265e he characterizes this procedure as an art of efficient butchery, and distinguishes the good carver of discourse from the bad by his ability to cut the body at its natural joints. The association of dialectic with dismemberment and food production doesn't strike me as innocent, and there's no reason why it should: its ultimate destination is an account of the techniques that improve logography and help extend its practice into private life. Socrates first introduces the method of division after suggesting that the "good" or dialectical rhetorician knows how to deceive people by making the just appear unjust and the good bad (263a-b).

Socrates will conclude his account of soul-writing at 278c by condemning all types of logography unless they are informed by truth, and—here's the rub—unless the writer who composed them can support them by refuting them and "has the power to show by his own speech that the written words are of little worth" (278c). That is, those who know the truth also know that it cannot be transmitted, cannot be defended against misinterpretation, by writing; and if this is part of the truth they know, one may legitimately ask why they bothered to write in the first place. The answer suggested in several dialogues is that they confused their desire to perpetuate the truth with their desire to perpetuate themselves. If so, since they are not themselves immortal, since they can't hang around forever to defend their writing, they foolishly chose the wrong medium; their mastery of the dialectical art went for naught, and that mastery is itself placed in question by the fact that, having divided the written truth from the spoken truth, and writing on scrolls from writing on souls, they chose the wrong division.

At 277b-c Socrates recalls and summarizes the earlier discussion of dialectical logography. He then goes on to assert, first, that it is a disgrace for any writer to believe his writing has great certainty and clarity, and second, that it is a disgrace to be ignorant "of what is a waking vision and what is a dream-image [I follow Hackforth here] of the just and the unjust, the bad and the good, . . . even if the whole mob applaud it" (277d-e). Here again, if you connect the two assertions, the implication is that a written image of the just and the good is itself unjust and bad, that—or perhaps I should say *because*—the writer is motivated by the desire for applause and power as well as by his self-defeating belief in the clarity and certainty of the medium. The final version of the soul-writing formula at 278a focuses more intensely than before on the father's problematic relation to his project: "only in things said for the sake of teaching and learning about the just and also about the beautiful and the good, and really written in a soul, is there clearness and completeness and serious value; and . . . such *logoi* should be considered the speaker's own legitimate offspring, first the one within himself, if it be found there, and secondly such of its children and brothers as may have sprung up worthily in the souls of others. That man who renounces all other *logoi* is likely, Phaedrus, to be such as you and I might pray that we may become." I note in passing the hesitation of "if it be found there," the conditional softening of "such . . . as may have sprung up," and the uncompromising accent of "renounces all other *logoi*." But what most attracts my attention is the statement that the speaker is the father of the *logos* inscribed in his own soul. Wasn't there a prior father? Is his *logos* autonomous and self-generated? Since talk about the just, the beautiful, and the good uniquely characterizes Socratic discourse, I'm inclined to think he is proposing his own anomalous practice and its *telos* as a model. Did he then conceive or invent his ethical *logos*, first teaching himself, learning from himself, inseminating himself, and inscribing himself until he came to "see" its truth at last, fixed clearly, unambiguously, in his soul? If so, inscription would scarcely be possible. For either the *logos* he transmits is the product of that process or it is the process itself. If it is the product, it would be inscribed in another without the method of self-insemination that would enable the learner to produce and defend his own legitimate offspring. If the *logos* is the process, then each new father displaces his predecessor and generates his own *logos* in terms of *his* conception of the truth about the just and the good and the beautiful—terms about whose positive content the Socratic father could hardly be said to be overly forthcoming. The result of the first scenario would be filicide, and, of the second, parricide. Both scenarios are aporetic in the sense that they imply that the pathway of inscription is blocked. And the passage as a whole remains perplexing because the ambiguity of the term *logos* defends against decisive interpretation.

In spite of all uncertainty, however, Socrates's repeated formulations of the ideal keep his official advocacy of soul-writing in the foreground. But the more he rephrases and insists on the ideal, the more he sows seeds of doubt as to its viability. As he pushes the argument for inscription aggressively forward, something in his language resists it and shrinks away from it, progressively undermines it. So when he ends on the up-beat and carries the now enthusiastic Phaedrus along with him, any voyeur looking down at the text from the Plato-tree under which Socrates and Phaedrus are, in their different ways, lying, is likely to feel a certain uneasiness about what Phaedrus hasn't heard. And the feeling is not diminished by the way Socrates more or less abruptly shuts off the discussion: "we've already played around long enough with talk about *logoi*." Then, as Griswold notes, "he sends

Phaedrus off to deliver to Lysias and all composers of discourses, to Homer and all the poets, to Solon and all the law writers, a report of their dialogue," but an incomplete report, one restricted to the logography discussion, since Phaedrus is shown to have understood little of what went on in the speech- and myth-making it followed. But if Socrates releases Phaedrus to the circle of inscription, Phaedrus—Griswold adds—"is sent by Plato out into the world under cover of a text" whose "message is far more complex than that which Phaedrus is charged by Socrates with delivering" (217). Phaedrus will deliver an anecdote whose secret message is not given out. Plato represents Socrates as uttering *logoi* that can only be given out to an audience beyond his power to reach, and given out thanks to the resources of the medium he rejects.

The increasing dissonance between what Socrates says and Phaedrus seems to hear leads me to imagine a touch of anger or bitterness in his words, as if he has resigned himself to telling Phaedrus what Phaedrus wants to hear. I can imagine, for example, that he puts forth the rigorous concept of soul-writing as a kind of sardonic hyperbole expressing what he would have to do to secure his *logos*, or mimicking what those who think of themselves as his friends want from the great teacher. They want exactly what he refuses to give them, and they want it in the way that would destroy what he does have to give them. They want to be sites of Socratic logography, just as they are already sites of sophistical, poetic, nomothetic, and rhetorical logography. But they also want to control the content of inscription. Socrates is to be their speechwriter, supplying them with zero-sum *logoi* for all occasions; *logoi* to make them performers, entertainers, and politicians; *logoi* to help them get the better of their fellow citizens, their households, their lovers, their parents, their children, and themselves; *logoi* to protect them from their fear of death, of each other, of themselves.

Because I believe Vlastos is right in the account of Socrates's disavowal of knowledge and teaching I cited earlier, I can't subscribe to a straight reading of the inscription passage. On the other hand, I can't fully agree with Vlastos's assertion that "Socrates would want to say he is a teacher, the best of teachers in his time, the only true teacher." At least I would need to know whether "best" is meant as the superlative of a Socratic or a Protagorean good. Socrates, and I mean Plato's Socrates, is hardly the most successful teacher in his time, and I don't think he would want to say that he is. I am more inclined to agree with Derrida's statement that Plato "*writes from out of* . . . Socrates's death," that is, writes from out of "the sterility of the Socratic seed left to its own devices."[40]

But I would add some riders to this statement and turn its head in a different direction. First, Plato *represents* that sterility. Second, he represents

Socrates as aware of the sterility, and in the *Phaedrus* this awareness is signaled by his subversive conduct of the inscription *logos*. Third, when Socrates says the arguments never come from him, he may not merely be stating his principle of dialogical modesty; he may be voicing a complaint or confession, acknowledging that the sterility that makes him a midwife derives from his failure to get free of the circle of inscription. After his long struggle to circumvent the defenses of Phaedrus, he might well be expected to toy with the idea that if he could write directly on the soul the arguments would always come from him. If you can't beat the circle, why not join it? of course, if he is in the circle and is unable to get out of it he must be an inscribee as well as an inscriber. But inscription has one saving feature: it is a reversible process. That is, although the process is clearly described as operating from the past to the future, there is no reason why that logic isn't reversible too. Why couldn't Socrates be describing what he does, for example, to Protagoras in the *Theaetetus*, or to Achilles in the *Apology*, or to Homer and Hesiod in a number of dialogues? Or what Plato does to him? If philosophy is an art of dying, that could mean it is part of the maieutic process of being killed by reverse inscriptions—by arguments coming from others in the future.

It could also mean, as Kant might say, that it is an art of curtailing knowledge and its inscription to make room for interpretation. It could mean being inscribed in a revisionary structure of inscriptions that undo themselves and foreclose closure. It could mean refusing to resign oneself to the genealogical tyranny of the future and fighting the good fight for the control of the future perfect. Although the living who flee obliteration seek to be perpetuated or resurrected, they may have to settle for revision, for Hegelian *Aufhebung* appropriated by Nietzsche in the Eternal Return of the Different. I conclude that if Platonic philosophy is an art of dying and a desire for death, and if that is taken to be a desire for sublation and appropriation, then it is a desire not for immortality but for textuality; a desire not to be concluded.

NOTES

[1] This is a revised and much expanded version of an essay with the same title published in *Textual Fidelity and Textual Disregard*, ed. Bernard P. Dauenhauer (New York: Peter Lang, 1990), 81-103.

[2] Jacques Derrida, "Plato's Pharmacy," in *Dissemination*, trans. Barbara Johnson (Chicago: University of Chicago Press, 1981), 149.

[3] *Theaetetus* 161b; see 149b-151d for the discussion of midwifery, or maieutics.

[4] My translation, though some of my word choices were influenced by the following translators: H.N. Fowler in Volume One of the Loeb Classical Library bilingual editions of the dialogues (1914; rpt. Cambridge: Harvard University Press, 1960), 565-67; R. Hackforth, *Plato's "Phaedrus"* (1952; rpt. Cambridge: Cambridge University Press, 1972), 158; C.J. Rowe, *Plato: "Phaedrus"* second edition (Warminster: Aris and Phillips, 1988), 125. Future translations from the *Phaedrus* rely mainly on Fowler, with some help from Hackforth, but I haven't hesitated to vary or ignore their renderings in order to get closer to particular meaning effects in the Greek text.

[5] See the hilarious and scintillating speculations on this theme in Jacques Derrida, *The Post Card: From Socrates to Freud and Beyond*, trans. Alan Bass (Chicago: University of Chicago Press, 1987).

[6] Gregory Vlastos, "Socrates' Disavowal of Knowledge," *Philosophical Quarterly* 35 (1985): 8-9.

[7] Pierre Bourdieu, *Outline of a Theory of Practice*, trans. Richard Nice (Cambridge: Cambridge University Press, 1977), 218.

[8] Eric A. Havelock, *Preface to Plato* (Harvard: Harvard University Press, 1963), 141.

[9] *Republic* 377a, 382d, 382c, 377a-b, 378e. Translation based on that of Allan Bloom, *The Republic of Plato* (New York: Basic Books, 1968), 54-60, but freely revised; choice of words occasionally influenced by the translation of Paul Shorey for the Loeb Classical Library *Republic*, revised edition (1937; rpt. Cambridge: Harvard University Press, 1953).

[10] See my "Facing Sophists: Socrates' Charismatic Bondage in *Protagoras*," *Representations* 5 (1984), 66-91.

[11] *Protagoras* 323a-c. On *aidôs* as a species of *deos* (fear, anxiety), see *Euthyphro* 12a-c.

[12] *Protagoras* 325c-326b. My translation, though I have consulted those by W.R.M. Lamb and C.C.W. Taylor in the Loeb Classical LIbrary and the Clarendon Plato series respectively.

[13] *Prot.* 329a.

[14] "The Canon," trans. J. Chadwick and W.N. Mann, in *Hippocratic Writings*, ed. G.E.R. Lloyd (1950; rpt. and rev. Harmondsworth: Penguin Books, 1978), 68.

[15] See Ronna Burger, *Plato's "Phaedrus": A Defense of a Philosophic Art of Writing* (University, Alabama: University of Alabama Press, 1980), 84-86 for a different but not sharply enough focused account of the limits of the medical analogy.

[16] In this connection it is interesting that Akoumenos is thrice mentioned in the *Phaedrus* (227a, 268a, 269a)—interesting for me, at least, because when the name is shifted from a proper to a common noun it functions as a comment on both the knowledge and the reputation of doctors: *akoumenos*, "knowing by hearsay" and "being known by hearsay." Reincorporating the common property in the referent of the proper noun personifies the unreliability, the sophistry, of medical discourse and allows one to imagine the genealogy of its transmission from father to son to *paidika*. I am grateful to my colleague Daniel Selden for help on this point.

[17] I discuss this topic at greater length in "Plato's Flying Philosopher," *The Philosophical Forum* 13 (1982): 385-407.

[18] See Burger, *Plato's "Phaedrus"* 84 and 144 n.34. See also Socrates's Anaxagorean parody at 246b-d: the fully winged soul "mounts upward and governs the whole world"—*meteôroporei te kai panta ton kosmon dioikei*—but when it loses its wings it falls and takes hold of a body. This Icarian trajectory resembles that of the fate of Anaxagoras's (theory of) *nous* in the *Phaedo*. See "Plato's Flying Philosopher" 393-96. At *Phaedrus* 246e Zeus becomes the Anaxagorean place-holder: the *megas hegemôn* in the sky goes first, *diakosmôn panta kai epimeloumenos* ("ordering and ordering for all things").

[19] *Laws* 810e-811a, trans. R.G. Bury (Loeb Classical Library).

[20] Quoted passages from the translation of Thomas L. Pangle, *The Laws of Plato* (New York Basic Books, 1980), 36-37.

[21] Trans. R.G. Bury (Loeb Classical Library).

[22] In the *Timaeus*, when Critias promises—or threatens—to tell about the ancient Athenian exploit (against Atlantis) that he learned from his grandfather, who learned it from his father, who learned it from Solon, Socrates tartly responds, "Excellent! But come now [*alla dê*], just what was this exploit described by Critias [the grandfather] following Solon's *akoên* [report or hearsay] as a thing not verbally recorded although actually performed by this city long ago" (21a, Bury's translation modified). This response rings with the same, skeptical irony as the statement to Phaedrus.

The *Timaeus* and *Critias* bring out the affinity between Egyptian and Eupatrid values and strategies lurking in the background of this section of the *Phaedrus*. Critias continues by describing the occasion on which he heard Solon's Egyptian tale: the *Koureôtis*, the day during the Dionysian festival of the *Apatouria* on which newly-born male children of Eupatrid fathers were enrolled in the clan. The ceremony gave the elders an opportunity to inscribe older sons with Family Values by having contests in recitation in which "many poems of many poets were recited" and, "since the poems of Solon were at that time new, many of us children chanted them" (21b). After finishing his account of how he went about recovering the true story he had heard many years ago in that initiatory context, Critias exclaims on the truth of the old saying "that what we learn in childhood has a wonderful hold on the memory," for the story "the old man was eager to tell me is stamped indelibly on my mind like an encaustic painting" (27b).

The *graphê* has been imprinted by fire so that it can't be washed out by water (*enkaumata anekplytou*), and it is destruction by water that most threatens the continuity and accomplishments of ancestral rule, bypassing the illiterate rustics in the mountains but sweeping away the lower-lying urban centers of culture and aristocracy (22b-23d) like Atlantis and the Old Athenian warrior community. Critias's tale of Atlantis is a symbolic reenactment, an attempt by an embittered

Eupatrid to restore the lost power and glory of pre-democratic Athens. The whole episode vividly dramatizes what is behind Socrates's comment and Egyptian tale in the *Phaedrus*.

Phaedrus has just enthusiastically endorsed as *pankalôs* Socrates's advice to Tisias that the wise man will practice the art of rhetoric primarily in order to be able to please the gods; he should strive to please "not his fellow slaves, except as a secondary consideration, but his good and noble masters" (273e-274a), and this locution—*alla despotais agathois te kai ex agathôn*—is standard Socratic code for new and old *agathoi* and wouldbe tyrants (see, for example, *Euthyphro* 14a-15d). A few interchanges later Socrates prefaces his Egyptian tale by asking Phaedrus whether he knows how to act or speak about *logoi* so as best to please god, and it is after this that he says he has heard something on the subject from *tôn proterôn*, "but whether it is true, they only know. But if we ourselves should find this out, should we care any longer for human opinions?" (274c), for, presumably, we should have made ourselves gods and other humans our slaves.

The rhetoricians and sophists admired by Phaedrus, and especially Tisias, on whom Phaedrus is an expert, could not find a better way to make their dream of inscriptive power come true than to study the career and teachings of Thamus, the king who became a god and whom Protagoras might well number among the disguised sophists of ancient times. For Critias and Thamus—and for Phaedrus, who was hoping at the beginning of the dialogue to exercise his memory by reciting Lysias's speech—authoritative truth is constituted by the domination and dominance of memory: its domination and appropriation by institutionalized despotism, and its dominance not only as a mode of reception that validates its contents as "received knowledge, wisdom, truth," etc., but also as a rhetorical mode, since to produce *the effect of memory* is a standard strategy for naturalizing or authorizing whatever *logoi* one wants to put into play.

Finally, a word about G.R.F. Ferrari's interesting and sophisticated argument that the myth is about the cause of the loss of that innocence that would make it possible to accept the myth at face value and believe its truth (*Listening to the Cicadas: A Study of Plato's "Phaedrus"* [Cambridge: Cambridge University Press, 1987], 214-22). Implicit but not stressed in Ferrari's balanced interpretation of the mechanical and ethical relations of speech and writing is the thesis that the emergence and awareness of inscription as logography is an important factor in destroying "the innocence of an earlier age" that Socrates values because of its "unconcern with questions of pedigree and status where this is irrelevant to truth" (217). But what Ferrari fails to consider is that this Socratic "ideal" is itself represented as a naturalized fiction, a tale of bygone innocence thinly enough disguised as a deposit of memory for Phaedrus to complain that "you easily make up stories of Egypt or any country you please" (275b). Socrates replies that to Phaedrus, unlike the innocents of old, "it makes a difference who the speaker is and where he comes from, for you do not consider only whether or not his words have truth" (275b-c). Ferrari argues that although this admonition seems disingenuous because in Socrates's day "considerations of pedigree" do matter, it nevertheless "offers the best means of both incorporating and going beyond the lost simplicity of that earlier time," for it enables Socrates "both to enunciate and to put into action the very ideal that the people of oak and rock themselves exhibited, but could not enunciate "—because, as he had noted earlier, "pedigree and truth had not yet been sundered in their society" (217-18). Yet the ideal Ferrari attributes to Socrates and unwittingly hints at in the preceding statement is that pedigree *is* and *determines* truth. For what criterion governed the ancients who were "content in their simplicity to hear an oak or a rock, provided only that it spoke the truth" (275b-c)? The criterion is location in a holy shrine: "those at the sanctuary of Zeus of Dodona said the words of an oak were the first prophetic utterances" (275b, trans. Rowe). A myth, Ferrari states, "is just a story that has been accepted on the grounds of pedigree and tradition . . . rather than truth" (217); rather, it has been accepted on those grounds *as* truth, the truth placed in the god's mouth by the human medium through whom speak those with the power to construct and ventriloquate the gods. For Phaedrus to accept Socrates's rebuke is to betray his commitment to, his respect for, his fear and desire of, the new criteria of pedigree, status, and tradition that dominate public opinion: the logographic criteria that establish the rhetorician as the modern purveyor or mystifier of truth, heir to the oracle, the oak, the rock, and the god.

[23] *Timaeus* 22e-23b.

[24] See Burger 146, notes 14 and 20. For a compact description of the priestly role see Helmust von den Steinem, "Plato in Egypt," *Bulletin of the Faculty of Arts of the Fouad I University Faculty of Letters* (Cairo), 13 (1951): 116-18, 123. Von den Steinem distinguishes ordinary writing from *hiera grammatica*—hieroglyphs—in an effort to reconcile the difference between this passage and the priest's interests in the written work in the *Timaeus*. This at least has the virtue of reminding us that if Plato had seen hieroglyphs he could have considered them in the category of visual art and seen them as obscurantist symbols serving the political purposes of the priests. The hieroglyphs, von den Steinem writes, "bear in themselves mystical powers, that is, they can be interpreted only by priests who are inspired from mouth to mouth, from living soul to living soul through cosmic knowledge" (123). Von den Steinem finds Plato in sympathy with this. My view is that the author gives a very clear statement of an ideology that Plato represents as the enemy Socrates contends with.

[25] *Philebus* 18b-c.

[26] Inventions and/or discoveries: between 273b and 275a some form or compound of *heuriskein* appears seven times: two refer to the art of Tisias, one to the activity of the "true" rhetorician, one to Socrates and Phaedrus, and four to the works of Theuth. The puzzle about the term is that it bears the contrary meanings of "to discover" and "to create or invent." Those who claim to know the truth and discover likenesses already in existence can point to something beyond themselves—perhaps the god in whose name the discovery as such is authorized. Those who want to claim such authority for their own inventions can rename them discoveries—unless, of course, they are or proclaim themselves gods, in which case the difference between invention and discovery falls away.

[27] Derrida, and Ronna Burger after him (99), identify the legitimate *logos* with Platonic writing. Burger argues that Plato represents the limits of Socrates's commitment to oral discourse and the limits of the appreciation of writing which that commitment causes, but that the Platonic dialogue also acknowledges its own limitations as writing. Substantially the same position is argued by Charles L. Griswold Jr. in *Self-Knowledge in Plato's "Phaedrus"* (New Haven: Yale University Press, 1986). Burger and Griswold both insist that Plato's dialogues transcend the limits of writing specified in the *Phaedrus*, and become bearers of the true *logos*. Griswold asserts that "Plato's dialogues themselves recant their authority as *written* in order to return the reader to the life of ensouled discourse" (225). In Burger's view the "Platonic defense of dialectic writing against Socrates' apparent commitment to the *erôs* of living speech is established through the 'internalizable' written logoi which point to the dangers of the written word" (109). The point is interestingly argued by both authors, and the only problem is that they both avoid the implications of the inscription metaphor. Burger's term, "internalizable" doesn't mean the same as "inscribed," while Griswold's "life of ensouled discourse" would emit a less airy resonance if it had been "life of inscribed discourse."

[28] Trans. H.N. Fowler, Loeb Classical Library, Volume Seven of Plato's dialogues.

[29] See Ferrari, *Listening to the Cicadas* 91-95.

It should be noted that Lysias's speech in effect praises the power of the beloved. The so-called passive partner, the object of predation and penetration, is not only the speaker's quarry but also the father of his *logos*. The speech celebrates the beloved's mastery over his lovers in what is actually mutual seduction. The beloved inspires the madness the speaker describes as well as the deception he perpetrates. This is worth mentioning because Phaedrus positions himself both in this dialogue and in the *Symposium* as a beloved. In the *Symposium*, as Griswold notes (19), he is called the father of the *logos* by his lover Eryximachus, and his own speech is a defense of the primacy of the beloved. Socrates plays on the paradoxical interchange of passive and active roles between lover and beloved throughout the dialogue, and he does so for what should by now be an obvious reason: the interchange is a bipolar version of the circle of inscription.

[30] Ferrari points out that Plato has Socrates "correct the age of the beloved to whom the speech is addressed: 'there was once a boy (*pais*)—or rather, a young man (*meirakiskos*) . . .' (237b2). The ethical stance in Socrates' speech is more suitable for one who is old enough to appreciate a principled resistance to pleasure, where Lysias' non-lover appeals only to a relatively childish scheming towards the maximum of selfish satisfaction" (253).

[31] See especially Ferrari 96-99. He makes the important observation that Socrates's speaker differs from Lysias's in that his speech manifests self-hate (98). This insight, which I find substantiated by the text, strikingly qualifies one's impression of the speech: Socrates's lipsmacking excoriation of lovers as a host of pleonectic marauders becomes not only a strategic act of self-concealment but also, and hiding behind that disguise, a voyeuristic act of self-flagellation.

[32] Lysias is famous especially for writing speeches to be delivered in court cases (forensics) and public assemblies (deliberative). Most of his extant speeches fall in the first category, and in public cases occasioned for the most part by the political struggles taking place at the end of the fifth century in Athens. Lysias is mentioned in the dialogue as the son of Cephalus, the old man in whose house the discussion reported in the *Republic* takes place. Cephalus and his family appear to have been resident aliens who did not have rights of citizenship but did have privileges denied other aliens. Ferrari notes the irony of the situation in which, excluded by his status from direct participation in politics, he devoted most of his professional activity to writing speeches for others: "Lysias the professional in court—just as he is the voice concealed beneath Phaedrus's cloak—cannot appear in that forum even when the summons is directed to him in person" (228).(One exception to this occurred when he was briefly granted citizenship after the overthrow of the thirty tyrants, and at this time he delivered one speech in person.) He can only exercise his art and arguments through others, but this constraint is a source of power; at the same time, the fact that he was so successful indicates that he knew how to appeal to, how to reflect and imitate, the sentiments of the many who comprised the juries and deliberative assemblies.

[33] As K.J. Dover puts it, love—*philia*, not *erôs*—"inspired by admiration and gratitude towards the erastes, coupled with compassion, induces the eromenos to grant the 'favors' and perform the 'services' which the erastes so obviously and passionately desires": *Greek Homosexuality* (Cambridge: Harvard University Press, 1978), 53. See also David M Halperin, *One Hundred Years of Homosexuality* (New York: Routledge, 1990), 75-151.

[34] When Socrates mockingly imitates Phaedrus's reaction to the speech he is reading, he says "I am dumbstruck because, looking at you, I saw that you were gladdened by the speech as you read. So . . . I, following, shared in the frenzy with you, the divine head" (234e). I translate the idiom, *tês theias kephalês*, literally in order to bring out Socrates's innuendo: a transmission of enthusiasm, similar to that described in the *Ion*, is here superimposed on the circle of inscription. From Lysias's divine head, the words flowing like wine gladden and enthuse his votary. This means that the effect of Lysias's writing on Phaedrus is precisely that which the nonlover's speech condemns. The anonymous "I" and "you" of the written discourse converge with Lysias and Phaedrus. The former's words have unstrung their speaker and made him the medium of further conquests. Thus the dissembling lover's seduction of his auditor is enacted in a recitation that aims to pass the spell on to the next auditor, a confessed "lover of *logos*." What began as a text and a fiction invades actuality when it is embodied, reincorporated, by speakers and auditors.

[35] Alexander Sesonske, "Plato's Apology: *Republic* I," *Phronesis* 6 (1961): 35-36.

[36] C.J. Rowe, "The Argument and Structure of Plato's *Phaedrus,*" *Proceedings of the Cambridge Philological Society*, 212, n.s. 32 (1986): 120.

[37] See Griswold, *Self-Knowledge* 55, for an astute account of the meaning of Socrates's hiding his head in his cloak.

[38] R. Hackforth, *Plato's Phaedrus* 160 n.3.

[39] See my "Plato's Flying Philosopher" 400-406.

[40] "Plato's Pharmacy" 153-54.

by Djelal Kadir

On the *ars combinatoria* of Plato's *Cratylus* and Its Latest Peripeties

I have speculated with some delight on the possibility that the enterprise engendering this volume of essays might have its own genesis in the first two lines of the *Cratylus:*

> *Hermogenes*: Suppose we make Socrates a party to the argument.
> *Cratylus*: If you please.

If not here, clearly the editor of this felicitous volume must have his prompting somewhere in Plato. I fancy the possibility, all the same, that the efficient, if not the primal cause of the present endeavor on Plato and Postmodernism might lie in the incipit of this particular dialogue. To ask why would be begging the question, and so I shall spare you the prompter and explain.

In synoptic terms, which I shall hasten to dilate presently, the *Cratylus* has always struck me as somewhat anomalous within the Platonic corpus, if not in kind, certainly in degree. The measure of that deviation from the Socratic norm, if the Socrates of this particular dialogue would not protest unduly at such imputation of normativity to his extemporized enthusiasm, the measure of this digression is what makes the *Cratylus* hospitable to a Postmodernist overture. The nature of this breach resides principally in the drift of this dialogue from the *dialectic*, which we are all taught to recognize in the Socratic project, to the *enantiomorphic,* which is a fluid, if not a volatile turn that would be considered somewhat inconsistent with the mainstream Socratic metaphysics we have been conditioned to anticipate.

In the ternary waystations of a dialectical schema, we are taught to expect the antithetical coefficients whose contredanse moves to the querying and contestatory tune, usually in an ironic key, of a shuttling Socrates, weaving now from one, now from another direction to the warp and weft of a synthetic argument, or an open-ended suggestion that binds and abides nonetheless. An *enantiomorphêmê*, on the other hand, and I shall endeavor to describe it variously, an *enantiomorphêmê* describes an incommensurable encounter between mirrored figures that have been double-crossed, in the sense that, although they be mirrored, they are dissymmetrically reversed, a *contretemps*, if you will, that interdicts their jiving. Physicists who work in crystallography would recognize, no doubt, the rhetorical and ideational correlative of a physical phenomenon. In rhetorical terms, we could call this enantiomorphic matter a chiasmus that strayed into catachresis. The example that most readily comes to mind, if you will forgive my Postmodernist ecumenicity, is from Marx, Graucho Marx: "Outside of a dog, a book is a man's best friend. Inside of a dog, it's too dark to read." Such a strange encounter of antithetical figures clearly throws into question the entire oppositional relationship of dialectical binaries, leaving reason's colloquy and colloquy's reasoning to cut strange cloth, not to say a mixed metaphor. In the *Cratylus,* this is emphatically a cloth whose knots are of water and whose threads, while unwinding, refuse to entwine or abide. It is a cloth of language that Socrates and his interlocutors seek to articulate in and with language. And the fugacity of their subject, which is also their instrument, comes closest to a subterfuge of metaphysical discourse and its customary Socratic constancy. Socrates, of course, sides in the argument between Hermogenes and Cratylus with the former, asserting the conventionality, as opposed to the natural character, of language. At the same time, however, what their discussion demonstrates, not necessarily in its discursive claims but by its symptomatic illustration, is that Socrates vindicates Cratylus by demonstration as much as he seconds Hermogenes by assertion. This is so inasmuch as the dialogue we know as the *Cratylus* displays the traits that are endemic to the nature of its object, namely the nature of language as fluid and indomitable, as virtually indeterminate combinatorial phenomenon. (It would be interesting to speculate why the dialogue is not known as the "Hermogenes." Perchance, the paronomasia may be a dialectical ruse, a mirrored lexical inverse of the "true" nominal configuration.) In this sense, then, the dialectic as such is mooted by paradox, a paradoxical entailment that ironically undermines dichotomous discourse and binarist ideation, suspending any possible resolution by maintaining the viability of incommensurable coefficients in simultaneity. Socrates is not but he also is Cratylian at once; Cratylus is contravened, but he is also vindicated; Hermogenes is seconded, but his argument cannot logically maintain its own defence, lest it undermine by demonstration its own argument. Socrates seeks the truth, but he finds it *through* and *as* falsehood embedded in the voluble combinations of language and in the ruses of his own questionable and circuitous etymologizing. In the end, they all capitulate to Heraclitan mutability and inconstancy's flux, but their dialogue persists as trialogue that betrays them all. But, at the same time, that indomitable colloquy and its voluble argument are fully capable of adumbrating the principal conundrums of a cultural debate of a time some two millennia hence, that is, our time. For the paradoxical predicament embodied in the *Cratylus,* as you no doubt have gathered, and as I shall be explaining less cryptically in short order, has us shading into what are recognizably some of the characteristic quandaries of our Postmodernism.

Considered thus, Plato's *Cratylus* could be read as dramatic triangulation of a Postmodern poetics, not only as formal aesthetic, but also as social and political discourse whose narrative brings into question some of the very issues that vex our Postmodern epoch. I shall refer to a few of these issues shortly. Allow me first, however, to recapitulate the foregoing observations through yet another tact to be sure that the claims I make for the *Cratylus* have not been overwhelmed by the enthusiasm with which they compel me to make them.

In brief, conditioned to view Hermogenes and Cratylus as antithetical prosopopeias, a view that conforms to our canonical expectations of a "Socratic dialogue," we tend to overlook the sundering of dialectic into an ironic and paradoxical drama of irresolution. In the *Cratylus,* this open-ended deferral, as the language of our post-structuralist discourse would have it, is a function of the Socratic intervention whose mediation interdicts a resolute closure (an eschatology), an epiphanic aperture (an apocalypsis), or an apodictic truth (a resolute metaphysics). The counter-postures represented by Cratylus and Hermogenes come off not as *antithesis* but as *enantion,* in other words, not as mutually exclusive alterities, but as co-existent and incommensurable reflections, or as interfaced reversals. The end of this adversative, by which I do not mean adversarial or binary, confrontation does not come down to a dénouement; that is to say, the encounter does not end in a *katastrophê* whereby one of the articulated positions reduces or subsumes the other. Rather, Socrates mediates the encounter in a way that interdicts such catastrophizing, leaving the discussion open and unending. With studied élan and winking irony, Socrates, despite his contrary claims at the end (439b) that would indeed privilege a metaphysics, demures to the Heraclitan flow in whose indomitable spirit he etymologizes so elaborately, and so ironically, particularly on the genesis of divinity, the etymons of truth, and the lexes of language itself. Socrates would have his interlocutors and, by example, us, his readers, demure likewise to the inexorable combinatorial mutabilities of Heraclitus. Our Postmodernism may well be our way of finally heeding the wink of that Socratic beckoning.

I see us heeding that summons through what Alan Wilde terms a *suspensive irony.* In his book *Horizons of Assent: Modernism, Postmodernism, and the Ironic Imagination* (Johns Hopkins University Press, 1981), Wilde distinguishes between *suspensive irony* and *disjunctive irony.* Whereas the latter, Wilde claims, corresponds to a crisis of consciousness that is the Modernist's bedeviling sense of an irreducible breach between a need for order, or mastery, and the disorderliness of reality, *suspensive irony* is a mellow perspicacity that "turned down" Modernism's "rage for order," if I may borrow from Wallace Stevens' "The Idea of Order at Key West." And the pathos of the Modernist's angst has been displaced by an understated and ironic acceptance of a "manageably chaotic" world (44). In a succinct way, the *disjunctive irony* of the Modernist, whose oppositional aporia is at the root of Modernism's self-seeking consciousness and anxious reflexivity, had been assuaged already by what is recognizably a *suspensive irony* in the

Cratylus, where language does indeed sally to seek itself, pursuing at one point the language of language, more specifically, the *name* of the *name,* and finding that what the pursuit yields is the pursuit itself: *onoma*, Socrates notes, scans etymologically as a compression of *on hou zêtêma*, meaning, "being for which there is a search" (421a). Related to the parsing of the name of *name* is the etymon of truth, *alêtheia,* and falsity, *pseudos*. Because, Socrates insists, if *name* indicates a real existence for which there is seeking *(on hou masma), alêtheia,* or truth, is also an agglomeration of seeking and motion—*theia alê,* "divine wandering" (421b). Falsehood, on the other hand, derives from stagnation, inaction, which compares to sleep, *heudein*, a word disguised to become falsehood by the addition of the letter *psi* as prefix. Now, where *alêtheia* and the truth of all this etymologizing are concerned, Socrates is being either ironic or conveniently forgetful or, most likely, both. His guise is certainly not the disguise of falsehood, so he must be both *lethic and* an *eirôn* when it comes to this version of *alêtheia* by which he garbs the unconcealed, the *a-lêtheia*, in another guise of expedient concealment in order to make his point.

And the paradox of all this lies in the manner by which Socrates's procedure belies itself. This is so by virtue of the fact that Socrates has arrived at truth's root as *theia alê* by way of a divine motion, a Socratic gesture of remembering to forget *alêtheia*'s true etymology. In that ironic suspension of memory, or in the limitless virtuality of forgetfulness, which is another name for *lêtheia*, Socrates has come upon truth, *alêtheia.* Clearly, this strategy is not the proverbial ruse of the *docta ignorantia*, but a strategic move to render the volatile and "manageably chaotic" into a congenial dwelling of the ironically and self-knowingly perplexed. In the end, of course, Socrates will counsel paradoxically that he and his young friends Hermogenes and Cratylus yield irresolutely to the irresolvable. Because, though his final panegyric is to metaphysical knowledge which is abiding, for otherwise, he says, "there will be no one to know and nothing to be known" (439b), Socrates and his interlocutors do move on willy-nilly, promising to resume the inconclusive discussion yet another day. After all, not only truth is a form of divine wandering, but being itself, that is *on*, we are told at 421b, is also moving on, that is, *ion*.

Motion, of course, has its peripeties, and Socrates knew it well. And that is why he always sought to counsel the constancy of reason and the immutability of truth. But once loosed from its moorings, metaphysical or lexical, at the paradoxical end of the *Cratylus*, there is no saying where the streams of Heraclitus will carry the seekers or their sought-after object. And there is no gainsaying the unpredictable turns such an adventure might yield. Our Postmodernism is one of the waystations of that meandering and its peripeties.

I have recently come across our *Cratylus* in such a Postmodernist context, where the issues raised by Plato's *Cratylus* are confronted and appropriated as problematic legacy by an exuberantly Postmodern novelist, the Mexican Carlos Fuentes, in his hilariously Heraclitan novel *Cristóbal Nonato*, 1987 (*Christopher Unborn*, 1989). In this peripatetic accommodation, Fuentes's novel opens with a dramatic reference to *Cratylus* 402b, with his heroine supine on a paradisal beach Xenophon never dreamed of, and if he did, certainly never admitted to it. She is Edenically naked, except for her face which is covered by a green tome that happens to be a copy of Plato's Collected Dialogues, that, of course, happens to be open to the *Cratylus*, and, specifically, to that part of the *Cratylus* (402b) where Homer (*Iliad*, XIV:201) and Xenephon (*Anabasis:* "Thalassa! Thalassa!") happen to meet. Throughout the five-hundred-sixty-some pages of the novel that ensue, the Cratylic juxtapositions become a leitmotif. There is particular focus in Fuentes's opus on *Cratylus* 392-93, where the issues of language, genesis, and gender are dramatized with persiflage, irreverent mirth, and an iconoclastic critique of the Modernist ethos and its phallogocentric mythoi. It is not likely that Plato had imagined an avatar of his own concerns in a New World beyond his own Atlantis. And it is fitting, nonetheless, that he should have been discussed on the occasion that yielded this volume of essays in a well-born city of the New World so Cratylistically named, Eugene, naturally. (I am referring, of course, to the symposium at the University of Oregon that was the original occasion for a version of these comments).

In appropriating the *Cratylus,* Carlos Fuentes is recapitulating as well a high Modernist appropriation of Homer, Plato, and Xenophon at once. When Socrates invokes at 402b of the *Cratylus*, "Oceanus, the origin of the Gods," he knows he is citing Homer (*Iliad* XIV: 201). James Joyce knew to be citing both, in turn, on page 309 of *Finnegans Wake* when the Homeric sententia diaphoretically transmutes into "birth of an otion that was breeder to sweatoslaves," and there is little question and much evidence concerning the *Wakes'* influence having washed into Fuentes's Pacific shore. Joyce had already conflated all of these headwaters on the Heraclitan streams in the opening pages of the Telemachiad, the first episode of his *Ulysses,* with scatological irreverence: "The snotgreen sea. The scrotumtightening sea. *Epi oinôpa ponton* ["Over the wine-dark sea," *Odyssey* II: 420]. Ah, Dedalus, the Greeks. I must teach you. You must read them in the original. Thalatta! Thalatta! She is our great sweet mother."

Fuentes's accommodation of all this streaming influx distinguishes itself as Postmodern principally because, unlike Joyce, he has no anxieties and little concern about reading or citing "the Greeks in the original" because that form of privilege or authentication is moot and perennially mooted by the circumstantial, the differential, and the worldly banal. In the Postmodernist self-divestment of those anxieties for the original voice or master narrative, the Homeric, or Cratylic, or Xenophonic takes on contingent specificity, a human scale, a local voice, and experiential immediacy, not to say compelling urgency, as in the case of Fuentes's priapic *pater familias* and father of the novel's hero who blithers, as he slithers, hot and heavy, toward the hero's supine mother, "coño origen de los dioses." The couple's ensuing intercourse, linguistic and otherwise, has the hero's mother invoking the arguments in the text that covers the face of her otherwise *dis*-covered body, namely, *Cratylus* 392a-393a. It is here that Socrates and his young friends explore the differentiations between the language of the gods' and the language of humans.

That discussion, if I may turn your attention for a moment from Fuentes's lubricious couple, refers to book XIV, line 291 of the *Iliad*, where Homer speaks of a bird "called 'chalkis' by the gods, by men 'kymindis'," and to book XX, lines 73-74 that refer to a "mighty eddying river,/ Xanthos to the gods, to men Skamánder." And she says, as she is being churned by desire's urgency, "[y]ou and I call the sea sea, but who knows what its real name might be, the name the gods utter when they want to churn it up and to say to themselves 'Thalassa. Thalassa. The sea is our source'" (12). But Angeles, that's her name, who uncannily manages, body and soul, more than one activity at the same time, has an even more compelling interest in what might be one of our most pressing concerns in the Postmodern era: gendered language. *Cratylus* (392d) may well be one of the first instances in which this vital political and social issue is entertained. It has to do, as Socrates says, with "the names of Hector's son [which] are more within the range of human faculties." Hermogenes remembers the lines from the *Iliad*, book XXII, line 507. Scamandrius is what the Trojan women called the boy; Astyanax was the men's name for him. Socrates queries Hermogenes: "And must not Homer have imagined the Trojans to be wiser than their wives?" To which Hermogenes replies, "To be sure." "Then," asks Socrates, "he must have thought Astyanax to be a more correct name for the boy than Scamandrius?" "Clearly," concurs Hermogenes.

Of course, the history of the last two millennia has clouded the issue. And, unquestionably, in our Postmodern era, the certainty of Socrates and Hermogenes have come into question. It is one of our most urgent concerns and it points to a more timely phase of our Postmodernism. We may not be wiser than Socrates, but we do question what was unquestionably beyond question for him, as a number of scholars who deal with Plato and the feminine in this collection of essays make abundantly clear. As for definitive answers beyond the urgency of the ethical behavior implied by such issues, our Postmodern epoch still resonates with Socrates's own admission at *Cratylus* 392b: "Now, I think that this is beyond the understanding of you and me." Definitive understanding, fortunately, does not have to be a *sine qua non* of ethical practices in our social and intellectual life. And while we continue our peripeties in the itinerant colloquy set in motion by Socrates and his interlocutors in the *Cratylus,* we might do well to recall the virtue of uncertainty as willed to us by the Socratic deference to the indeterminate and the mutable. I leave you with this and with those primal New World protagonists on a Mexican beach, or at least, with the latter-day textual avatar of Plato's *Cratylus* which is, in part, Fuentes's novel.

by Douglass H. Thomson

Plato's Cratylus in the Light of Postmodernism

Listen to how anachronistic H. N. Fowler's estimate of the *Cratylus* sounds today in the context of postmodernism: "The *Cratylus* cannot be said to be of great importance to the development of the Platonic system, as it treats of a special subject [the correctness of names and the nature of language] somewhat apart from general philosophic theory."[1] One cannot help noting Fowler's traditional metaphysical bias in favor of "system" and "theory" over (and unknowingly against) such an apparently trivial and too specialized topic as language! Since Derrida raided Plato's pharmacy and unwrote the prescription for philosophy, the issue of writing, especially Socrates' reservation about the written word in the *Phaedrus*, has occupied center stage in recent reappraisals of the Platonic achievement.[2] Actually, it would be more accurate to say that Derrida's emphasis is only one perspective—the poststructuralist—among the many voices of postmodernism that have restored attention to the rhetorical and figural dimensions of the dialogues as a counterpoint to the powerful tradition of metaphysical commentary. The ongoing reappraisal of the sophistic movement; the rereading of Plato in the context of the orality and literacy debate; the new emphasis on the function of myth in the dialogues; feminist interpretation of language and gender in these myths—all these postmodernist voices, wary of received "systems," have worked to make the problem of language a crucial concern in any reassessment of Plato. The *Cratylus* provides an important context for this reassessment. Not only its subject—the nature of language—but its figurative and eristic strategies make the dialogue a central doctrine in the decentering of Platonism. Furthermore, the formal divisions and irresolutions of the *Cratylus* echo and provide a forum for the debate within postmodernism itself.

The debate within postmodernism has yielded two sharply opposed approaches to the rereading of Plato. On the one hand, we find readers who regard Plato as the archê-enemy of the postmodern, who in his devotion to the spoken word denigrated writing and began philosophy's long flight from the recursive dimension of its own progress. On the other hand, postmodernism has afforded us a new way of reading the dialogues, restoring or insisting upon their rhetorical and dramatic character over and against their paraphrasable philosophical content.

The anti-Platonic stream of commentary numbers among its advocates some of the best known voices of postmodernism: 1) Richard Rorty and the new pragmatism, which tends to regard any idealist or essentialist metaphysics as an unfortunate aberration in the history of philosophy.[3] Against the freighted final vocabularies and unambiguous ideals of such platonisms, the social constructivist sees truth as a matter of agreement and accommodation, preferring theory—if there must be one at all—based on coherence rather than correspondence to some sacred construct. 2) In a related phenomenon—related because the new pragmatism echoes the longstanding pluralism of the rhetorical tradition—we witness the ongoing reappraisal of the sophistic movement, an attempt to lift the stigma of Platonic denigration from those first philosophers of language and to question the fairness and sanity of Socrates' anxiety about rhetoric and writing.[4] 3) Feminists, often productively divided within and, at times, against the postmodern, have been fairly consistent in their reading of Plato as one of the seminal patriarchs of phallocentrism. Irigaray's and Gilbert and Gubar's importantly subversive readings of the allegory of the cave are among a number of studies which demonstrate how philosophy attempts to sublimate or marginalize the feminine as a condition of its getting down to business.[5] 4) And, of course, there is Derrida, in the *Grammatology* and especially "Plato's Pharmacy," focusing on how the phonocentric bias of the *Phaedrus* translates into a logocentrism that suppresses the play (and playfulness) of writing and ambiguity. This anti-Platonic side of postmodernism, in summary, regards Plato as a too serious thinker: an entrenched enemy of pluralism, playfulness, the feminine, and the disseminating character of writing. Where once we debated the Platonic achievement in terms of *mimêsis*, *nomos*, and the Forms, we now regard the Platonic attacks on the mimetic, the poets, the sophists, and Theuth's gift of alphabetic literacy as unified expression of his anxiety about writing. So much so that an editor of a recent literary criticism textbook can proclaim that poststructuralism furnishes "the ultimate vindication of poetry against Plato's attack. For it is the poets, celebrating the free play of the signifier, who have had the right notion of language, and the philosophers, aiming for precision of terminology, who have been pursuing the will o' the wisp."[6]

That is *one* way postmodernism regards Plato. But from many quarters, including Derrida as he characteristically cuts across the grain of his own argument, comes a different picture: Socrates as *pharmarkeus*, a magician of wordplay and irony, highly suspicious of final vocabularies; the dialogues as aporetic, self-divided, open-ended, frequently undercutting and qualifying their alleged ontotheological conclusions. This kind of interpretation entails what Barbara Johnson calls "unfolding those dimensions of Plato's *text* that work against the grain of (Plato's own) Platonism"[7]—a strategy familiar to deconstructive reading. But the possibility of such a reading comes from many sources, some unexpected: 1) Leo Strauss, a political philosopher, who considered the dialogues "radically fictive," dramatic, and even "comic."[8] He coined the phrase "aporetic dialogue" long before post-structuralism had used *aporia* to dislodge *alêtheia* as the key term in interpretation. 2) G. B. Kerferd, a Cambridge classicist, who makes an argument that would have most confounded the magesterial tradition of Platonic commentary: Socrates *as* sophist[9]. Kerferd traces the profound debt of the Socratic method to the sophistic arts of *antilogikoi*, *eristic*, and *elenchus*. And Derrida, too, wonders aloud in the "Pharmacy": "isn't Socrates the spitting image of the sophist?"[10] 3) From the orality-literacy debate comes a reading utterly antithetical to the one regarding Plato as an enemy of writing. Havelock argues that Plato's quarrel is not with the poets or sophists *per se* but with the old, mnemonic, oral method of education.[11] Socrates—"he who does not write"[12]—occupies a transitional role between oral and literate cultures; he is a bit distrustful of the new writing but anticipates in his speech that kind of logical reasoning associated with a fully literate age and so well exploited by Plato in *his* writing. 4) And, finally, the old tradition of Plato *as* a poet, given new urgency by Julius Elias in his provocatively entitled *Plato's Defense of Poetry*: his is an intricate argument, but essentially Elias believes Plato had come to doubt the efficacy of dialectic and logic and turned to myth to convey "the indemonstrable first premises" of his philosophy.[13] As distinguished from the anti-Platonic stream of postmodernism, these interpretations discover not the Idealist philosophy of institutionalized Platonism but self-divided and wonderfully fluid dialogues, offering positional truth rather than the Truth. These various readings seek to rehabilitate and even to appropriate Plato as anticipating many major concerns and strategies of postmodernism.

The *Cratylus* provides a perfect context for considering the merits of this productive debate within postmodernism. Its subject, which reaches far beyond "the correctness of names" to include the origins, integrity, and place of language in philosophy, naturally reflects the intense linguistic scrutiny of poststructuralism, especially in the way Socrates relies upon a rhetorical or conventional view of language to undermine a theory of its referential correctness. This Platonic debate between the rhetorical and ontological positions on language has produced from commentators equally sharply divided interpretations of the dialogue. Some readers have found in Socrates' management of the investigation an impossibly rationalistic approach to the correctness of language: Kerferd, for one, complains that "Plato resolved the problem of correct language by altering reality [through an appeal to the Forms] to fit the needs of language, instead of the reverse."[14] Others have interpreted the dialogue as one of Plato's zaniest, rife with delightfully conscious irony and parody from a Socrates "fooling at the top of his bent"[15]; one recent critic, A. C. Kelly, has even suggested we read it as a satire of the philosophical method.[16] Four of the dialogue's most puzzling features provide touchstones for a means of gauging the merits of these sharply conflicting interpretations: its form; its manic, crazy cap etymologies; its myth of the legislator as original namer; its concluding remark that "no man of any sense will like to put himself or the education of his mind in the power of names" (229). In considering these four elements in the dialogue, I want to examine not only how Plato comes to terms with language in the *Cratylus* but how postmodernism comes to terms with Plato.

First the question of form and method, which reminds me of a question one of my students asked the other day: if the Socratic method is synonymous with an open, back-and-forth, argumentative exchange of ideas, why does it always seem Socrates knows the answers beforehand and his listener plays the fool or sounding board? Perhaps that's a bit overstated, but postmodernist focus on the method and form of the dialogues, especially following Strauss, has called for revisions in our way of reading them. Many critics have found the form of the *Cratylus* craftily staged to Socrates' advantage, with his authority assured and his final word inevitable.

In the dialogue, Socrates is asked to mediate an argument between Hermogenes, who holds that names are merely conventional, something agreed upon by usage and custom, and Cratylus, who is said to advocate a belief in their natural correctness, a fitness based on reference of name to thing. The first thing worth noting is that Hermogenes and Cratylus never debate. Their argument takes place before or outside of the dialogue. Socrates first considers the merits of the "natural view" in an attempt to explain to Hermogenes what Cratylus apparently has not explained; then, in a more formal eristic vein, he cross-examines and rather too easily demolishes Cratylus' argument for the natural view. One could complain there's something too stagy here, as Socrates, in preempting and directing the terms of the debate, actually prevents a real engagement of the rhetorical and ontological positions on language.

Moreover, the participants in this erstwhile dialogue seem awfully easy targets for Socratic logic and irony. Hermogenes, like so many other pro-rhetoric speakers in the dialogues, provides actually a caricature of the conventional view. He's easily bewildered and a bit dull-witted, as the joke on his name implies. Cratylus had perplexed poor Hermogenes by informing him that "if all the world were to call you Hermogenes that would not be your name" (173). Socrates supplies the rationale for what he calls "the joke": Hermogenes can be "no true son of Hermes" because he is "always looking after a fortune and never in luck" (173-174). The joke, coupled with other instances of Hermogenes' gullibility, economically serves to discredit the conventional view *ad hominem*.[17] Socrates regrets that Hermogenes has yet to come into his inheritance so that he could purchase the wisdom of the sophists or at least the "reputation" of wisdom "rather too dearly bought" (181) by his brother Callias, a great patron of the sophists. Socrates also regrets not having the money himself to have taken the fifty-drachma course from Prodicus on the correctness of names. But both regrets are, of course, couched in unmistakable irony, relying upon Socrates' most persistent denigration of the sophists: the equation of their wisdom with how much one can afford to pay for it. As a bit of a dimwit standing in for the real target of Socrates' reservations, the sophists, and affording him an easy opportunity to discredit their views on language, Hermogenes allows Socrates to step around the more disturbing, Heraclitean aspects of the conventional argument. He is a perfect example of Kerferd's complaint about how persistently Plato misrepresents the serious arguments of the sophists. Prodicus and Protagoras had taught and written about the correctness of names,[18] but we will not hear their arguments in the person of the easily perplexed Hermogenes.

Cratylus does not fare much better. As proponent of the natural view, he goes further in advocating a referential fitness for language than anyone could expect. Consider again, for example, Cratylus' explanation of why "Hermogenes" is a wrong name. Yes, this is part of Plato's fun with the advocate of the conventional view, as understood through Socrates' "joke." But the joke actually discredits both positions. Hermogenes might not live up to his name, but all by "convention" and "custom" agree to identify him by it. To contend, as Cratylus apparently has done and later insists on doing (221), that Hermogenes is not his name quickly brings the "natural" view to its *reductio ad absurdum*. And throughout Cratylus' defense of the natural view, we find similar examples of his naive literalism and spotty logic. He even is taken in, hook, line, and sinker, by the rationale guiding Socrates' outrageous etymologies! Socrates has no trouble demolishing the logic of Cratylus' position, although one might stress that he is actually unravelling the line of argument that he, Socrates, attributed to Cratylus in the debate with Hermogenes. An anti-Platonist could understandably complain that the deck has been stacked in favor of Socrates: he holds all the cards. One could also complain that instead of really engaging the conflict between the conventional and ontological positions on language, Plato has burlesqued both. The form of the dialogue allows Socrates to define and to control the terms of the debate about the terms of language; his two antagonists, mere parodies of serious positions debated by the sophists, are no match for him and were no match for him from the start.

A more congenial reading of the dialogue might stress a different approach to its form: the form, after all, places Socrates *between* the conventional and natural views. And this is where many postmodernist studies want to situate him: not as the unproblematic advocate of philosophy in its ancient quarrel with rhetoric and poetry, but as a figure in the middle of the debate. At first we might expect Socrates to support Cratylus' view of language against one stressing its arbitrariness because of his characteristic objection to arbitrary, man-made, relativistic doctrines. But exactly the opposite is the case. After getting Cratylus to admit certain words are intelligible only by custom, Socrates freely concedes the merit of the conventional position: "I fear that this dragging in of resemblance is a shabby thing, which has to be supplemented by the mechanical aid of convention with a view to correctness" (224). This concession has been perhaps the single greatest reason the once neglected dialogue has gained the interest of postmodernist critics, as Socrates seems to anticipate the insistent anti-referentiality of structuralism. But, as he makes clear later, this "mechanical aid of convention" is really too obvious to matter much and does not really address or solve the problem of the *logos* in its relation to truth.

From his position in between the natural and conventional views, Socrates may control the terms of the debate, but this formal strategy actually allows Plato to subvert these terms. For when Socrates argues in defense of the natural view against Hermogenes—with fruitless arguments by analogy and appeals to the gods, the names in Homer, and the Legislator—he is actually undermining the natural view, anticipating his dismantling of Cratylus' positions *later* in the dialogue. And as he demolishes Cratylus' position, he concedes the merits of the conventional view but undermines it by declaring its obviousness and by questioning its usefulness. Far from a neat dialectic structure in which Socrates reconciles thesis (the natural view) with antithesis (the conventional view), the form of the dialogue more nearly resembles a *chiasmus*: as Socrates first interrogates the conventional view (Hermogenes), he anticipates and crosses over to the problems of the natural view; as he addresses the natural view (in the second half of the dialogue with Cratylus), he crosses back and reflects upon the inadequacy of the conventional view. This crossing back and forth allows Socrates an incredible range of irony and rhetorical playfulness to counterbalance the serious endeavor of ascertaining the truth about language. Or, to put it another way, Plato's endeavor to determine the correctness of names already acknowledges, through the formal ingenuity of the dialogue, the playful character of the *logos.*

Equally important as its rhetorical playfulness is the note of uncertainty upon which the dialogue ends. After making his more typical appeal to "a standard . . . without employing names" (227) as the ultimate basis of truth, Socrates tells Cratylus: "This may be true . . . but it is also very likely to be untrue; and therefore I would not have you easily persuaded of it. Reflect well and like a man, and do not easily accept such a doctrine" (229). Even more unsettling is the conclusion Cratylus draws from all of the foregoing discussion: he now inclines to the Heraclitean view (229). These and other features have encouraged many critics to number the *Cratylus* among the aporetic dialogues in the canon. An anti-Platonist may complain that its form and terms have been predisposed in Socrates' favor, but he does not have the final say (Cratylus does) as the dialogue ends with the issue to be reopened. Indeed, the dialogue ends suggestively, with Hermogenes setting

Cratylus on his way into the country. Perhaps only on vacation or in the pastoral can such a conflict about language be ameliorated—or forgotten.

The second feature I want to examine, the etymologies, comprise the single most prominent formal element of the dialogue, dominating the first half of the discussion. Even, or maybe especially, from those who would see Socrates fearful of the disseminating play of language, there appears something almost poignant about this manic ransacking of etymologies to discover a referential logic in naming. Socrates begins with the names of the gods in Homer and other proper names, moves on to names of the virtues, then other words, down on to syllables and finally letters themselves—all in an attempt to demonstrate their natural fitness. Earlier commentators were a bit bewildered or even bored by this Sisyphean effort. One could argue from the anti-Platonist perspective of postmodernism that one can find no clearer example of the self-defeating nature of Socrates' rationalism than in his desperate search for a natural logic in the maze of words. Even Hermogenes must occasionally object to "a very shabby etymology" (203), and, when things don't fit, Socrates ruefully admits to a too obviously expedient device: "the device of a foreign origin" (205).

In truth, however, and in support of those postmodernists who would stress Plato's playfulness, the entire etymological foray, allegedly in defense of the ontological view, is one sustained prank, an ironic joke of almost epic proportions and of decidedly mock-epic purpose. Even Jowett's headnotes for the sustained etymological warfare run "Solemn nonsense," "Socrates fooling at the top of his bent," and "more and more absurd etymologies." As a formal feature, their sheer accumulation—their number, the overreaches, the qualifications, the often downright silliness—serves to disrupt the referential theory. Within them we find obvious highjinks: "'o' is the sign of roundness and therefore there is plenty of 'o' mixed up [in the Greek word for *round*]" (216). There is also a broad swipe at the sophists in an "improved" etymology for one of the few that survive translation: *hero* from *eros. Hero* might also come from the word meaning "to put the question." This dubious etymology leads to an equally ridiculous surmise: "in Attic dialect the heroes turn out to be rhetoricians and questioners. All this is easy enough [quips Socrates]—the noble breed of heroes are a tribe of sophists and rhetoricians" (188). There's no doubting the mock-heroic tenor of this passage! And, finally, we have the fun and games with the source of Socrates' inspiration for this etymological conjuring, an inspiration caught from the great Euthyphro of the Prospaltian *dêmos*, who has ravished his soul and whose superhuman power supposedly works through Socrates in his investigation of names (186). Not coincidentally, Socrates attributes to himself the same kind of *enthousiasmos* for which he criticized the poets and rhapsodes in the *Ion*. Apparently the only way to search out the referents for names is to be out of one's mind—or, to put it in a more telling way, one must be out of one's mind to begin such an inquiry in the first place. A postmodernist defender of the sophists and poets on the issue of language might object to these potshots Socrates levels against the competing theories during his etymologies. But in truth the real purpose of the manic ransacking of etymologies has been to parody the natural, ontological view espoused by Cratylus and the too serious thinker. Socrates' lesson in etymologies bears resemblance to his lengthy and equally dubious defense of Simonides in the *Protagoras*, in which he offers a competing literary interpretation, ostensibly to clear the poet's name but really to expose the forced ingenuities of the sophistic art. As he tells Hermogenes that tomorrow he will seek some "priest or sophist" to purge him of this "enchanting ravishment" (186) that has inspired his etymological conjuring, the terms and the target of Socrates' parody become all too clear.

Those who would still accuse Socrates of being too serious a thinker might find a supreme example for their argument in the third feature I want to examine: Socrates' conjuring of an original Namer, the Legislator, "who of all skilled artisans in the world is the rarest" (179) and who once upon a time insured the natural correctness of names. One is tempted to think of what a follower of Lacan would make of such a figure, at once the primordial namer and lawgiver. He certainly recalls Lacan's "Nom-du-Pere," the namer through no-no, whom the young child experiences as the authority for naming as he or she enters into the symbolic order of language and realizes desires can be repressed or masked through words. The appeal to such an authority reveals Socrates' awareness that an originary, ideal link between words and things has been ruptured: as the etymologies amply suggest, the children must wrestle with the bewildering code left by the absent Father of language. One, I suppose, could argue that Plato wants to delay the entry of philosophy into the symbolic order of language unless one can appeal to an original Namer or Lawgiver who can insure a referential grounding for that order—in short, Plato is guilty of phallocentrism: the legislation of a paternal order that represses ambiguity and preempts the play of debate and interpretation by appeal to an ur-namer, the father of language.[19]

Yet to offer such a reading would again ignore the trenchant Socratic irony that undercuts presentation of the Legislator. This Law-giver has been summoned to support the natural view, the very view Socrates so intricately works to refute. Socrates eventually casts doubt about the ability of this Legislator "to make and give all names with a view to the ideal name" (179), suggesting that a dialectician must be his guide "if the names are to be rightly given" (180). Again, one could read this as Plato insisting that philosophy be given control of language: an ideal code would be based on a logical order of referentiality determined by dialectical reasoning. But the terms of the myth are so far-fetched, not to mention anachronistic (Solon and a dialectician?), that it is impossible to take Socrates seriously. Indeed, after some wayward etymologies, Socrates concludes that if a legislator were responsible for naming, he did not do a very good job of it. The myth is just one more element of the joke at Hermogenes' expense and against the natural view.

So far my review of the *Cratylus* may seem to question the fairness of the anti-Platonic strain of postmodernism, suggesting the portrait of Socrates as an enemy of writing can be drawn only if we ignore the ironic and figurative dimensions of Plato's writing. But actually Socrates' ironic unravelling of the natural view and his fun and games with the conventional view in the *Cratylus* have carefully steered the dialogue to a predictably strong metaphysical conclusion: because investigations into the nature of language are so uncertain, "every man should expend his chief thought and attention on the consideration of his first principles" (225). The logic guiding this argument is one familiar to Platonism: because names are mere images (often unreliable ones) of an uncertain phenomenal world, they cannot be a starting point for an inquiry into the nature of truth, which exists, unchanging, beyond the reversals of that phenomenal world and, thus, even more so, beyond the mimesis of that world by language. Socrates vaguely appeals to "another standard . . . without employing names" (227), some non- or extra-linguistic authority, as the ultimate basis of truth. With this appeal to a stable center beyond the reach of writing, we return to the kind of Platonic mystification most severely critiqued by poststructuralism. One cannot fault G. B. Kerferd for complaining that "Plato resolved the problem of correct language by altering reality to fit the needs of language, instead of the reverse" (77).

We've come upon a very large, crucial problem which continues to shape the course of postmodernist debate about Plato: to what extent can we merely extract the grammar of philosophical content from a dialogue whose rhetorical and figurative features work to qualify understanding of that content? In defense of Plato against his own Platonism, one could list a number of things. In the *Cratylus* Socrates specifically labels his search for "absolute existence" a "dream of mine" (228), not something finalized upon which he can rely as a means of logic to refute the opposition. There is also the remarkable degree of uncertainty ending the dialogue. And the conclusion also contains, as a counterpoint, some of the most remarkable statements Socrates offers anywhere on the *limits* of knowing—he even goes so far as to admit that the very word "knowledge" is ambiguous (226).

But whatever we make of these apologies for Plato, it seems to me there remain several ways to read the surest conclusion Socrates can draw from all of his foregoing discussion: "No man of sense will like to put himself or the education of his mind in the power of names" (229).

If we privilege the metaphysical Plato who has incurred the displeasure of postmodernism, we can read this conclusion simply as one parting shot at the rhetorical tradition and the sophists, those competing educators whom Socrates constantly battled and belittled. Indeed one can read the conclusion in the specific context of Socrates' quarrel with those advocates of the conventional view, Hermogenes and his brother Callias, the latter of whom "too dearly bought the reputation of wisdom" (181) in his education by the sophists. This reading would return us to the old and, by now, unfavorable portrait of Plato as the defender of an inarticulate Ideal against the unfairly portrayed first philosophers of language.

Or one can take this concluding remark in a different spirit: could not Socrates' ending reservation about the "power of names" more specifically address the potential dangers of the natural view of language advocated by Cratylus? The remark, after all, is addressed to him. If one subscribes to an incarnational view of language, if one believes in the correspondence of name to reality, if one believes, as Cratylus says he does, that "he who knows the name also knows the things which are expressed by them" (224), the possessor of such knowledge will lack the kind of reflection and questioning scrutiny crucial to the formation of values. He will fall under the "power of names" (much like an initiate of the oral tradition) without the ability to question their hold on him. He will, in short, lack the recursive consciousness of the conventional view advocated by the rhetorical tradition and amply demonstrated by the figural *tour de force* of Plato's own dialogue.

And yet there's another way, the one I prefer, to interpret "No man of sense will like to put himself or the education of his mind in the power of names." Reminded that, for Plato, education is above all a supremely moral issue, we can more gently read the conclusion in terms of something postmodernism has yet to come to *terms* with: ethical understanding. Socrates could simply be saying that an education predicated upon names will be unprincipled if the end is merely to exert power over words through learning the tricks of the trade. A principled education will include the search for ontological certainty counterbalanced by the reflective scrutiny of rhetoric, a scrutiny Socrates has clearly exercised in this dialogue. The important thing to note about this reading is that a moral education proceeds *not* from fidelity to some radiant, unambiguous ideal but from occupying the position between the natural and conventional views—between the search for ontic certainty and the recursive consciousness of writing.

Thus, we discover in the surest conclusion Socrates can draw from his investigation of language an ambiguity, a productive uncertainty as to just what he means in warning us about "the power of names." Whether this uncertainty is more a product of the postmodernist penchant for discovering paradoxes in the text or a characteristic of the Platonic achievement I leave for the reader to decide. One *can* read the remark as unfairly dismissive of the sophists and the rhetorical tradition, returning us again to the portrait so often invoked by the contrarian spirit of postmodernism: Plato, the enemy of writing and all it entails. Or one *can* appropriate Plato as a vanguard of the postmodern, warning us about the dangerously totemic power of words for those who read them, like Cratylus, uncritically and with blind literalism. Or, as I have suggested in my third interpretation, we can read Socrates' warning as ethically charged, a warning about the "power of names" not proceeding from an ontological "theory" or "system" but from an awareness of their potential for abuse from *either* the conventional or natural view. This last Plato needs to be heard from more often by postmodernism. Not the whipping boy of the anti-Platonic strain of poststructuralism, not the merely playful and ironic voice who seems congenial to the rehabilitative strain of postmodernism, this Plato stands as historically he has been most potent, challenging a new age to define the ethical character of its own undertaking. If, as seems the case in most postmodernist polemic, the ethical argument is one for pluralism, so be it, but one wonders how this could be post-anything, for the argument for pluralism, stemming clearly from the old rhetorical tradition, is as old as the hills. Perhaps it is time that postmodernism consider less fretfully its own notion of the true, the just, the good. Perhaps one will witness construction of something genuinely new after a stage of such thoroughgoing and valuable deconstruction. As today's readers demystify one of the most powerful of names—the name of Plato—postmodernism continues to come to terms with the character and even possibility of its own achievement.

NOTES

[1] H. N. Fowler, "Preface" to his translation of the *Cratylus* (London: Loeb Series, 1926), 3.

[2] Jacques Derrida, *Disseminations*, trans. Barbara Johnson (Chicago: University of Chicago Press, 1981), 67-151.

[3] Richard Rorty, *Philosophy and the Mirror of Nature* (Princeton: Princeton University Press, 1979).

[4] For the classic pluralist argument against Plato, see K. R. Popper's *The Open Society and Its Enemies* (London: Routledge, 1945). G. B. Kerferd in *The Sophistic*

Movement (Cambridge: Cambridge University Press, 1981) offers an excellent overview of recent reevalauations, many rehabilitative, of the sophists.

[5] Sandra M. Gilbert and Susan Gubar, *The Madwoman in the Attic* (New Haven: Yale University Press, 1979). Luce Irigaray, *Speculum of the Other Woman*, trans. Gillian C. Gill (Ithaca: Cornell University Press, 1985).

[6] David H. Richter, *The Critical Tradition: Classic Texts and Contemporary Trends* (New York: St. Martin's Press, 1989), 949.

[7] "Preface" to *Disseminations*, 7.

[8] Leo Strauss, *The City and the Man* (Chicago: Rand Mcnally, 1964), 55, 71.

[9] Kerferd, 55-57.

[10] Derrida, 117.

[11] Eric Havelock, *Preface to Plato* (Cambridge: Harvard Univerity Press, 1963).

[12] Frederich Nietzsche, "Auf dem Gedankenkreise der Geburt der Tragodie," trans. G. C. Spivak in her edition of Derrida's *Grammatology* (Baltimore: Johns Hopkins University Press, 1976).

[13] Julius A. Elias, *Plato's Defense of Poetry* (Albany: SUNY Press at Albany, 1985), 115.

[14] *The Sophistic Movement*, 77.

[15] Benjamin Jowett, "Headnote" to his edition of the *Cratylus* in *The Dialogues of Plato, Volume I* (New York: Random House, 1937), 205. All subsequent notations of the *Cratylus* refer to Jowett's translation and will be noted parathetically by page number in the text.

[16] "Swift's Satire Against Etymologists in *The Antiquity of the English Tongue*," *South Atlantic Review*, XLVIII (1983), 22.

[17] See also the further fun with Hermogones' name in the etymological section: after Socrates has discovered an "improved" etymology for Hermes as "contriver" or "speechmaker," Hermogones sheepishly replies, "I am very sure that Cratylus was quite right in saying that I was no true son of Hermes, for I am not a very good hand at speeches" (197). Nor, I have been arguing, is he a very good reader of Socratic irony.

[18] Prodicus was renowned for his treatment of synonyms, which Kerferd believes must have figured in his lecture *On the Correctness of Names*. Protagoras, among other accomplishments, distinguished the genders of names. For a discussion of how pervasive the problem of names was before Plato's treatment, see Kerferd, 68-74.

[19] Derrida suggests perversely or playfully—probably both—that Plato in writing about his dead father (Socrates), who had condemned writing, was performing, in effect, an act of patricide. In this vein, the Legislator, insuring the correctness of names, would, I suppose, figure as the Grand Father anticipating the cause of dispute between his descendants.

by Louis Orsini

An Act of Imaginative Oblivion: Eric Voegelin and the *Parmenides* of Plato

Edith Hamilton and Huntington Cairns, in their introduction to Cornford's translation of Plato's *Parmenides*, write that "the best Platonists differ about its meaning. The ordinary person will be hard put to it to discover any meaning at all."[1] It is, though, precisely this problem of "meaning" that is being addressed in the *Parmenides.* More to the point, if the *Parmenides*, as Hamilton and Cairns suggest, is written "in words that appear to make sense and yet convey nothing to the mind" (920), it also addresses the question of how language can arrive at meaning, and what that meaning is derived from. The seemingly endless convolutions, negations and outright nonsensical propositions call attention to themselves precisely as the philosopher's attempt to articulate meaning in language, and point to the snares that await any philosopher who would seek to articulate what must remain a given. I will return to this last point again.

The *Parmenides*, then, is a gross parody that Plato would have show what happens when the philosopher outsteps the boundaries of his own philosophizing, and not only reifies the experience which led to the philosophizing in the first place, but also reifies the very language the quest for meaning takes place in. In the *Parmenides*, that experience is the experience of the "one," and Plato would thus examine how that experience can destroy meaning when it is placed *in* the philosopher's consciousness as one of the *things* to be reflected upon. Thus contextualized it is, then, the notion of a philosophizing consciousness that is also very much at issue in the *Parmenides*, and furthermore, precisely *where* this consciousness stands in relation to the reality it would articulate.

I thus propose to examine the structure of consciousness in light of Eric Voegelin's analysis, and to apply this analysis to the *Parmenides* to show how Plato, too, was aware of this structure, and what happens to philosophy when the structure is, to use Voegelin's word, "deformed." Regarding the structure of consciousness, Voegelin writes:

> On the one hand we speak of consciousness as a something located in human beings in their bodily existence. In relation to this concretely embodied consciousness, reality assumes the position of an object intended. Moreover, by its position as an object intended by a consciousness that is bodily located, reality itself acquires a metaphorical touch of external thingness. On the other hand, we know the bodily located consciousness to be also real; and this concretely located consciousness does not belong to another genus of reality, but is part of the same reality that has moved,

> in its relation to man's consciousness, into the position of a thing reality. In this second sense, then, reality is not an object of consciousness, but the something in which consciousness occurs as an event of participation between partners in the community of being.[2]

The paradoxic nature of consciousness is thus that it not only intends reality as an object, but it also *occurs* in that same reality. The paradox is precisely that consciousness cannot get outside itself to observe its own occurrence, it can only *experience* it.[3] That which consciousness observes Voegelin terms the "thing reality." That which it can only experience its own participation in he terms the "It reality," or the "comprehending reality." It is the tension inherent in this paradox, consciousness experienced as "in between" that reality which it intends as an object and which it also experiences itself as part of, which Plato, says Voegelin, denotes by the term "metaxy." It is central to Voegelin's thought, as it is to Plato's as well, that "the poles of the tension must not be hypostatized into *objects* independent of the tension in which they are experienced as poles" (emphasis added).[4] If reality is assumed to be solely one *or* the other of the poles, the destruction of the tension assumes the form of what Voegelin terms an "act of imaginative oblivion" (*Search* 41); that is, consciousness forgets that it partakes of both poles and assigns truth to one and consigns the other to "oblivion." It is precisely this hypostasis which, I intend to show, occurs in the *Parmenides*.

Furthermore, as Voegelin points out, the philosopher's precarious balance "includes language and truth, together with consciousness and reality," because "there is no autonomous, nonparadoxic language ready to be used by man when he wants to refer to the paradoxic structure of reality and consciousness" (*Search* 17). Parmenides, however, insists that his language be nonparadoxic. In this context, then, Plato, in the *Parmenides*, points to the dangers inherent in language in its solely intentionalist mode, where a sign always equals a referent and both are seen as part of the thing reality. In fact, this conception of language is central to Parmenides' argument, for as he says:

> What I mean is this. When you use a word, you use it to stand for some*thing*. You can use it once or many times, but in either case *you are speaking of the thing* whose name it is. However many times you utter the same word, you must *always* mean the same thing. (147d) (emphasis added)

This obviously flies in the face of language as it is experienced because language does not always operate in a solely denotative mode. The tension of the metaxy is also inherent in language itself, which points toward the It reality when it is used symbolically, and the thing reality when it is used denotatively. "Words and their meanings are just as much a part of the reality to which they refer as the being things are partners in the comprehending reality" (*Search* 17). Parmenides, however, has hypostatized the poles of the tension by insisting that language be used only denotatively. Plato thus articulates the 'comedy of errors' which follows from such a notion as Parmenides pursues it to its reduction *ad absurdum*.

A short digression here may help to clarify Plato's 'meaning' in the *Parmenides*. On a very subtle level, Plato implies the tension of the metaxy as it is experienced in language by forcing the reader to confront contradictory conclusions arising from a single analysis. It is the reader's very perplexity, when confronted with "words that appear to make sense yet convey nothing to the mind," which underscores Plato's understanding of what Ricoeur calls the "ontological vehemence" of language, the simultaneity of its denotative and conotative modes, which is precisely its paradoxic nature. It is also a paradox that, as Voegelin says, "Plato . . . in the practice of his own philosophy, coped with . . . by using both conceptual analysis *and* mythic symbolization as *complementary* modes of thought in the quest for truth" (*Search* 17). The *Parmenides* is significant for the complete absence of language used in its symbolic mode, but then, this is in keeping with Parmenides' whole intentionalist approach, and the ground rules, so to speak, which he gives to Socrates *in no uncertain terms*. But, as Voegelin says, and as Plato understands, "the philosopher's understanding of language must not be confused with the linguists' conception of language as a system of signs" (*Search* 21).

This intentionalist deformity occurs, in the *Parmenides*, on the level of the consciousness complex also. I referred, at the beginning of this paper, to that which must remain a given. This given, for Plato, was the experience of the Beyond, the being beyond being which causes the prisoner in the cave to turn around and ascend toward the light. It is that which draws the philosopher into the quest for truth. It is thus an existential *event*, if we recall Voegelin's word, and forms the ground for all philosophizing. Moreover, as Voegelin says, "the ground is not to be found among *things* of the external world . . . but lies beyond this world. Plato has introduced the *symbol* of the beyond, the epikeina, into philosophical language as the criterion of the creative divine ground" (*Anamnesis* 96, emphasis added). The "One" of Parmenides is clearly that which is beyond for Plato. Yet the "One" that is analyzed by Parmenides is an *object* of consciousness, and thus constitutive of a corresponding loss of experience of the "One" as part of the field in which both the philosopher and the "One" participate in the tension of the metaxy. The tension no longer exists when the "One" is hypostatized into a thing by Parmenides' act of imaginative oblivion. Each proposition about the "One," as a thing, is subject to its opposite proposition. The dialogue becomes a parody of the paradox of the tension of the "complex consciousness-reality-language" (*Search* 16).

Let us turn, then, to the dialogue in more detail, to see what, if any, "meaning" can be found in Plato's characterization of Parmenides' relentless intentionalist approach; and also to see what consequences this approach has for philosophy as Plato would have the reader of the dialogue understand it.

Significantly, Plato portrays Socrates as a young man, and thus somewhat philosophically naive at this point in his life. It is, in fact, this naivete which allows Parmenides and Zeno to dominate the dialogue, and handily dispose of any of Socrates' objections to their method of dialectic. Socrates makes an attempt at placing the argument of the dialogue in the context of the It reality, or at least an attempt to draw the discussion out of the realm of intentionality, when he says, in speaking of the forms, "May it not be that each of these forms is a *thought* which cannot properly exist anywhere but in a *mind*? In that way each of them can be one and the statements that have just been made would no longer be true of it" (132b) (emphasis added). Socrates here intuits that something is amiss in Parmenides' method of analysis. If the forms are *thoughts*, then they exist in a consciousness, which is subject to the tensions of the complex consciousness-reality. However, instead of seeing this as a possible entreé into the realm of the It reality, the participation of thought in the realm which it intends, Parmenides returns the conversation purely to the level of thing reality when he asks, "Then, is each form one of those thoughts and yet a thought of nothing?" Socrates, in his naivete, replies, "No, that is impossible" (132b). Socrates' descent back to the level of intentionality is then seized upon by Parmenides, who assumes control of the dialogue again and re-directs it to thing reality when he says, "So it is a thought of something." The forms then, as objects, become subject to a deconstruction by Parmenides, who concludes, based on his intentionalist argument, that "we do not possess the forms themselves, nor can they exist in our world," to which Socrates, acceding to Parmenides' method, is forced to agree (134b).

Clearly, what Plato is doing here is not undermining his own theory of forms, as some would suggest, but rather he is deliberately hypostatizing the poles of the paradox of consciousness-reality-language and showing, as the dialogue proceeds, how this split leads to the contrariety of differential propositions existing in an intentionalist mode and, finally, to the negation of meaning.

This hypostatizing of the forms into objects to be speculated on "*delivers being to the libido dominandi* of the speculators and activists," as Voegelin says, and philosophy "derails into speculations of the theogonic or historico-dialectic type" (*Anamnesis* 127). The derailment into theogonic speculation will become evident in Parmenides' manipulation and application of terms centered on the concept of being as this analysis proceeds. For the present it is sufficient to note that Parmenides is clearly in control of the argument. But even though he dominates Socrates, Plato, as the author of the dialogue, "Pays (him) back in the same coin with something to spare" (128d), as Zeno has said of Parmenides' detractors, by showing the absurdities of the intentionalist method as the dialogue continues.

We recall that Parmenides, in ostensible control of the argument, has had Socrates naively accede to the hypostasis of his (Parmenides') conclusion that these "forms have no significance with reference to things in our world, nor have things in our world any significance with reference to them. *Each set has it only among themselves*" (134d) (emphasis added). The tension of the metaxy, in this statement, has been decisively resolved into two separate poles, each having nothing to do with the other. What follows is remarkable. Parmenides admits that his deconstruction has led to the conclusion that if "a man refuses to admit that forms of things exist or to distinguish a definite form in every case, he will have nothing on which to fix his thought, so long as he will not allow that each thing has a character which is always the same, and in so doing *he will completely destroy the significance of all discourse*" (135c) (emphasis added). After admitting this, Parmenides then asks Socrates what to do about philosophy, presumably because philosophy, as discourse, would be meaningless also. He remarks to Socrates that "there was one thing you said to him (Zeno) which impressed me very much—you would not allow the survey to be confined to visible things or to range only over that field; it was to extend to those objects which are *specially apprehended* by discourse and can be regarded as forms" (135e) (emphasis added). Once again the possibility exists for the dialogue to lift itself out of the mode of intentionality, as that 'special apprehension' can be seen to be the young Socrates' intuition of the It reality, so conspicuously absent in Parmenides' consciousness. The hypostatization of the poles of consciousness that had led to the aforementioned *separate* worlds of gods and men could have been reintegrated into the tension of the metaxy. Yet just the opposite occurs. Parmenides does not recognize the possibility of the "destruction of all meaning" in his own discourse. Parmenides finally and decisively directs the dialogue into that type of philosophy which Plato calls "eristics." Because of the limits Parmenides has placed on the nature of discourse, that is, language in a strictly conceptual, intentionalist mode, he is able to make the assertion that a philosopher "must not merely make the supposition that such a thing *is* and then consider the consequences; (he) must also take the supposition that the same *thing is not*" (136a) (emphasis added). In a deliberate act of imaginative oblivion Parmenides has performed a piece of "speculative magic by which the thinker brings the divine ground into his possession" (*Anamnesis* 109). The "One," the ground of all being and that which is the source of the philosopher's quest, is thus itself called into question because it is perceived as a thing rather than as an experience which philosophy participates in by way of the tension of the metaxy.

But, Voegelin reminds us, "philosophy in the classic sense is *not* a body of ideas or opinions about a divine ground dispensed by a person who calls himself a philosopher, but a man's responsive pursuit of his questioning unrest to the divine source that has aroused it" (*Anamnesis* 96). Parmenides has, in essence, as Voegelin would say, demoted the "One" to "doxa," or mere opinion. As opinion, then, the "One" becomes subject to the supposition that it "is not," for one "opinion" is as good as the next when the ground of the quest for truth has been undermined. The consequences of this are that "when the consciousness of the cosmic bond of being as the background of all philosophy declines, there arises the well known dangers of the de-divinized world and the unworldly God, the unworldly world as nothing but a nexus of relations between immanent things and the de-divinized God reduced to mere existence" (*Anamnesis* 79) or, in Parmenides' case, the *supposition* of mere existence.

It is precisely this "de-divinized world" and the "unworldly God" that Parmenides has unwittingly referred to in the conclusion to his critique of the forms, for when the forms are perceived "intentionally" "the gods' mastership can never be exercised over us, nor their knowledge know us or anything in our world. Just as we do not rule over them by virtue of rule as it exists in our world and *we know nothing that is divine* by our knowledge, so they, on the same principle, being *gods*, are not our masters *nor do they know anything of human concerns*" (134d-e) (emphasis added). The split is thus complete. Parmenides' concepts of "knowledge" and language preclude the possibility of the experiential aspect of consciousness because he has reified both knowledge as a quest, and the ground that determines the quest. As Voegelin says, "when the non-divine *things* provide the model for being, the predicates are derived from immanent existence, and even the *predicate being itself can apply to God only by way of analogy*. The aporias of this type are *not* soluble on the basis of objectivizing thought *about* being. In order to solve them, the philosopher *must* acknowledge that the figures of cosmic primary experience are still present in his thinking about being, and he *must* include the truth of the primary experience of a divine-worldly cosmos in his philosophy" (*Anamnesis* 78) (emphasis added).

The predicates of being in Parmenides' analysis are clearly derived from "immanent existence" since he emphasizes that the philosopher must question whether "such a *thing is*" and then take the supposition that the same "*thing is not.*" His philosophical method, then, has essentially immanentized the experience of the "One," of the beyond, and in so doing has placed the experience of the It reality into the field of the thing reality as an object to be manipulated or dominated; but as an object it forever remains an "other" which can only be speculated about. Parmenides thus exhibits what Voegelin calls a *deformed* consciousness (and keeping his deconstruction of the "forms" in mind, the pun is intentional). It is, then, this act of imaginative oblivion, this dissolving of the tension of the poles of consciousness by an immanentizing act, which, forming the basis of the rest of the dialogue, allows Parmenides to investigate the ontological status of the "One" as it can be manipulated in an intentional mode as subject to predicates of being and non-being, rather than that which consciousness participates *in* and responds *to.*

Plato perceives the irony inherent in this whole way of philosophizing; and when Zeno says to Socrates that "you cannot hit upon truth and gain understanding without ranging this way over the *whole field*" (136d-e) (emphasis added), the irony is precisely that he has not taken the "whole field" into account because he has not recognized the comprehending reality of which he is a part. He has, rather, hypostatized it into a principle to be "solved" on the basis of "objectivizing thought about being." Thus Parmenides starts his dialectic with the (mistaken, Plato would have us see) supposition "if there is a 'one'" (137c), and the meaning of the dialogue dissolves into the aforementioned "words that appear to make sense yet convey nothing to the mind."

As Hamilton and Cairns point out, Parmenides was "one of the greatest thinkers in the generation just before" Socrates. In the *Parmenides*, however, Plato takes this greatness of thought to task, and the *Parmenides* can be seen as an "act of resistance" to what Plato perceives as the philosophical disorder of his time, i.e., the tendency of philosophy toward eristics. As Steven Shankman has pointed out, "In the *Philebus* Plato has Socrates compare the divinely sanctioned noetic process with the kind of mental activity practiced by "the man who is considered wise"[5] in Plato's time; and the reference Shankman makes to the *Philebus* bears repeating here, as it can be seen to apply to the means and method of the dialectic practiced by Parmenides who

> while making his one—or his many, as the case may be—more quickly or more slowly than is proper, when he has got his one proceeds to his unlimited number straightaway, allowing the intermediates to escape him, whereas it is the recognition of those intermediates that make all the difference in discussing problems in a philosophical manner rather than contentiously.[6]

Plato thus has the analysis of Parmenides proceed contentiously as a dialectic between the "one" and the "many." The intermediate, which, in the context I have been discussing it, is most certainly the metaxy, that which "makes all the difference." It is precisely the metaxy that Parmenides ignores, as he moves directly from the "one" to the "many" which "must be *unlimited* in multitude" (143a) (emphasis added).

The young Socrates must have learned something from Parmenides, though perhaps not that which Parmenides intended to teach. If there is a certain "madness" in Parmenides' method, there is also a certain "method" in Plato's seeming madness in writing the *Parmenides*. And that method is, as the mature Socrates says in the *Philebus*, that the philosopher must

> come to see not merely that the one that we started with is a one and an unlimited many, but also just how many it is. But *we are not to apply the character of unlimitedness to our plurality* until we have discerned the total number of forms the thing in question has intermediate between its one and its unlimited number. (*Philebus* 16d; emphasis added)

It would seem that Hamilton and Cairns are right in their assessment of the Parmenides; and *that*, Plato would have us see, is precisely the point. "Meaning" is properly to be found in the philosophers response to the experienced tension of the metaxy, and not in pointless intentionalist speculation on either of its poles: the "One" of the beyond, or the many of immanent existence. It is Parmenides' ignorance of the metaxy and his subsequent act of imaginative oblivion in reifying the one and applying to it predicates of being or non being, which, as Voegelin has said, "can apply to God only by way of analogy," which leads to the "conclusion" that

> whether there is or is not a one both that one and the others alike are and are not, and appear and do not appear to be all manner of things in all manner of ways, with respect to themselves and to one another. (166b)

It is *then*, for the first time in the dialogue, that the famous Socratic irony makes its appearance, as the young Socrates recognizes, finally, the babble of incoherence that the method of Parmenides' dialectic has produced. We can almost visualize the knowing smile on Socrates' face as Aristoteles replies, "Most true"; and the dialogue ends leaving a self-satisfied Parmenides in his ignorance, and Socrates, and the reader also Plato would hope, a slightly older but much wiser person.

NOTES

[1]Edith Hamilton and Huntington Cairns, ed., *The Collected Dialogues of Plato* (Princeton: Princeton University Press, 1987), 920. All quotes from the *Parmenides*, trans. F. A. Cornford, are from this edition.

[2]Eric Voegelin, *Order and History Vol. V—In Search of Order* (Baton Rouge: Louisiana State University Press, 1987), 15.

[3]The philosopher can, however, reflect on this experience, as long as it is remembered as an experience. Voegelin goes into great detail about what he terms this "reflective distance." Since Parmenides does not even recognize the experience as such, this aspect of Voegelin's thought is not of great import to the present discussion, though it certainly is for a more complete understanding of Voegelin's analysis.

[4]Eric Voegelin, *Anamnesis* (Notre Dame: Notre Dame University Press) 104.

[5]Steven Shankman, "Reason and Revelation in the Pre-Enlightenment: Eric Voegelin's Analysis and the Case of Swift," *Religion and Literature* 16:2 (1984), 5-6.

[6]Hamilton and Cairns, *Philebus*, trans. R. Hackforth, 1096.

Part Three:
Plato and the Feminine

by Linda Kintz

Plato, Kristeva, and the Chôra: Figuring the Unfigurable

In an article entitled "Postmodern Parataxis: Embodied Texts, Weightless Information," N. Katherine Hayles describes a distinguishing feature of postmodern culture:

> On the one hand, we all experience ourselves as embodied creatures, living in specific times and places and limited by the biological, cultural, and historical inheritances that define us. On the other, contemporary technology, especially informatics, has given us the sense that we can transcend these limitations and live a disembodied, free-floating existence made possible in part by the near-instantaneous transfer of information from one point on the globe to any other.[1]

Hayles argues that this juxtaposition causes us to live "a paratactic mode of experience," constantly relating a metaphoric sense of a figured, representable body in a specified place to a postmodern metonymic interpretation of the world according to pieces of information that are simply found next to each other. Such information comes to us the way it does when we flip through channels with the remote control; it is no longer arranged according to some overarching, transcendent meaning or accessible to judgment from a clearly locatable, guaranteed vantage point.

I shall argue that Julia Kristeva's revision of the *chôra,* a concept introduced by Plato in the *Timaeus*, provides a way to investigate what Hayles calls a "disjuncture of reals" through a theory of representation that challenges information technology and the commodification of information. Such a theory might be able to take into account Hayles' binary opposition between figurations of human subjects still limited by androcentric representation, on the one hand, and the weightlessness of information, on the other. Yet it might also allow a theoretical move beyond such an impasse.

In the *Timaeus* Plato tells a story of the creation of the universe, of a cosmos that is self-inclusive, complete, and harmonious, and in this story he comes to rely on the *chôra,* the medium within which Platonic intelligible forms, or paradigms, are phenomenalized in their relationship to the world *in its order*. This *chôra* is, in Plato's version, not matter but space. Kristeva's revision of it, which I will follow in some detail later, conceptualizes the *chôra* not as space but as spac*ing*. This development of Kristeva's own concept of the *chôra* is part of an early stage of her study of the effects produced by Western metaphysics on theories of language, as she develops a methodology for historicizing the various textual ideologemes, or typologies, of the

Sign, tracing the vagaries of the historical shifts in the relationship between the signifier and the signified. Her discussion and reinterpretation of Plato's *chôra* was developed in *Revolution in Poetic Language* in an attempt to show how certain theories of language, among them Husserl's, Hjelmslev's, and Frege's, resulted in what she calls an idealized linguistics that could not account for the materiality of language as performed by embodied subjects.[2] She then moves through theories of materiality, in particular those of Hegel and Marx, in order to discuss the relationship between language and matter, and she ends by developing her own theory of sociolinguistics that draws on the work of Freud and Lacan. Yet through this study, she also revises a number of the key concepts of psychoanalytic theory, in particular Lacan's theory of the mirror stage, and suggests that textual and poetic forms can be linked through psychoanalytic theory to the social structure, power relations, and the mode of production.

The important point in her revision of Plato's *chôra* , which is also called the semiotic, is her definition of it as spacing, rather than as space—as the site of an aesthetic wobble that shows up in English in the postmodern grammatical form of choice, the gerund with its *-ing* to suggest that textuality or interpretation never stops but is always in process. The aesthetic wobble is the ground of meaning through which bodies (the real which is always present but never available in unmediated form) and signs (the "real") are mediated; this is a ground that is paradoxically in motion, a moving dialectic or wavering between the body of the subject and the historical train of symbols and signs through which that subject has come to identify itself as a human subject. In this process the symbolic level of culture (its institutions, language, visual sign systems, power relations) is linked to the specificity of each subject, ensuring that there is no such thing as a universal humanness but, rather, historically specific experiences of humanness mediated by particular, specific, gendered constructions in culture. The implications of such a linkage are that the interpretation and living of such experiences can best be described as an aesthetic or textual process, for the relationship between culture and subject rests, like poetic meaning, on an aesthetic, unfixed, dialectical wavering between real and representation, making them forever indistinguishable yet requiring infinite interpretation.

Kristeva's revision of Plato's *chôra* significantly brings this aesthetic element into play by focusing on the performance of philosophy, which, like linguistics, must be retheorized in order to show the ways its abstractions have repressed "the laws of the production of meaning, precisely insofar as meaning emerges from (and in) matter."[3] But this "matter" itself must be historicized, for it drags along its own metaphysical history, its reconsideration requiring a look at philosophy.

We might ask why Kristeva and those French go on so about philosophy, given that in an American context philosophy has never seemed to carry the kind of weight it does in France. Yet philosophy as a discipline, the knowledge of knowledge, has provided the models in Greco-Judaeo-Christian cultures for telling the history of human bodies, the history of human subjectivity, the very history of history—those things that we take to be real. Though philosophers may not feel quite so powerful as all that today, philosophy has participated in organizing the historically variable relations between that deceptively simple duo, the signifier and the signified—the signifier as a symbol for something, and the signified as what that symbol represents or means. This is where the postmodern problematic, its critique of representation, situates itself and where the shifting valences in the relationship between signifier and signified allow for Kristeva's history of the Sign.[4]

Timaeus *and the Story of the Cosmos*

Plato's *Timaeus* is variously described as a mythological text, a theological one, a text whose originality lies in its description of the rationality of the universe and of nature. It is the story of the origin of the cosmos told by Timaeus, who is an expert in astronomy, and the story of the origin of the cosmos is the story of the universe in its order.[5] The initial project of the divine creator, characterized as a kind of Demiurge or divine Craftsman was, says Timaeus, to distinguish between Being (that which always is and never becomes, is eternally the same, and apprehensible by intelligence) and Becoming (that which is always becoming and never is, the object of opinion and irrational sensation, that which is coming to be and ceasing to be.)

The origin of the universe was located not in Becoming but in Being, which took precedence, just as truth took precedence over belief. This Craftsman acted on the cosmos, but it ostensibly did not act on him. The shape of the cosmos, a shape suitable for its nature as a perfect One, was a rounded sphere with all its extremes harmoniously equidistant in all directions from its center. It was designed as a kind of perfect "body," a whole of complete parts, single, with nothing left over, ageless, free from disease, finding nourishment from its own decay, "a single spherical universe in circular motion, alone but because of its excellence needing no company other than itself, and satisfied to be its own acquaintance and friend."[6]

After the planets and the sun had been created in their spheres of Same and Different and following the creation of an intermediate tier of gods came the creation of human beings, whose entry introduced confusion because of the fact that their immortal souls were located in mortal bodies. The disturbances caused by the sensations damaged the soul's harmonious circles which could barely hold together, such disturbances causing difficulty in judgments about the categories of Same or Different in the external world. This difficulty led to the need for philosophers, whose purpose was to know and teach the intelligible but not immediately visible forms and to help order the body to resemble the soul.

This human body was at first spherical, consisting only of the head, the most divine part which eventually came to control all the rest: "To prevent the head from rolling about on the earth, unable to get over or out of its many heights and hollows, [the gods] provided that the body should act as a convenient vehicle. And after the arms and legs, the most important organs were the eyes" (44d-e). It is the eyes, says Timaeus, that have made available to us the greatest gift of all, philosophy, which is derived from the sight of the stars, the sun and heaven whose observation gave us the months, the equinoxes, the invention of number, the notion of time, and made us inquire into the nature of the universe.

The philosopher, the privileged observer, is thus figured and situated in relation to two things: a circular universe that is self-contained rather than infinite, and the privilege of vision, though Plato reverses that privilege so that appearances, the objects of the senses, are not what are seen as real. Rather, it is the philosopher's *mind's* eye that sees the mathematical and geometric truths. The philosopher locates himself and his identifiable body in relation to a universe that is out there within a spherical enclosure divided visually into the celestial and the terrestrial, the sky above, the earth below, his own position vertical to other men.

But in this text, the important terms of Being and Becoming do not stay in relationship without some kind of dialectical glue to hold them together, some kind of field or medium within which they can retain a decipherable interaction, and that glue is the *chôra.* For, as Timaeus says, "We did not distinguish a third form [other than Being and Becoming] considering two would be enough; but now the argument compels us to try to describe in words a form that is difficult and obscure" (49a). The *chôra* is first characterized as a receptacle, the nurse of all becoming and change. Because the real is not directly accessible, the interpreter or philosopher-knower will have to situate a thing as *this* thing, this particular thing, these "things" functioning primarily as positions or sites where thingness takes place, or takes a place, as Kristeva might say. The unchanging form or paradigm (the real) and the phenomenon (which is not real) momentarily coincide in an abstract space of intelligibility. But such a space is made possible only because of the availability of a broader category of space called the *chôra*, where necessity is also located.

The *chôra* holds open the space of intelligibility to allow thingness to "take a place"; it is the natural receptacle of all phenomenal bodies: "For [the *chôra*] continues to receive all things, and never itself takes a permanent impress from any of the things that enter it; it is a kind of neutral plastic material on which changing impressions are stamped by the things which enter it, making it appear different at different times" (50b-c).

Here the text arrives at a point at which Plato must turn to particular human figurations to tell the truth of Being and Becoming, these figurations related to historically specific kinds of socialized bodies, that is, bodies as represented at a particular historical moment. A socialized body, its representation or figuration, grounds *any* grammatical statement, as any enunciation arises out of a *thetic* place—a historically specific, represented place from which a thesis is set out, even though that place and that thesis ultimately prove to be constructions. In the Western metaphysical tradition's insistence on identity, the thetic "I," or speaking position, is part of a theological system which grounds what Kristeva calls the "phantasmatic necessity on the part of speaking beings to provide themselves with a representation (animal, female, male, parental) *in place of* what constitutes them as such, symbolization."[7] The very logic of Plato's text both requires this hierarchical figuration and necessitates the socialized body of a masculine philosopher-speaker. As Foucault says: "[T]o describe a formulation [as a] statement does not consist in analyzing the relations between the author and what he says (or wanted to say, or said without wanting to); but in determining what position can and must be occupied by any individual if he is to be the subject of [the statement]."[8] To point this out is merely to historicize the performance.

The kind of embodiment, or phantasm, "spoken" here is that of an unquestionably masculine speaking subject who interprets Being, or that which is resembled and which in this constellation is analogous to the father. That which becomes is the offspring, or son, and that in which it becomes is the receptacle, womb, nurse, mother. And in terms of the latter, the receptacle or the womb, Plato says: "Anything that is to receive in itself every kind of character must be devoid of all characteristics" (70). Thus the medium, the dialectical glue, between the first two, Being and Becoming, is space, the *chôra*, now figured as the nurse or mother. Eternal and indestructible, it provides a position for everything that comes to be and passes away and can be apprehended only by a kind of bastard reasoning. It is a medium that is hard to believe in (unlike truth or true opinion) and can only be looked at in a kind of dreamlike state. This story and its masculine speaking subject prove to require a writing surface that is written on and in and that is, very importantly, unchanged by that writing. Such a surface is not itself worthy of interpretation nor of being read for itself; its function is simply to enable a reading, to make it possible to read something else whose interpretation is actually important. It is an amorphous surface whose existence is fundamental to the interpretation of truth but exists only *to be read from or not read* as it foregrounds what is legible.[9]

And in order to write on this surface, the Craftsman in Plato's account transforms matter from chaos to cosmos by shaping it into a kind of language made up of basic elements, a distinct configuration of shape and numbers—the triangles that make up the four disorderly states of water, air, fire, and earth. They consist of tetrahedra, octahedra, and icosahedra, which constitute a kind of geometric alphabet that translates from the data of the senses to a language understandable by the soul. This geometric alphabet had to do, says Gregory Vlastos, with "measuring, numbering, weighing so the philosopher will not be at the mercy of phenomena, which are held suspect till proved innnocent by rational judgement."[10]

Perhaps the central tenet of deconstruction and Lacanian readings of Freud is that it is in and through language itself, through language as the space of intelligibility, that what we come to know as the real and as history are constructed; it is in language as the space of intelligibility that the real and history take place. Language, of course, does not work like a window pane we simply look through. That is, it is not only through semantics or content that words work, but through the very way language (or languages) divide up and establish some kind of order, for example, through syntax, rhythm, condensation and displacement, articulation (as sound divided up into units) to make process readable. Here in Plato's language of geometry, the Craftsman "writes" the universe in triangles, arranging it in a readable order and in a very particular androcentric form of geometry that does not include relativity or infinity and presumes a geocentric cosmos with a self-identical observer who knows who and where he is. Such a geometry privileges a specific kind of vision, the mind's eye, and provides the alphabet of intelligibility, while the reasonable Soul functions as the ideal reader and the *chôra* (now thoroughly coded as passive, receptive, feminine though "devoid of all characteristics") provides the writing surface, to be read from—or not read.

Seeing Space: Victor Burgin, Geometry, and Fantasy

But how to get from Plato's geocentric, androcentric, unchanging *chôra* and *space* to Kristeva's *chôra* and a culturally, materially determined concept of *spacing*? What is at stake here is the need to displace the mind's eye and to disrupt the opposition with which this discussion began, between androcentric metaphors of embodiment, on the one hand, and the metonymic weightlessness of information, on the other. A move toward such a displacement might follow a trajectory described by Victor Burgin in an article entitled "Geometry and Abjection" that traces geometry as a language that both describes space and constitutes the spacing of intelligibility linking intellection and perception, for space, like humanness, has a history.[11] Burgin argues that in the history of space in the West and, as a result, the history of vision, perspective, and the situatedness of the observer, a classical or pre-modern notion of bounded space was imported into the modern period, though its physics and technology had long since abandoned it.

In a curious way, systems of representation circumscribed by the birth of perspective in Brunelleschi's cone of vision, intersected by a plane surface, were contradicted by two things: the non-geocentric, boundless infinity that Galileo and Euclidean geometry described and the entrepreneurial humanism (Burgin's term for mercantile capitalism during the Renaissance that was in many ways enabled by a conceptual shift from theological explanations of the world to humanist beliefs in the earthly capacities of human reason and activity) with its "boundlessness" of a world to be explored. Thus while Euclidean geometry, on the one hand, altered the practices of science and the exploration of the world, on the other hand, systems of representation in the early modern period of the Renaissance continued to work according to Euclidean optics based on a model of vision with certain boundaries that were similar to those of the *Timaeus.* Though the cosmos as conceptualized in the early modern period was no longer thought of as geocentric, it nevertheless remained egocentric and androcentric, as its figurations and optics contradicted its geometry. (This is a time-lag of representation that still haunts us, for as Roland Barthes argued, even today interpretation remains androcentric and egocentric, still presuming "a subject (author, reader, spectator, voyeur) [casting] his gaze towards a horizon on which he cuts out the base of a triangle, his eye (or mind) forming the apex.")[12]

In the postmodern period Hayles speaks of, this noncoincidence of geometry and representation takes another turn. Space is no longer the space of industrial capitalism but of financial capitalism, as postmodern space implodes in the abstract span of the market which, as Burgin says, "had to destroy the autonomy and quality of places . . . eliminating geographic distance to reproduce distance internally as spectacular separation."[13] Spectacle here refers to a characteristic of postmodern culture in which images and media determine much of what counts as reality and information. We live in a period of mass-mediated culture that is no longer best described in relation to a mode of production and manufacturing but rather according to a mode of information whose commodity is information. This is information that comes to us in the form of spectacles—for example, the omnipresence of media in which culture and economy become indistinguishable, the public relations of political campaigns, the media staging of the Gulf War, advertising, global computerized markets. Burgin draws on the theory of spectacle in its relationship to financial capitalism, media, and commodity culture as articulated by the Situationist theorist, Guy Debord. For Debord, spectacle is the cultural site "where the tangible world is replaced by a selection of images which exist above it, and which simultaneously impose themselves as the tangible [itself]."[14]

Within this space of financial capitalism and the mode of information, the concept of *space traversed* (a concept historically quantified in certain ways, as, for example, what we drive through or fly over or deprive prisoners of) shifts to *time traversed,* a process no longer governed by the mechanical speed of machines like airplanes but by the electronic speed of machines like computers—at nearly the speed of light. As Paul Virilio says, "the space-time of electronic communication may finally approach the perceptions of physics . . . Technological space is not a geographic space but a space of time."[15]

But what concerns Burgin is the way the pre-modern world view of bounded, emplaced embodiment with its androcentric privileging of a specific kind of vision still similar to the mind's eye of the *Timaeus* continues to haunt modern and postmodern representations, contradicting Einsteinian and particle physics as well as financial capitalism and the mode of information. As Foucault says, "Contemporary space is perhaps still not entirely desanctified (apparently unlike time, it would seem, which was detached from the sacred in the nineteenth century)."[16]

In order to talk about representation in a way that more accurately takes into account postmodern economy and technology, Burgin's interest is in a theory of something called "psychical reality," (I'd call it postaesthetic aesthetics[17]) which refers to the space of intelligibility where psychological fantasies "take a place." To repeat Kristeva's formulation, the site of the "phantasmatic necessity on the part of speaking beings to provide themselves with a representation." The mobile ground of this spacing, this wavering between perception and intellection which is fantasy is described by Kaja Silverman in this way: "Fantasy might thus be said to confer psychical reality upon the objects which stand in metaphorically for what is sacrificed to meaning—the subject's very 'life'."[18] And it links symbolization, the mode of production, subjectivity, and the materiality of the body. To discuss psychical reality, Burgin thus draws on a broadly expanded notion of psychoanalysis that brings together psychoanalytic theory's formal descriptions to an analysis of the power relations of the *socius,* or Symbolic.

But in order to draw on the resources of psychoanalytic theory, Burgin must first critique the privileging of the visual in Freud's theory, for it is Freud who has, he argues, "conflated psychical space with the space of visual perception . . .," the site/sight of the Oedipal son's gaze.[19] A reconsideration of this ocular privileging is part of Kristeva's revision of the *chôra*, opening up the description of the construction of the human subject within culture by describing its relation to the maternal body prior to the infant's entry into Lacan's mirror stage—before the illusory unifed image and the son's eye assumes its power and before the distinction between subject and object.

Kristeva's Semiotic Chôra: Inscriptions Instead of Images

This revisionary *chôra* becomes the basis for Kristeva's theory of negativity, which she develops in order to account for what is heterogeneous to language: the materiality of the body, the unconscious, the drives and their ordering, history, death, semiosis. The speaking subject does not simply speak out in an abstract field of language; rather, the physicality of her body (not simply its visual identifications but also the composite history of its tactile and sensual interpretations) interacts with the history of the physicality and materiality of other bodies, a history that is both sedimented and disrupted in language. Its description is inherently also a theory of the performative, for it necessitates a reading of the conditions of the production of discourse, or rather a rereading of what has hitherto functioned only as a background or a medium to help read something else. The conditions of the production of discourse can now be read as traces of the materiality of actual bodies and, in particular, of the feminized materiality that has in the *Timaeus* simply been dismissed as receptacle, womb, the neutral imprinting surface on which to read the father's meaning. This feminized matter turns out to be what has all along been read from or not read, the background or the matter that has consistently dropped out in Western metaphysics, as it has in the *Timaeus,* leaving behind only what has been read. And what has been read is Being, the ostensibly static grammar, the product, the father's meaning.

Reconceptualizing the *chôra* as negativity or medium whose articulations must be deciphered and learned isolates a clear distinction between Kristeva's version and the amorphous and ontologized *chôra* of Plato with its unchanging status, always available to hold the imprinting of Soul though ostensibly never changed by or exerting any influence on that imprinting. Plato's amorphous space is one of constant, unreadable but necessary motility, but unlike his, Kristeva's *chôra* has to do with a necessary motility that is *already* socially constructed and constrained, these constraints interacting and altering what is written on it. Its fluid motility is not readable in terms of the Symbolic because it is not yet language, but neither is it simply a neutral space of free play. It is already riven by historical factors whose articulations must be deciphered and codified much more carefully. Its inscriptions (the semiotic) have to be learned, for there is something to be read prior to the entry into the Symbolic, or language, where the infant's body is already being organized in particular ways that ground its bodily experience in a relationship to culturally constructed femininity, a body experienced through the mediation of activities of care which articulate systems of touch, smell, sight, and especially rhythm.[20] Though this cannot yet be called language because there is as yet no subject—the infant has not differentiated its own body and image from that of the mother—the infant's drives are, however, already encountering stases and movement which produce markings. These are traces that are pre-linguistic (they occur prior to the entry into language), but they are not pre-cultural.

The infant's drives are in a state of motility that is historical: "Discrete quantities of energy move through the body of the subject who is not yet constituted as such and, in the course of [its] development, [these quantities of energy] are arranged according to the various constraints imposed on this body—always already involved in a semiotic process—by family and social structures: it is already regulated, its vocal and gestural organization is subject to what we shall call an objective ordering . . . dictated by natural or socio-historical constraints such as the biological difference between the [bodies of the] sexes or family structure."[21] In this way the drives, which are 'energy' charges as well as '*psychical*' marks, articulate what we call a *chôra* : a nonexpressive totality formed by the drives and their stases in a motility that is as full of movement as it is regulated."[22]

Kristeva continues: "We may therefore posit that social organization, always already symbolic, imprints its constraint in a mediated form which organizes the *chôra* not according to a *law* (a term we reserve for the symbolic) but through an *ordering*," or a series of articulations or spacings. And, she continues, it is the "mother's body [that] mediates the symbolic law organizing social relations and becomes the ordering principle of the semiotic *chôra*," which is "the place where the subject is both generated and negated, the place where [its] unity succumbs before the process of charges and stases that produce [it]."[23] The *chôra* and the Symbolic are not so much in Hegelian dialectical opposition or Freudian negation as in an inextricable mixture structured by the constant negativity of process, semiosis, being alive, moving toward death.

What becomes very clear is that the matter or medium that Plato determinedly insisted had no characteristics of its own but whose function was simply to function as a writing surface is precisely the matter or medium whose inscriptions Kristeva insists be read, a surface directly related to the maternal body. Such a reading will require a very different way of thinking about language, for it is negativity's irruptions, the semiotic that is not yet organized into symbolic language but is nevertheless not pre-cultural, that must be deciphered in the form of other languages such as gesture, rhythm, ellipsis, touch, the paralinguistic features or languages of bodies, the poetic characteristics of language, as well as non-Western languages and the trickster or "signifying" strategies for dealing with dominant languages.[24]

Negativity is thus a fundamental concept for Kristeva, whose use of it distinguishes her from other poststructuralists like Derrida, for she recodes negativity to suggest that it provides the evidence of materiality rather than the proof of an absolute alienation from it. In her version, negativity is not exactly negative in the old sense. Instead it undoes attempts to make meaning static, but it is also a constantly fleeting marker of the real and of feminized matter, the marker of the constant intrusion of the materiality of the body into the necessary abstractions of signs.[25] That is, negativity is the inescapable but unreachable proof of matter, which language, by definition, must inevitably exclude in order to organize meaning, its exclusions enunciated, however, only by subjects living in material bodies. The interruptions and intrusions of negativity, or materiality, make language what it is, a constant and infinite construction and deconstruction of meaning.

This negativity, or evidence of materiality, has historically served as dialectical glue to keep the dialectic from getting out of control, though it has been symbolically excluded or repressed. The historically specific nature of that glue, however, can now be traced in Kristeva's *chôra,* its early ordering of the body that is not yet writing but an ordering mixed up or coagulated with the infant's reading of the mother's desire as well as the tactile relationship to her body. In linking Plato's philosophical text describing the *chôra* to its use by Kristeva to theorize the way cultural texts have produced the systems of representation by which human subjects come to identify themselves as human, what emerges is the way the meaning of the father (Being and the philosopher's knowledge in the case of Plato and the father's law in the case of psychoanalysis) is perched very precariously on feminized matter and desire, the tenuous structure of the father's meaning resting on the certainty that its background or writing surface is dependably secure and has no characteristics or influence of its own. The very notion of the speaking subject, the generic "I", has come down to us as the purified position of a masculine speaker, its body "cleaned up," as are the father and son of Plato's figurations in the *Timaeus*, of the traces of the maternal body, of "all that we must shed and that we must distance ourselves from in order to be," as Kristeva says.[26]

In this symbolic organization the traces of the maternal body are excluded but that exclusion is unenforceable, and to deal with that unenforceablity, the inevitable failure of prohibition, those traces are coded as defiled and abject when they reappear. And reappear they do, in the form of ambiguous and threatening signs of mixture and fluidity that threaten to overrun the unenforceable boundaries of clear categories and clear gender, racial, sexual, bodily boundaries that are increasingly phobically protected by dominant groups. What such a phobic subject protects against are mixture, language, and non-identity.[27]

Fantasmatic Ethics, or Postaesthetic Aesthetics

We have finally circled back around to a third position other than Plato's ontologized neutral medium of intelligibility and Hayles' binary opposition between two kinds of bodily experience, the one androcentric, the other weightless. For the fact that Kristeva's *chôra* focuses on the very specific kinds of bodies in every performance means that, in the case of Plato's *chôra,* there simply could *be* no amorphous, disembodied medium, for all interpretation whether read, thought, felt, or spoken, is performed or enacted by embodied persons who articulate that interpretation, including philosopher-knowers. And neither could there be any information that is weightless. In the latter case, a mode of production and a Third World are required, with mostly female assemblers of computer chips adding bodily "weight" to the free-flow of weightless information.[28] And finally, Burgin's argument suggests that in the present system of representation the cultural metaphors of embodiment available to us are still constrained and limited by the androcentric philosopher's mind's eye.

But Kristeva's theory of the relationship between materiality and representation takes yet another step in this long dissection of that mind's eye. For she connects this theory of the semiotic *chôra* to the Western theological, phantasmatic need for representation by proposing an ethics that supersedes Western religion even as it takes advantage of its resources, an ethics that shifts that phantasmatic necessity from sacred representation to the deconstruction and reconstruction of secular aesthetic representation. Such an ethics locates itself in what she calls aesthetic practices, which are grounded precisely where Burgin found them, in fantasy as the spacing between perception and intellection—where symbolization is both produced and dissolved. "It seems to me," Kristeva argues, "that the role of what is usually called aesthetic practices must increase—not only to counterbalance the storage and uniformity of information by present-day mass media, data-bank systems, and, in particular, modern communications technology—but also to *demystify the identity of the symbolic bond itself* . . ."[29] That is, what must be demystified is the belief that there is a universal language community to which "we" all come equally, that there is a kind of generic "I," a universal identity that equalizes and humanizes each and every one of us alike within the space of intelligibility that is language, and that a woman could equally have been the speaking subject of the *Timaeus*. The links between relations of power and the space of intelligibility which is language are such that were a woman to be the speaking subject of the *Timaeus*, an entire power structure and world would have to have been rearranged. Language, politics, and power relations are intimately and intricately related.

Such a demystification of the common identity of speakers within the symbolic community might also displace the androcentric mind's eye so that what could become more readable is "the *singularity* of each person and, even more, along with the multiplicity of every person's possible identifications (with atoms, for example, stretching from the family to the stars)—*the relativity of his/her symbolic as well as biological existence*, according to the variation in his/her specific symbolic capacities."[30] Such singularity would rest not only on identifications and samenesses isolated in the field of Oedipal vision or the identity of the ego but on a multiplicity of other kinds of identifications, such as touch, sound, gesture, other forms of vision not encapsulated by the Oedipal gaze of the son's eye. What would be readable would be not the origin but the originality of every subject along with a more precise register of the constraining influences of the symbolic community upon that subject's ability to make itself heard. The "symbolic capacities" of each subject are linked as much to that subject's ability to be heard by dominant groups as they are to the ability to speak.[31]

Aesthetic practices, or rather what must by now be called postaesthetic aesthetics, which have to do precisely with this fantasmatic spacing of intelligibility, with learning to listen to and read the traces or inscriptions of *what has been read from or not read* instead of the images and geometries located in the mind's eye, are "undoubtedly nothing other than the modern reply to the eternal question of morality." For if it is true that symbolic language, by definition, must inevitably separate itself from bodies and the real, perhaps within the Western logic of purity that locates blame on women and feminized groups such as people of color, people living in poverty, and Jews, learning to read differently can relocate the site of blame for the inevitability of non-identity and for meaning's incompleteness. For that site of blame is language itself—not the other, nor the other sex, but language.

Kristeva's revision of the *chôra* at least points us toward the possibility of another corporeal and desiring space, or spacing, that does not rest on identity and that might—ethically—interrupt, in both anthropomorphic figuration and weightless information, the anachronistic vision of the philosopher's mind's eye.

NOTES

[1]N. Katherine Hayles, "Postmodern Parataxis: Embodied Texts, Weightless Information," *American Literary History* 2.3 (Fall 1990), 394.

[2]Julia Kristeva, *Revolution in Poetic Language*, trans. Leon Roudiez (New York: Columbia University Press, 1984). *La révolution du langage poétique* (Paris: Editions du Seuil, 1974).

[3]Oswald Ducrot and Tzvetan Todorov, "Toward A Critique of the Sign: The Text as Productivity," *Encyclopedic Dictionary of the Sciences of Language*, trans. Catherine Porter (Baltimore: The Johns Hopkins University Press, 1979), 365.

[4]Deconstruction in the United States requires a somewhat different analysis because of the different weight philosophy carries here. What is needed here is an analysis of the step that has followed deconstruction, and that is the reconstruction of transparent meaning. Reconstruction is now the dominant rhetoric in political campaigns and advertising, and it exerts a strong influence on academic backlashes against feminism, multiculturalism, and poststructuralism.

[5]Gregory Vlastos traces the history of the verb, *kosmeô*, which means "to set in order, to marshal, to arrange" and is used to describe ordering that "strikes the eye or the mind as pleasingly fitting: as setting, or keeping, or putting back, things in their proper order. There is a marked aesthetic component here, which leads to a derivative use of *kosmos* to mean not *order* as such, but *ornament, adornment*; this survives in the English derivative, *cosmetic*, which, I dare say, no one, without knowledge of Greek, would recognize as a blood-relation of *cosmic*." *Plato's Universe* (Seattle: University of Washington Press, 1975), 3.

[6]Plato, *Timaeus*, trans. H.D.P. Lee (Baltimore: Penguin Books, 1965), 34a. Further references will be cited in the text.

[7]Julia Kristeva, "Women's Time," *Signs* 7.1 (Autumn 1981) 32. See also Kaja Silverman's painstaking discussion of the fantasmatic and its relationship to the ego and the first person pronoun in *Male Subjectivity at the Margins* (New York: Routledge, 1992), especially the first chapter, "The Dominant Fiction," 15-51.

[8]Michel Foucault, *The Archaeology of Knowledge*, trans. A.M. Sheridan Smith (New York: Harper and Row, 1972), 95.

[9]The questions raised here about Plato's writing surface are influenced by Cynthia Chase's discussion of unread writing surfaces in "Primary Narcissism and the Giving of Figure," in *Abjection, Melancholia and Love: The Work of Julia Kristeva*, eds. John Fletcher and Andrew Benjamin (London: Routledge, 1990), 124-36; and "Desire and Identification in Lacan and Kristeva" in *Feminism and Psychoanalysis*, ed. Judith Roof (Ithaca: Cornell University Press, 1989), 65-83.

[10]Gregory Vlastos, Appendix, Section M, 112. *Plato's Universe*. See especially Chapter 3 in this volume, a discussion of Plato's development of the atomist concept of *stoicheia*, or "letters," in his theory of the structure of matter in the *Timaeus*.

Anne Freire Ashbaugh's *Plato's Theory of Explanation* (Albany: State University of New York Press, 1988) deals with verisimilar explanation in the *Timaeus* and the importance of aesthetic relations in interpreting Plato's theory of matter, helping situate the *chôra* as an aesthetic "space of intelligibility."

[11]Victor Burgin, "Geometry and Abjection," *Abjection, Melancholia, and Love: The Work of Julia Kristeva*, eds. John Fletcher and Andrew Benjamin (New York: Routledge, 1990).

[12]Quoted by Burgin, 104.

[13]Debord, quoted by Burgin, 109.

[14]Guy Debord, *Society of the Spectacle* (Detroit: Black and Red, 1983) Passage 36. The term "mass-mediated culture" is developed by Ian Angus and Sut Jhally in their introduction to *Cultural Politics in Contemporary America* (New York: Routledge, 1989), 5.

[15]Quoted by Burgin, 108.

[16]Michel Foucault, "Of Other Spaces," *Diacritics* (Spring 1986), 23.

[17]Clyde Taylor has suggested the term "postaesthetics," which he defines as "the refusal to accept at face value the western-originated notion of the aesthetic and the lines of interpretation that flow from it." "The Master Text and the Jeddi Doctrine," *Screen* 29.4 (Autumn 1988), 96.

A postaesthetic aesthetics would historicize that western aesthetic, as Pierre Bourdieu does, on the way toward theorizing other aesthetics arising out of "other spaces."

[18] Silverman, *Male Subjectivity at the Margins*, 20.

[19]In feminist literary and film theory, discussions of the visual have long been focused on the surveillance or sadistic nature of the Oedipal gaze; that focus is now giving way to much finer distinctions in the way vision influences representation. In particular, see Silverman's discussion of the distinction between the gaze and the look in *Male Subjectivity at the Margins* and Rey Chow's "Postmodern Automatons" in *Feminists Theorize the Political*, eds. Judith Butler and Joan Scott (New York: Routledge, 1992), 101-17.

[20]The semiotic stage chronologically precedes the Symbolic in terms of the development of subjectivity, but it is only accessible to be read or interpreted retroactively through the Symbolic level of culture.

[21]Julia Kristeva, *Revolution in Poetic Language*, trans. Margaret Waller (New York: Columbia University Press, 1984), 25. *La révolution du langage poétique* (Paris: Editions du Seuil, 1974).

[22]Kristeva, *Revolution*, 27.

[23]Kristeva's phrase in the French is this: "Lieu d'engendrement du sujet, la *chôra* sémiotique est pour lui le lieu de sa négation, où son unité cède devant le procès de charges et de stases la produisant" (27). She uses the masculine pronoun to refer to the subject because of the historical project she engages in, a description of the place of the "legitimate" speaking subject. Perhaps her project will find itself at an historical point where she can use the feminine pronoun, something she at least approaches in her discussions of Marguerite Duras in *Black Sun: Depression and Melancholia*, trans. Leon S. Roudiez (New York: Columbia University Press, 1989).

[24]Henry Louis Gates, *The Signifying Monkey: A Theory of African-American Literary Criticism* (New York: Oxford University Press, 1988).

[25]The connection between femininity and materiality is not an essentialist one but rather the result of the Symbolic's historical coding and construction of both. Looking at the different ways negativity shows up in the texts of different artists might lead to a way to isolate cultural differences, in particular those differently gendered treatments, both thematic and formal, of fluidity. See my "Gendering the Critique of Representation: Fascism, the Purified Body, and Theater in Adorno, Artaud, and Maria Irene Fornes," *Rethinking Marxism* 4.3 (Fall 1991), 83-100.

[26]Burgin, 117.

[27]Kristeva develops this cultural logic of purity and its relation to both Greek and Biblical logic in *Powers of Horror: An Essay in Abjection* (New York: Columbia University Press, 1982).

[28]Jennifer Wicke has developed this point in "Postmodernism: The Perfume of Information," *Yale Journal of Criticism* 1.2 (Spring, 1988), 145-59.

[29]Kristeva, "Women's Time," 34.

[30]Kristeva, "Women's Time," 35.

[31]See Nancy Fraser's "Rethinking the Public Sphere: A Contribution to the Critique of Actually Existing Democracy "in *Social Text: Theory/ Culture/ Ideology* 25-26 (1990), 56-80. Fraser studies Jurgen Habermas's notion of the public sphere of democratic discourse in order to historicize the ways in which a masculine, seemingly objective and neutral style in such discourse has been privileged in opposition to a number of other equally public discourses that have, nevertheless, been dismissed because of the illegimate "style" of their articulation. The symbolic capacities of speakers who speak in other styles are judged inadequate; they are not heard in the same way as are speakers trained in the dominant form of public discourse.

by Sharon Larisch

Plato's Practice: Genealogy and Mathematics

Although in recent years Plato's social and political theory has enjoyed a guardedly positive reception by feminist critics, prompting one prominent scholar to question whether Plato was perhaps a protofeminist,[1] his views on discourse and dialectic have not been accorded similar approbation. The dialogues, it is argued, are structured by binary and hierarchized oppositions that effectively work to suppress the feminine; the critic's task, then, is one of retrieval, of searching for the concealed traces of the feminine in the dialogues and in dialectics. Irigaray's discussion of the cave allegory seeks to uncover the glassed-over depths of the maternal cave.[2] Page duBois argues that the Platonic appropriation of reproduction erases the maternal presence.[3] For Derrida, the dialogues seek to limit the functioning of the second term of a number of oppositions, among them the distinction male/female.[4] Even Kristeva's analysis, which complicates the opposition between the symbolic and semiotic, harbors the same suspicion: Plato, she suggests, attempts to conceal the motility of the semiotic *chôra*.[5]

These revisionist readings vary in focus and in the scope and intent of their oppositional strategy, but they share the basic assumption that Plato's dialogues seek to establish binary hierarchies.[6] As a perhaps necessary consequence, then, the arguments themselves are structured by the same hierarchies examined in Plato's texts. The readings address only the problem of otherness or opposition in the dialogues, and, given this focus, the more general activities of combination—the slippage of the *pharmakon*, the linking of copula or the shifting *chôra*—can only be seen as subversive of Plato's intent. If, however, we approach the Platonic corpus with the assumption that the structuring principle is not otherness but, rather, combination, Plato's treatment of the feminine in language takes on a different cast. Such an approach does not ignore the existence of gender-based hierarchical oppositions in the Platonic corpus, but seeks to recognize as well the consistent and *unconcealed* presence of the equalizing force of combination. To explore this problem I will distinguish between two models for dialectics proposed in the Platonic corpus. The first is a genealogical model, which is based in hierarchized oppositions and often couched in terms of paternity. This model is the object of many feminist critiques. The second is a mathematical model, based in combination and couched in terms of the feminine and maternity. Since these models are not mutually exclusive and both depend ultimately on judgment and the processes of separation and combination, my goal is not to refine this distinction. Rather, I will seek to show how Plato constantly moves back and forth between these two poles and how their harmony and tension ultimately constitute both the problem and procedure of dialectics. My discussion will therefore focus on those moments when mathematics and genealogy participate in the engendering of dialectic.

Plato's Practice: Genealogy and Mathematics

An early nexus of genealogy and mathematics occurs in the figure of the matchmaker. In the *Theaetetus*, Socrates first describes himself as a midwife who aids in the birth of ideas which he himself cannot engender, but adds that the midwife's role is not limited to selection among others' offspring; it can also include matchmaking to produce the best possible progeny. Indeed, Socrates says that midwives are "the cleverest matchmakers, having an unerring skill in selecting a pair whose marriage will produce the best children."[7] Again, midwives do not produce the seed—they do not "father" in that sense—but they can mix and combine elements to produce a favorable birth resulting from a good combination: eugenics produces *euporia*, the resolution of doubts and difficulties in discourse or the successful outcome of maternity.

With the extension of midwifery to include matchmaking, the Platonic genealogical system embraces an implicit mathematic model, and genetics, especially eugenics, becomes a model for dialectical collection and division, just as midwifery in the narrower sense of aiding a soul in labor provides a model of dialectics as question and answer. It is in the *Phaedrus* that Socrates first defines himself as a "lover of...divisions and collections," claiming to share this quality with all dialecticians (266b), and this doctrine seems to be based in part on the Hippocratic practice previously alluded to in the *Charmides* (156c) of treating the whole body rather than simply the affected part. Following Hippocrates' organic and therapeutic practice, Socrates elaborates a discursive practice based on the combination of units (simple objects) among themselves and division into parts. This employment of the part and the whole or the one and the many as a method lays the groundwork for his use in the *Theatetus* of the Hippocratic theory of genetics to describe the activities of the dialectician as matchmaker. Again, the organic practice of genetics can be transferred into discursive practice. As Robert S. Brumbaugh has shown, Hippocrates' incipient theory of genetics is adaptable to a matrix scheme similar to the geometric and algebraic schemata inherent in the construction of Platonic argumentation as well as in the generation of the cosmos in the *Timaeus*.[8] The resultant matrix specifies parts as well as possible combinations:[9]

		MALE PARENT			
		M	m	F	f
FEMALE	M	MM	Mm	MF	Mf
	m	mM	mm	mF	mf
	F	FM	Fm	FF	Ff
	f	fM	fm	fF	ff

In the Hippocratic system both the male and the female parents can produce four types of seed: the male (M) and female (F) seeds which dominate and the male (m) and female (f) seeds which are dominated. Of the possible combinations detailed above, some are impossible, since only one seed can dominate (thus, for example, MM would not be a possibility) and a male seed from a male parent cannot be dominated by the male seed donated by the female parent, nor can a female seed from a female parent be dominated by a female seed from the male parent. Even given these restrictions, however, this charting out of combination contrasts sharply with the view of gender and engendering implied by the Pythagorean table of opposites that posits the separation of opposed terms and the dominance of the limit, associated with the male, over the unlimited, associated with the female:[10]

limit	*unlimited*
odd	even
one	multitude
right	left
male	female
resting	moving
straight	twisted
light	darkness
good	bad
square	oblong

(Aristotle, *Metaphysics* 986a)

The terms and the arrangement of this table are, of course, familiar. Many critics, especially those who read Plato through Aristotle, have privileged the Pythagorean influence on Plato's thought, and this schema of dominance has been the object of intelligent feminist scrutiny. This table, however, does not provide for any notion of combination or passage, and therefore cannot account for the functioning of a dialectical procedure based on the complementary processes of collection and division.

The inadequacy of this Pythagorean conception of hierarchized opposites and the necessity of a notion of combination is evident in the *Philebus* when the problem broached in the *Phaedrus* of the One and the Many is again taken up in the context of Socrates' definition of correct dialectical method. Confronted with the mysteries of the One and the Many, the limit and the unlimited, unity and plurality, Socrates proposes to his interlocutors that they solve the problem through collection (moving from the Many to the One) and division (moving from the One to the Many). Thus, he says, the gods have "committed to us the task of inquiry, of learning, and of teaching one another" (l6c-l7a). As a method of inquiry and teaching, however, we see here that dialectic process mimics its problem. Collection and division is the acting out of the problem of the One and the Many, and it is only through this enactment that the dialectician can seek to know their conjunction. This enactment, however, has nothing to do with stable, rigid knowledge; it is suitable, as Socrates says, for the *activities* of inquiry, teaching and learning, a moving through the Many in which the One is seen as the beginning of division and the end of collection. Here Socrates posits a kinetic view of knowledge through the processes of collection and division that do not depend on issue or reproduction and will not yield a system of dominance. It is an open-ended process of combination without a set sum.[11]

This type of combination is essential to Plato's practice of dialectic. As Plato's numerical fictions perhaps unwittingly demonstrate, dialectic must be abandoned if calculation is used to restrain combination and to produce a fixed sum. Such reckoning necessarily uses numbers non-dialogically, as a sort of transcription of a higher truth that defies investigation. The so-called "nuptial number" in the *Republic* is a particularly interesting example of Plato's non-dialogical reckoning because in this case the sum number also has genealogical implications. Because the rulers of the ideal state constructed in the *Republic* will be unable to ascertain the "laws of prosperous birth or infertility" and will, therefore, at times "beget children out of season" (546b), Socrates must reckon a sort of matchmakers' guide for the rulers of the *Republic*:

> Now for divine begettings there is a period comprehended by a perfect number, and for mortal by the first in which augmentations dominating and dominated when they have attained to three distances and four limits of the assimilating and the dissimilating, the waxing and the waning, render all things conversable and commensurable with one another, whereof a basal four thirds wedded to the pempad yields two harmonies at the third augmentation, the one the product of equal factors taken one hundred times, the other of equal length one way but oblong—one dimension of a hundred numbers determined by the rational diameters of the pempad lacking one in each case, or of the irrational lacking two; the other dimension of a hundred cubes of the triad. (546b-c)

Here the matchmaker's genetic (and, therefore, mathematical) dilemma is apparently solved mathematically—assuming, of course, that Socrates' interlocutors could unravel the mathematical complexities of this passage. Calculations of the nuptial number have differed, and the common solution of 12,960,000 has recently been challenged by Brumbaugh. But we must wonder, with Brumbaugh, if the correct calculation of the "sum" is what is at stake here. This number can be "proven" several times over to be the solution to the mathematical problem, but its meaning for the practice of genetics would still be in question, and it could not be a very useful guide to a matchmaker. But this fiction is instructive in that it illustrates a use of numbers *as* language as well as a certain use of language. Here, Plato seems to be assuming that his numerical fiction is transcribing or reflecting a higher truth; in this sense, it is like the myth of Rhadamanthus, the set story of otherworldly revelation and justice which he evokes in the *Gorgias* to prove that tyrants are not happy. The mode of transcription is simply numbers rather than letters. These fictions, both the myth and the numerical "proof," "stand in" for an idea that defies dialectic proof. The numerical proof, however, can only indicate a solution non-numerically, i.e., through a non-mathematical interpretation of a mathematical construction. We still have to say what 12,960,000 *means*. But in neither case do we have anything like an inquiry; rather, these fictions are offered as a kind of doxa or proof that must be accepted unconditionally, and are, indeed, most often called into play to counter the effects of "bad" figures of combination: sexual excess, the chameleon changes of the sophist, the protean power of the tyrant (in another numerical fiction Socrates proves that the philosopher king lives 729 times more happily than the tyrant).

Although numerical fictions enforce the limits of combination, they do so at the expense of dialogue, and it is therefore not surprising that collection and division as processes that do not necessarily lead to a final summation come to play a dominant role in the dialogues. If, however, combination is posited as the basis of dialectic, the Pythagorean notion of otherness and difference must be redefined. This task is assumed by the Stranger and Theatetus in the *Sophist*. The discussion in this dialogue centers on participation and mingling among the forms, and the Stranger and Theatetus affirm, as Socrates does in the *Philebus*, that the problem of blending is the problem of dialectics. Is this blending limited or can all forms mingle? In order to discover this, the Stranger and Theaetetus do not consider all the forms "for fear of getting confused in such a multitude" (254c), but only the most important: existence, rest and motion. They are then forced to add sameness and what has been variously translated as "other" or "difference" [*heteron*] to account for the fact that "some [things] are spoken of as ...being what they are with reference to other things" (255c). Difference or otherness is important, therefore, because "whatever is different [or "other": *heteron*], as a necessary consequence, is what it is with reference to another" (255d); or, to use Fowler's translation that preserves the repetition of *heteron*, "And other is always relative to other." Difference or otherness, they find, "pervades all the forms, for each one is other from the rest, not by virtue of its own nature, but because it partakes of the character of the other" (255e). Here, "other" or "difference" does not establish a series of binary oppositions like those we see on the Pythagorean table. Rather, it is recast as a principle of relation that can produce a form through spacing; at the same time, however, it represents the process of combination: all of the forms "partake" of otherness. In the *Sophist*, then, otherness or difference goes beyond the problem of otherness as opposition and encompasses the entire range of combination. The hierarchized Pythagorean distinctions yield to a notion of difference that can allow for the functioning of discourse. If, as the Stranger claims, the "isolation of everything from everything else means a complete abolition of all discourse, for any discourse we can have owes its existence to the weaving together of forms" (259c-260), it follows that the strictly enforced oppositions of the Pythagorean scheme could not serve as a model for discursive practice; *heteron* resides in the process of spacing, not in the oppositions that potentially arise as products of spacing.

This redefinition of *heteron* allows the Stranger and Theatetus to violate Parmenides' dictum: "Never shall this be proved that things that are not, are" (258d). If *heteron* is spacing rather than opposition, Non-being is simply the other of being and can be granted existence: "when we speak of that which is not," the Stranger reasons, "it seems we do not mean something contrary to what exists but only something that is different" (257b-258c). Since in this dialogue the Stranger and Theatetus are mainly concerned with relationships among the forms, especially in discourse, the problem of the role (or existence) of Non-being in creation or in the general structuring of the cosmos is not raised. These issues are central, however, to the *Timaeus*, and coming from the Sophist one might naturally ask what position Non-being occupies with respect to the bipartite division of Being and Becoming. That this question is not fully answered in the *Timaeus* is a function of its focus: creation here is not *ex nihilo*, from Non-being; the dialogue is concerned only with the combination and positioning of existing elements of the cosmos. And yet the place of Non-being is "filled" in the *Timaeus*: the possible triad of Being, Non-being and Becoming is replaced by the triad of Being, Space or Place (*hê chôra*) and Becoming.

Critias first couches his story of creation in terms of three elements when he is forced to make a new beginning in order to account for the complexity of his subject. For his former exposition, Critias tells us, two elements were sufficient: "one of them being assumed as a Model Form, intelligible and ever uniformly existent, and the second as the model's Copy, subject to becoming and visible" (48e-49a). The third element is termed a baffling and obscure form (*chalepon kai amydron eidos*), but Critias provides us with a number of guidelines for differentiating its function in relation to Being and Becoming. It is first called the "receptacle, and as it were the nurse, of all Becoming (*pasês...geneseôs hypodochên autên, hoion tithênên*)" (49a) or the "Wherein" Becoming becomes as opposed to the "source 'Wherefrom' the Becoming is copied and produced" (50c-d). In genealogical terms, Critias maintains that "it is proper to liken the Recipient to the Mother, the Source to the Father, and what is engendered between these two to the Offspring" (50d). Finally, he characterizes the three elements as to their generation, their relation to otherness, and their mode of being apprehended:

> we must agree that One Kind is the self-identical Form, ungenerated and indestructible, neither receiving into itself any other from any quarter nor itself passing anywhither into another, invisible and in all ways imperceptible by sense, it being the object which it is the province of Reason to contemplate; and a second Kind is that which is named after the former and similar thereto, an object perceptible by sense, generated, ever carried about, becoming in a place and out of it again perishing, apprehensible by Opinion with the aid of Sensation; and a third Kind is ever-existing Place, which admits not of destruction, and provides room for all things that have birth, itself being apprehensible by a kind of bastard reasoning by the aid of non-sensation, barely an object of belief; for when we regard this we dimly dream and affirm that it is somehow necessary that all that exists should exist in some spot and occupying some place (*en tini topôi kai katechon chôran tina*), and that that which is neither on earth nor anywhere in the Heaven is nothing (*ouden*). (52a-b)

The oppositions of Being and Becoming, Reason and Opinion, Mind and Sensation are familiar ones. The interpolation of space into these binary oppositions creates problems similar to those posed previously by Non-being. In the *Sophist* the difficulty is how to talk about Non-being since the grammatical categories of singular and plural and the copula "to be" all assign to Non-being something seemingly alien to it, Being. In the *Timaeus* the problem is understanding or apprehending space. Certainly it has an identity. Critias maintains that the various instantiations that occur in the receptacle can only be termed "such" for they are constantly reformulated and recombined, but the receptacle itself is a "this," possessing an essential nature. Its "thisness," however, is void of all form(s). Critias uses the analogy of a material to be stamped or the base for perfumes to explain that if space had a specific form it would intrude upon or interfere with the forms produced within it. Therefore, he describes the receptacle as a "Kind invisible and unshaped, all-receptive" (51b). Space allows for Becoming and prevents instantiation from being *nothing*, but it—or she, given the association of the receptacle with the mother—is neither Non-being nor Becoming nor Being. However, just as the Stranger through his recognition of the importance of Difference or Otherness grants the status of being (partaking of being) to Non-being, Critias ascribes being, a "thisness," to the Receptacle as the space of combination and differentiation, and, once again, numbers are implicated in this strange otherness.

The functioning of *chôra* can perhaps best be illustrated by using Critias's own analogy: the winnowing machine. In his tale the Receptacle receives earth and air, fire and water and is set in motion by the imbalance of the elements, separating like from unlike:

> And the forms, as they are moved, fly continually in various directions and are dissipated; just as the particles that are shaken and winnowed by the sieves and other instruments used for the cleansing of corn fall in one place if they are solid and heavy, but fly off and settle elsewhere if they are spongy and light. So it was also with the Four Kinds when shaken by the Recipient: her motion, like an instrument which causes shaking, was separating farthest from one another the dissimilar, and pushing most closely together the similar; wherefore also these Kinds occupied different places (*chôran*) even before that the Universe was organized and generated out of them. (52e-53a)

It is with this primary spacing or placing of the four Kinds that the Demiurge then sets to work "by first marking them out into shapes (*dieschêmatisato*) by means of forms and numbers" (53b). His activities are thus an extension of the differentiating movements of the Receptacle, and as such a prefiguration of the dialectician's collection and division. The important model for this phase of creation, however, remains the Receptacle. Here, place or space is the locus of kinesis, of movement and activity.

The idea of a location for a principle of movement is a difficult one, and might explain the problems Critias has in apprehending the role of space in creation, for space is often seen as a static element that is then occupied. The latter view will allow some critics to dismiss *chôra* in order to maintain the Pythagorean hierarchy. I'm thinking here of J.N. Findlay who argues that the "dualism of archai, of basic Principles [the Model/Father/Being and the Receptacle/Mother/*chôra*], really reduces to monism. One of the archai is really no arche at all, but a mere shadow of the other. The One is really responsible for everything, and the Indefinite Dyad which opposes it is merely what it needs to be itself."[12] *Chôra*, for Findlay, "runs behind" instantiation "in the ontological stakes"; it is "the utterly non-existent"; the Receptacle is a "dance of death."

Findlay's argument depends first on the association of *chôra* with Non-being and second on a definition of Non-Being as the opposite of Being, as death and non-existence. It is significant, however, that Plato chose to use *chôra*, partially occupied space, instead of *kenon*, the void of space, which would perhaps have approached more fully the notion of Non-being, and that the redefinition of otherness and difference in the *Sophist* causes the Stranger to grant existence to Non-being. For Plato the most familiar model for understanding *chôra* as the locus of activity would not necessarily have been death-like nonexistence; he possessed another possible model in the union of numbers, which, we have seen, constitute a principle of movement in the dialogues, with space.

We might best understand the union of numbers and space by appealing to figured or geometrized numbers, the arrangement of a certain number of dots (or, earlier, pebbles) in the shape of figures. The dots or pebbles were said to define a field, a *chôra*, a term also used for the spaces of the abacus and the chess board.[13] In the famous passage of the *Meno* (82b), the figure traced in the sand is termed a *chorion*, a diminutive of *chôra* and the related word *chôros* is also used by Euclid in *The Data* for area or enclosed space as opposed to lines and angles.[14] The activity of spacing that defines space is expressed by *chôrizein*, a very common verb in Plato meaning to separate or distinguish that serves as a description of dialectic. Aristotle tells us that the "Pythagoreans too asserted the existence of the void (*apeirou*) and declared that it entered the heavens out of the limitless breath—regarding the heavens as breathing the very vacancy—which vacancy 'distinguishes' (*chôrismou*) natural objects, as constituting a kind of separation and division between things next to each other, its prime seat being in numbers, since it is this void that delimits their nature."[15] (*Physics* 213b 24-28). Thus, at least in the Aristotelian reception, the process of separation and (numerical) difference first distinguishes "things" to the point that some idea of occupying a space can be formulated.

But *chôra* was also a troublesome concept. On the Pythagorean table of opposites odd numbers were included on the "good" side. This seems to be due to a possible abolition or occupation of the space or spacing that defined objects in the first place. A fragment from Aristoxenos, a disciple of Aristotle, defines "even numbers as those which are divided into equal parts, while odd numbers are divided into unequal parts and have a middle term."[16] The significance of this middle term can be seen by later references to odd and even. Plutarch tells us that when "the odd is divided into two equal parts, a unit is left over in the middle; but when the even is so divided, an empty field (*chôra*) is left, without a master (*adespotos*) and without a number (*anarithmos*), showing that it is defective and incomplete (*atelous*)"; "In the division of numbers, the even, when parted in any direction, leaves as it were within itself...a field (*chôran*)."[17] It would seem, then, that number is called into play both as a gap that differentiates and as a potential master to stop gapping by occupying the empty space. An even number is endlessly divisible, creating more minute differentiations, multiplying but never mastering *chôra*. In the case of the odd number, number itself takes a stand against division.

The Aristotelian description of Pythagorean number theory and Plutarch's account of the mastery of the middle term can be seen as interested; indeed, several centuries later Nicomachus, while admitting that the definition detailed above is commonly accepted, claims that according to the Pythagoreans an even number was simply "that which is divided, by one and the same operation, into the greatest and the least parts, greatest in size but least in quantity, in accordance with a natural reciprocity of the two species, while an odd number cannot be so divided but is only divisible into two unequal parts."[18] This discussion of the problem of even and odd numbers, however, can help us delineate the difference between the vision of the feminine space projected by the Pythagorean table of opposites and the concept of the feminine in the mathematical space of dialectic. The maintenance of gender-based hierarchized divisions depends on the control of a static space, the territory between the dominant and the dominated terms that must be maintained (or "occupied") in the interests of the dominant term. Dialectic as collection and division, however, necessitates an endless process of spacing. Therefore the activities of *chôra* and numbers cannot be hidden or occupied by number. These activities, rather, must be staged because with numbers, too, there is a certain reflexivity of subject and method. The problem of the One and the Many is indicated and enacted by *chôrizein*, the method of the One and the Many. It can be played out, but it cannot be definitively resolved. Numbers tied to feminized space (*chôrizein*) provide a model for the workings of dialectic, equivalent in this sense to the "gift of the gods" described in the *Philebus*.

This model, however, coexists with the notion of a possible control of combination. It is undeniable that Plato at times attempts to curb circulation, often by appealing to a genealogical model of production in the image of the father. This side of Platonic doctrine has been privileged by the philosophic tradition (but not always by the literary tradition) and has been subjected to a useful and perceptive feminist critique. But it also seems to me undeniable that Plato is aware that when circulation ends, when the movement and exchange associated with the feminine is arrested, dialogue yields to doxa. His notion of the feminine, of numbers tied to space, is, I believe, intended to counter the restricting force of the genealogical model. Unwilling to relinquish either a notion of control or a notion of combination, Plato constantly reenacts their tension by the process of *chôrizein*, seeking to grasp the trace—if not exactly the transubstantiation—of a certain plurality, a "such," always in the process of exchange.

NOTES

[1]See Gregory Vlastos , "Was Plato a Feminist?" *TLS* March 17-23 (1989). Plato's intent in this regard, however, remains an open question. Vlastos, among others, has suggested that Plato did indeed accept a greater role for exceptional women in society: "In a triumph of imaginative impartiality [Plato] separated the character his inherited prejudices imputed to the mass of women in his own society from the character which, he reasoned, a few exceptional women could develop under ideal conditions of equal nurture, awarding to them what his own theory of social justice required: status commensurate with the greatest contributions each of them could make personally to their own society and therefore equal in all respects to that of men" (277). Susan Okin, however, claims that Plato's apparently progressive ideas vis a vis women in the *Republic* are determined only by the logic of his argument in that dialogue and are abandoned in the *Laws*. See Susan Okin, *Women in Western Political Thought* (Princeton: Princeton University Press, 1979).

[2]Luce Irigaray, "Plato's Hystera," in *Speculum of the Other Woman*, trans. Gillian C. Gill (Ithaca: Cornell University Press, 1974).

[3]Page duBois, "The Platonic Appropriation of Reproduction," in *Sowing the Body: Psychoanalysis and Ancient Representations of Women* (Chicago: University of Chicago Press, 1988).

[4]Jacques Derrida, "Plato's Pharmacy," in *Dissemination*, trans. Barbara Johnson (Chicago: University of Chicago Press, 1982).

[5]Julia Kristeva, *Revolution in Poetic Language*, trans. Margaret Waller (New York: Columbia University Press, 1984).

[6]Again, the question of Plato's intent is left unresolved. Only Derrida treats this problem explicitly, and ultimately questions the possibility of broaching the question at all: "Plato does not make a show of the chain of significations we are trying progressively to dig up. If there were any sense in asking such a question, which we don't believe, it would be impossible to say to what extent he manipulates it voluntarily or consciously, and at what point he is subject to constraints weighing upon his discourse from 'language.' The word 'language,' through all that binds it to everything we are putting in question here, is not of any pertinent assistance, and to follow the constraints of a language would not exclude the possibility that Plato is playing with them, even if his game is neither representative nor voluntary. It is in the back room, in the shadows of the pharmacy, prior to the oppositions between conscious and unconscious, freedom and constraint,voluntary and involuntary, speech and language, that these textual 'operations' occur.... Only the chain is concealed, and, to an inappreciable extent, concealed from the author himself, if any such thing exists" ("Plato's Pharmacy," trans. B. Johnson, in Dissemination [Chicago: University of Chicago Press], 129).

[7]Theaetetus 149d. All translations of Plato's dialogues are from Plato, *Collected Dialogues,* ed. Edith Hamilton and Huntington Cairns (Princeton: Princeton University Press, 1983) or *Dialogues*, trans. R.G. Bury et al. (London: Heinemann, 1914-1935). Further references cited in the text.

[8]Robert S. Brumbaugh, *Plato's Mathematical Imagination* (Bloomington: Indiana University Press, 1977).

[9]Adapted from Brumbaugh, 77.

[10]Aristotle, *Metaphysics*, 986a.

[11]My discussion of Platonic number theory owes a great deal to Hans-Georg Gadamer's essays in *Dialogue and Dialectic: Eight Hermeneutical Studies on Plato*, trans. P. Christopher Smith (New Haven: Yale University Press, 1980). Gadamer's analysis, however, implicitly privileges the mean; I would leave the field more open.

[12]J.N. Findlay, *Plato: The Written and Unwritten Doctrines* (New York: Humanities Press, 1974), 324.

[13]See John Burnet, *Early Greek Philosophy* (New York: Meridian, 1930), 104; Sir Thomas Heath, *A History of Greek Mathematics* (New York: Dover, 1981), 1: 76-84; and Ivor Thomas, trans. *Greek Mathematical Works* (London: Heinemann, 1939), 1: 87-100.

[14]See *Greek Mathematical Works*, 1:479.

[15]Aristotle, *Physics* 213b 24-28.

[16]See Brunet, 288.

[17]See Brunet, 288.

[18]See *Greek Mathematical Works*, 1:73.

BIBLIOGRAPHY

Abrams, M. H. "How To Do Things With Texts," in *Critical Theory Since 1965*, eds. Hazard Adams and Leroy Searle. University of Florida Press, 1986.

Annas, Julia. "Plato's *Republic* and Feminism," *Philosophy* 51 (1976), 307-321.

Ashbaugh, Anne Freire. *Plato's Theory of Explanation*. Albany: State University of New York Press, 1988.

Bacon, Helen H. "Socrates Crowned," *Virginia Quarterly Review*, 35 (1959), 415-30.

Berger, Harry Jr. "Facing Sophists: Socrates' Charismatic Bondage in *Protagoras*," *Representations* 5 (1984), 66-91.

——, "Plato's Flying Philosopher," *The Philosophical Forum* 13 (1982), 385-407.

Bloom, Harold. *The Art of the Critic*. New York: Chelsea House, 1985.

Blumenberg, Hans. *The Legitimacy of the Modern Age*. Translated by Robert M. Wallace. Cambridge: MIT Press, 1983.

Bourdieu, Pierre. *Outline of a Theory of Practice*. Translated by Richard Nice. Cambridge: Cambridge University Press, 1977.

Brentlinger, John A. "The Cycle of Becoming in the *Symposium*," in Suzy Q. Groden, trans., *The Symposium of Plato*. Amherst: University of Massachusetts Press, 1970, 1-31.

Brumbaugh, Robert S. *Plato's Mathematical Imagination*. Bloomington: Indiana University Press, 1977.

Burger, Ronna. *Plato's "Phaedrus": A Defense of a Philosophic Art of Writing*. University, Alabama: University of Alabama Press, 1980.

Burnet, John. *Early Greek Philosophy*. New York: Meridian, 1930.

Cherniss, Harold. "Ancient Forms of Philosophic Discourse," in *Selected Papers*, ed. Leonardo Tarán. Leiden: Brill, 1977.

Clay, Diskin. "The Tragic and Comic Poet of the *Symposium*," in *Essays in Ancient Greek Philosophy: Volume Two*, ed. John P. Anton and Anthony Preus. Albany: State University of New York Press, 1983.

Debord, Guy. *Society of the Spectacle*. Detroit: Black and Red, 1983.

Derrida, Jacques. "La différance," in [Ouvrage collecti] *Théorie d'ensemble*. Paris: Éditions du Seuil, 1968.

——. *La Dissémination*. Paris: Éditions du Seuil, 1972. Translated by Barbara Johnson. *Dissemination*. Chicago: University of Chicago Press, 1982.

——. *Of Grammatology*. Translated by G. Spivak. Baltimore and London: Johns Hopkins University Press, 1974.

——. *The Post Card: From Socrates to Freud and Beyond*. Translated by Alan Bass. Chicago: University of Chicago Press, 1987.

duBois, Page. *Sowing the Body: Psychoanalysis and Ancient Representations of Women*. Chicago: University of Chicago Press, 1988.

Ducrot, Oswald and Todorov, Tzvetan, "Toward a Critique of the Sign: The Text as Productivity," *Encyclopedic Dictionary of the Sciences of Language*.

Translated by Catherine Porter. Baltimore: The Johns Hopkins University Press, 1979.

Elias, Julius A. *Plato's Defense of Poetry*. Albany: State University of New York Press, 1984.

Ferrari, G.R.F. *Listening to the Cicadas: A Study of Plato's PHAEDRUS*. Cambridge: Cambridge University Press, 1987.

Findlay, J.N. *Plato: The Written and Unwritten Doctrines*. New York: Humanities Press, 1974.

Fletcher, John and Benjamin, Andrew, eds. *Abjection, Melancholia and Love: The Work of Julia Kristeva*. London: Routledge, 1990.

Foucault, Michel. *The Archaeology of Knowledge*. Translated by A.M. Sheridan Smith. New York: Harper and Row, 1972.

——. "Of Other Spaces," *Diacritics* (Spring 1986), 1-23.

Friedlander, Paul. *Plato: An Introduction*. Translated by Hans

Meyerhoff. Princeton: Princeton University Press, 1973.

Gadamer, Hans-Georg. *Dialogue and Dialectic: Eight Hermeneutical Studies on Plato*. Translated by P. Christopher Smith. New Haven: Yale University Press, 1980.

——. *Truth and Method*. New York: Seabury Press, 1975.

Gallavotti, Carlo. "Sulle classificazioni dei generi letterari nell' estetica antica," *Athenaeum*, n.s. 6 (1928), 356-66.

Gilbert, Sandra M. and Gubar, Susan. *The Madwoman in the Attic*. New Haven: Yale University Press, 1979.

Glidden, David K. "The *Lysis* on Loving One's Own," *Classical Quarterly*, 31 (1981), 39-59.

Griswold, Charles L., ed. *Platonic Writings, Platonic Readings*. New York: Routledge, 1988.

——. *Self-Knowledge in Plato's Phaedrus*. New Haven and London: Yale University Press, 1986.

Hackforth, R. "Immortality in Plato's *Symposium*," *Classical Review*, 64 (1950), 43-45.

Halperin, David M. *One Hundred Years of Homosexuality and Other Essays on Greek Love*. New York: Routledge, 1990.

——. "Plato and Erotic Reciprocity," *Classical Antiquity*, 5 (1986), 60-80.

——. "Platonic *Eros* and What Men Call Love," *Ancient Philosophy*, 5 (1985), 168-84.

Havelock, Eric A. *Preface to Plato*. Cambridge: Harvard University Press, 1963.

Hayles, N. Katherine. "Postmodern Parataxis: Embodied Texts, Weightless Information," *American Literary History* 2.3 (1990), 394-421.

Hearne, Vicki. *Adam's Task: Calling Animals by Name*. New York: Knopf, 1986.

Heidegger, Martin. *Existence and Being*. Translated by R.F.C. Hull and Alan Crick.

London: Vision Press, 1949.

Hornsby, Roger. "Significant Action in the *Symposium*," *Classical Journal*, 52 (1956/57), 37-40.

BIBILIOGRAPHY

Irigaray, Luce. *Speculum de l'autre femme*. Paris: Les Éditions de Minuit. Translated by Gillian C. Gill. *Speculum of the Other Woman*. Ithaca: Cornell University Press, 1985.

Jaeger, Werner. *Paideia: The Ideals of Greek Culture*. Translated by Gilbert Highet. New York: Oxford University Press, 1943.

Jameson, Fredric. *Postmodernism, or the Cultural Logic of Late Capitalism*. Durham, N.C.: Duke University Press, 1991.

Kahn, Charles. "Drama and Dialectic in Plato's *Gorgias*," *Oxford Studies in Ancient Philosophy*, 1 (1983), 75-121.

Kastely, James L. "In Defense of Plato's *Gorgias*." *PMLA*, vol. 106, no. 1, January 1991, 96-109.

Kerferd, G.B. *The Sophistic Movement*. Cambridge: Cambridge University Press, 1981.

Kristeva, Julia. *Black Sun: Depression and Melancholia*. Translated by Leon S. Roudiez. New York: Columbia University Press, 1989.

——. *Powers of Horror: An Essay in Abjection*. New York: Columbia University Press, 1982.

——. *Revolution in Poetic Language*. Translated by Leon Roudiez. New York: Columbia University Press, 1984.

——. "Women's Time," *Signs* 7.1 (Autumn 1981), 1-32.

Lonergan, Bernard. *Insight: A Study of Human Understanding*. New York: Philosophical Library, 1970.

Lowenstam, Steven. "Paradoxes in Plato's *Symposium*," *Ramus*, 14 (1985), 85-104.

Luce, J.V. "Immortality in Plato's *Symposium*: A Reply," *Classical Review*, n.s. 2 (1952), 137-41.

Lyotard, Jean-Francois. *Heidegger et "les juifs."* Paris: Galilée, 1988.

——. *Innovation/Renovation*. Madison: University of Wisconsin Press, 1983.

——. *The Postmodernist Condition*. Minneapolis: University of Minnesota Press, 1984.

——. "Réponse à la question: qu'est-ce que le postmoderne?" *Critique*, 35, no. 419, April, 1982, 360-75.

Mac Intyre, Alasdair. *After Virtue*. Notre Dame, Indiana: Notre Dame University Press, 1982.

Man, Paul de. *Allegories of Reading: Figural Language in Rousseau, Nietzsche, Rilke, and Proust*. New Haven: Yale University Press, 1979.

——. *Blindness and Insight: Essays in the Rhetoric of Contemporary Criticism*. Minneapolis: University of Minnesota Press, 1983.

McFarland, Thomas. "Involute and Symbol," in *Coleridge, Keats, and the Imagination*, eds. Barth and Mahoney. Columbia and London: University of Missouri Press, 1990.

McGowan, John. *Postmodernism and its Critics*. Ithaca and London: Cornell University Press, 1991.

Melville, Stephen W. *Philosophy Beside Itself: On Deconstruction and Modernism.* Minneapolis: University of Minnesota Press, 1986.

Neel, Jasper. *Plato, Derrida, and Writing.* Carbondale and Edwardsville: Southern Illinois University Press, 1988.

Nussbaum, Martha. *The Fragility of Goodness: Luck and Ethics in Greek Tragedy and Philosophy.* Cambridge: Cambridge University Press, 1986.

——. *Love's Knowledge: Essays on Philosophy and Literature.* New York and Oxford: Oxford University Press, 1990.

Plato. *The Collected Dialogues of Plato.* Edited by Edith Hamilton and Huntington Cairns. Bollingen Series LXXI. 1961. Reprint. Princeton: Princeton University Press, 1971.

——. *Platonis Opera.* Edited by J. Burnett. 5 vols. Oxford: Clarendon Press, 1905.

Popper, K.R. *The Open Society and Its Enemies.* London: Routledge, 1945.

Richter, David H. *The Critical Tradition: Classic Texts and Contemporary Trends.* New York: St. Martin's Press, 1989.

Ricoeur, Paul. *Freud and Philosophy: An Essay in Interpretation.* Translated by Denis Savage. New Haven and London: Yale University Press, 1970.

Roochnik, David L. "Plato's Critique of Postmodernism." *Philosophy and Literature,* 1987, 282-91.

Roof, Judith, ed. *Feminism and Psychoanalysis.* Ithaca: Cornell University Press, 1989.

Rorty, Richard. *Philosophy and the Mirror of Nature.* Princeton: Princeton University Press, 1979.

Rosen, Stanley. "Platonic Hermeneutics: On the Interpretation of a Platonic Dialogue," in *Proceedings of the Boston Area Colloquium in Ancient Philosophy,* vol. 1 (1985), ed. John J. Cleary. Lanham, Maryland: University Press of America, 1986.

Rowe, C.J. "The Argument and Structure of Plato's *Phaedrus,*" *Proceedings of the Cambridge Philological Society,* 212, n.s. 32 (1986).

Schabert, Tilo. "Modernity and History." *Diogenes,* No. 123, Fall 1983, 110-124.

Sesonske, Alexander. "Plato's Apology: *Republic* I," *Phronesis* 6 (1961), 35-36.

Shankman, Steven. "Reason and Revelation in the Pre- Enlightenment: Eric Voegelin's Analysis and the Case of Swift," *Religion and Literature* 16:2 (1984), 1-24.

Silverman, Kaja. *Male Subjectivity at the Margins.* New York: Routledge, 1992.

Stannard, Jerry. "Socratic Eros and Platonic Dialectic," *Phronesis,* 4 (1959), 120-34.

Steinem, Helmust von den. "Plato in Egypt," *Bulletin of the Faculty of Arts of the Fouad I University of Faculty of Letters* (Cairo), 13 (1951), 116-123.

Steinmetz, Peter. "Gattungen und Epochen der griechischen Literatur in der Sicht Quintilians," *Hermes,* 92 (1964), 454-66.

Straus, Leo. *The City and the Man.* Chicago: Rand Mcnally, 1964.

Taylor, Clyde. "The Master Text and the Jeddi Doctrine," *Screen* 29.4 (Autumn 1988), 75-98.

Trimpi, Wesley. *Muses of One Mind: The Literary Analysis of Experience and its Continuity*. Princeton: Princeton University Press, 1983.

Vlastos, Gregory. *Plato's Universe*. Seattle: University of Washington Press, 1975.

——. "Socrates' Disavowal of Knowledge," *Philosophical Quarterly*, 35 (1985), 1-31.

——. "The Socratic Elenchus," *Oxford Studies in Ancient Philosophy*, 1 (1983), 27-58.

——. "Was Plato a Feminist?" *Times Literary Supplement*, No. 4,485 (March 17-23, 1989), 276-289.

Voegelin, Eric. *Anamnesis*. Notre Dame: Notre Dame University Press, 1978.

——. *Autobiographical Reflections*. Baton Rouge and London: Louisiana State University Press, 1989.

——. *In Search of Order. Order and History*, vol. 5. Baton Rouge and London: Louisiana State University Press, 1987.

——. *The Ecumenic Age. Order and History*, vol. 4. Baton Rouge and London: Louisiana State University Press, 1974.

——. *Plato and Aristotle. Order and History*, vol. 3. Baton Rouge and London: Louisiana State University Press, 1957.

——. "Reason: The Classic Experience," *Southern Review*, 10 (1974), 237-64. Reprinted in *Anamnesis*, 89-115.

Webb, Eugene. *Eric Voegelin: Philosopher of History*. Seattle and London: University of Washington Press, 1987.

——. *Philosophers of Consciousness: Polanyi, Lonergan, Voegelin, Ricoeur, Girard, Kierkegaard.* Seattle and London: University of Washington Press, 1988.

Wicke, Jennifer. "Postmodernism: The Perfume of Information," *Yale Journal of Criticism* 1.2 (Spring 1988), 145-60.

Wittgenstein, Ludwig. *Wittgenstein und der Wiener Kreis: Aus dem Nachlass*. ed. B.F. McGuiness. Oxford: Basil Blackwell, 1967.

INDEX OF NAMES

INDEX OF SUBJECTS